2

The Wonderful Era of THE GREAT DANCE BANDS

The Wonderful Era of

A Windfall Book

DOUBLEDAY & COMPANY, INC.

THE GREAT
DANCE BANDS

by Leo Walker

GARDEN CITY, NEW YORK · 1972

Preface

Many books have been written on Jazz and the Jazz Musician. This is not another coverage of that complex, yet narrow and confined segment of America's musical history.

It would be unrealistic to say the story of baseball had been told if those who wrote it dealt only with its great pitchers or those who hit home runs. So, too, is it unrealistic to say our musical history is complete through the repetition of the feats of those accepted by the critics as Jazz Men.

No one has written about the Dance Bands which numerically were a much larger group and out of which most of the Jazz Men came.

This is an attempt to write that story recognizing that it is so big it could never be considered completely done.

The names of many Jazz Greats will be found in these pages. It would be impossible to write about America's music without including its Jazz Artists, for Jazz and Dance Music overlap and intermingle. Time was when they were considered one and the same. The modern version and its exponents insist that this shall not be. Consequently those accepted in the circle of Jazz as endorsed by this latter group who will be found here are those who at some period combined Jazz with Dance Music or intermittently worked with dance orchestras.

The primary qualification of the personalities selected for coverage here is that they enjoyed notable success in the dance field over an extended period of time, or made a contribution to the over-all cause in their attempts to achieve it. Those who made it are considered noteworthy since they could not have done so without the approval of a reasonably substantial segment of the public. The sole purpose of this book is to provide some of their millions of fans a source where they may find a nostalgic memory of their favorite dance orchestra from a great era now considered dead, despite periodic attempts to revive it.

There is no intention to editorialize or to endorse one musical style versus another beyond pointing out the degree of success of certain leaders, and their ability to survive the changing trends of the years.

In writing about a subject of this nature, the probing research of the early years encounters many conflicting versions of any given incident. The writer learns very quickly that to identify any individual as "the first" to start any particular trend is to stir up a hornet's nest. In many cases after checking all available sources of information, he can only sift out of it a version which seems most logical after fitting together the points agreed upon by the majority of those contacted.

Because of the scope of the subject the finished product must confine itself to being "a little bit about a lot of people." A great many were contacted, but not all of them responded. If you do not find your own favorite here he may be in this category. But most of the music people co-operated wholeheartedly, making the five years involved in personal interviews and correspondence a pleasant and memorable experience. To the hundreds of bandleaders, sidemen, personal managers, agency people, ballroom and hotel operators who contributed information and loaned pictures this opportunity is taken to express my sincere gratitude.

A special vote of thanks must be given to the following—

Barney McDevitt, dean of music publicity men, for the loan of many pictures, much material, and for providing an entree to many other sources.

Red Nichols and Anson Weeks, who each came up with a trunk full of clippings and pictures of all the important people of the twenties and thirties.

Muzzy Marcellino for his scrapbook loaded with prize pictures and for many helpful ideas.

Phil Harris, Freddy Martin, and Rudy Vallee for the loan of much material and for valuable suggestions.

Ralph Portnor, of the Lawrence Welk office, whose help was substantial.

Frank and Fred Monte of the Harry James office.

Insurance man Don Haynes, once the manager of Glenn Miller.

Andrew Karzas of Chicago's Aragon Ballroom.

Sterling Way and the management of the Hollywood Palladium.

Karl Kramer of Music Corporation of America for our many interesting exchanges of ideas.

Roger S. Littleford, Sam Abbott, and Bob McCluskey of Billboard Publishing Company.

Jack Hellman of *Variety*.

Max Herman, Ward Archer, Henry Joworski, Lou Wood, and other members of Local 47, American Federation of Musicians.

Russ Morgan, Will Osborne, Joe Rushton, Ronnie Kemper, Murray Williams, Freddie Large, Tony Briglia, Al King, and Elmer Eberhardt for unusual quantities of excellent pictorial material.

Mario Pitaro and his Duplicate Photo Service of Hollywood for excellent reproductions of the photographs borrowed from the foregoing people.

My secretary, Judy Forman, who spent her week ends typing the manuscript for very little reward beyond my promise to get her a starring role in the movie version.

LEO WALKER

Glendale, California
April, 1964

Table of Contents

SECTION ONE   GROWTH AND DECLINE OF A WONDERFUL
                 ENTERTAINMENT ERA

    Chapter I   THE FORMATIVE YEARS   9

    Chapter II   AFTER THE DEPRESSION CAME PROSPERITY   47

    Chapter III   WORLD WAR II AND THE POSTWAR BOOM PERIOD   83

    Chapter IV   THE DECLINE OF THE 'FIFTIES   113

SECTION TWO   THE DIVERSIFIED SEGMENTS OF THE BUSINESS

    Chapter I   RECORDS   139

    Chapter II   RADIO BUILT BANDS BUT TELEVISION HAD LITTLE NEED FOR THEM .   163

    Chapter III   PERSONAL APPEARANCES AND WHERE THEY MADE THEM . . .   189

    Chapter IV   THE MOVIES DISCOVERED THEM TOO!   221

    Chapter V   AGENCIES BUILT BANDS AND THEN FORGOT THEM   233

    Chapter VI   PUBLICITY WAS WHERE YOU FOUND IT   249

    Chapter VII   THE ROAD TRIPS WERE RUGGED!   271

    Chapter VIII   THE VOCALISTS MADE THEIR CONTRIBUTION   285

SECTION THREE   IN SUMMARY   301

INDEX   307

GEORGE OLSEN — Portland, Oregon, 1918. Group includes Wilbur Johnson, billed as the "world's only mellophone soloist." — *Photo courtesy of Anson Weeks.*

ART HICKMAN — Probably the first dance orchestra leader to attract national attention. — *Photo courtesy of Anson Weeks.*

WALTZ
(TOSTI)

ARRANGED
&
PLAYED
by
ART HICKMAN
AND HIS
HOTEL ST. FRANCIS
ORCHESTRA
6

The Formative Years

ONE OF THE favorite topics of cocktail party conversations in the late fifties and early sixties stemmed from an attempt to find an answer to this question, "What ever happened to the big dance band business?"

As a rule, nothing unusual was required for a conversation about music personalities to get under way — the host might start the records playing in the background — someone would make a request — and the reminiscing would take over. Nostalgia then fairly dripped as the "over thirty-five group" recalled the days when they went dancing to the music of Benny Goodman, Glenn Miller, Hal Kemp, Artie Shaw, Tommy and Jimmy Dorsey, or Glen Gray and his Casa Loma Orchestra.

A lot of other names and favorites would also be mentioned with the number governed by how long the party lasted and how far past thirty-five some of the group were. For the giants of their trade mentioned above were not the only stars of the Golden Era of Dance Bands, nor did they claim to be. At its peak the business had an imposing list of important names, plus hundreds of others who were contending for name status. Some of the latter group were the pioneers who during prior years firmly laid the groundwork for the prosperity which developed during the thirties and forties and who even though less well-known, outlasted, in many instances, the biggest names of that boom period.

Perhaps the best way to discover the answer to what contributed to the big band demise would be to look back farther than the period when the Goodmans, Millers, Dorseys, and others enjoyed their peak popularity and recall some of the people and forces responsible for raising it to the "big business" status which it ultimately attained.

So long as our friends at the cocktail party confined their reminiscing to the names and styles of their favorites in the past, they would be in safe territory. But let them try to identify one leader

° It became *jazz* in the early '20s.

as being the first to take music for dancing out of the sideline area and into the realm of professionalism, and nothing but an endless debate could result. None of the musical historians who have researched the subject exhaustively have been able to agree with one another on this point.

For in the beginning it was not a profession at all in the sense of providing full-time employment. Well into the twentieth century dance music was furnished by small groups assembled for each individual job rather than working together regularly. A great deal of the dancing was done at private functions since polite society did not permit itself to be seen in the public dance halls which existed at that time.

Most of the music produced by these groups was relatively simple, smooth, and for the most part, inoffensive. The instruments most commonly used were not those which would dominate later dance organizations. The violin, whose origin could be traced back to the middle of the sixteenth century, was usually the lead instrument. In most cases the violinist was assisted by a piano and drummer and occasionally a banjo player. Often, however, only a piano player and a drummer would set the tempo for the dancing couples.

Sometime between 1910 and 1920 this picture began to change rapidly. Dance music became more alive and dancers were starting to talk about "jass",° "syncopation", and "ragtime". As the interest in public dancing grew, the need for music could no longer be supplied by "pick-up" groups. It began to be a full-time job and all over the nation "organized bands" began to appear, some content to have a local following, but others who would eventually be known coast-to-coast and a few whose fame would extend to the European continent.

Historians often consider the marching bands of New Orleans to be the first bands whose personnel was constant. Since the function of these bands was not primarily to provide dance music, we must look elsewhere to find the first full-time, professional dance band although the point will never be proven regardless of who is named.

The candidate nominated by many is Wilbur Sweatman, who was playing regularly around the Chicago area and particularly at the Pekin Theatre as early as 1911. Yet most of the available material about him would indicate Sweatman was basically a vaudeville attraction during those early years. However, he billed himself as a "ragtime clarinetist", and one of his highly publicized talents was the ability to play three clarinets simultaneously although the musical importance of this feat was never made quite clear.

The Earl Dabney orchestra appears to have been operating equally as early as Sweatman's and is more clearly identified with dance music. He was playing such top New York spots as the Ziegfeld Roof as early as 1912 with a brand of music later to be identified as "Sweet Music" and a style not ordinarily identified with Negro groups.

In addition to Sweatman the Chicago area had Charlie Elgar who was working steadily with a five piece band at the Fountain Inn in 1912. That same year Erskine Tate was playing the Chicago dance spots and unverified stories indicate that Charlie Straight was also established as a Chicago leader by that time. Doubtless there are others whose beginnings can be traced back just as far.

But those who want to probe farther back into history than the years I have mentioned will have to make the trip without me. In reality, it makes no really great difference who was actually first. The supplying of dance music started to become a business sometime around the dates which I have used.

However, every story must start somewhere and to help get this one under way, I am going to relate the story of a band about whose origination more is known. Many credit this leader with having the first organized band, although this cannot be substantiated with dates. He certainly was one

PAUL WHITEMAN — Alexandria Hotel, Los Angeles, 1919. — *Photo courtesy of Paul Whiteman.*

Ted Lewis — His first musical group, 1916.—*Photo courtesy of Ted Lewis.*

Abe Lyman — In front of Ambassador Hotel, 1922. — *Photo courtesy of Anson Weeks.*

HERB WIEDOEFT (brother of Rudy) — This group was known as the "Cinderella Roof Orchestra" and after building a reputation in California, invaded the eastern market. — *Photo courtesy of Bill Stafford.*

CALIFORNIA RAMBLERS — Picture made at Monte Carlo, New York City, 1923. — *Photo courtesy of Joe Rushton.*

CALIFORNIA COLLEGIANS — Comedy was their stock in trade. — *Photo courtesy of Lou Wood.*

JACK BOWERING ad publicizing local appearance of Loring "Red" Nichols with Bowering for an Ogden, Utah, date on Washington's Birthday, 1922. — *Photo courtesy of Red Nichols.*

13

THE SYNCOPATING FIVE — Early 1920s. Their lively tempos created a great deal of attention on the East Coast. — *Photo courtesy of Red Nichols.*

THE ROYAL PALMS ORCHESTRA — Atlantic City, 1923. This was the Syncopating Five with Red Nichols added and would soon become the "Five Pennies". — *Photo courtesy of Red Nichols.*

of the pioneers and probably the first to enjoy national success.

This story begins in 1913 on the West Coast and in a baseball training camp. The San Francisco Seals were in the habit of taking their spring training at Boyes Hot Springs in Sonoma County, the area identified in Jack London's books as the Valley of the Moon. When the club assembled for their training that year, among the camp followers was a musician by the name of Art Hickman. If he needed any excuse for being there, the one he used was his enjoyment of fraternizing with a baseball team and with the newspaper correspondents who always covered the training period.

Shortly after his arrival in camp, he approached baseball manager Dell Howard with an idea for organizing a series of dances to prevent the evenings from dragging and to relieve the usual boredom of the long training season. Howard liked the idea and so Hickman got together a group of musicians for this purpose. By the time the training season was over the group was working together so well, and had received so much publicity from the newsmen, that they were booked into the St. Francis Hotel for the entire summer. This band consisted of six pieces: piano, trombone, trumpet, drums, and two banjos. Before long, a violin and string bass were added. Although many of Hickman's ideas would soon be copied by others trying to duplicate his success, his use of a string bass was not, for it would be another fifteen years before this instrument would attain popularity.

The band was booked back periodically into the St. Francis and was there all during 1915 when the San Francisco World's Fair was in progress. The next year, while his fame continued to spread, Hickman once more enlarged the group adding two saxophones. It was given a big lift by his writing of "Rose Room" which soon became a very popular hit. Some years later it would be used as a theme song by Phil Harris, another bandleader who first became well-known in San Francisco and went on to achieve world-wide fame.

Sometime during this period, Florenz Ziegfeld was visiting San Francisco and chanced to hear the music. He was very much impressed, so much so in fact that in 1919 he took the Hickman band to New York where they played first at the Biltmore Hotel and then at the Ziegfeld Roof. Hickman returned to San Francisco four months later and then went back to New York where his band worked for the entire run of the 1920 Ziegfeld's

Follies. This resulted in additional New York bookings at the Amsterdam Theater and the Amsterdam Roof, but towards the end of 1920 they gave up New York and its bright lights to return once again to San Francisco remaining this time for several months. In April of 1921 they were chosen to open the Cocoanut Grove at the Ambassador Hotel in Los Angeles where they enjoyed the same popularity they had found in San Francisco and New York. Soon after this Hickman tired of the band business and gave it up, turning the orchestra over to Frank Ellis who kept it going for several years under his own name.

From about 1916 until the time of his own retirement the Hickman band had been a ten man organization. This was larger than most groups which started prior to 1920 with most being small units of five or six men and a limited few having seven or eight. This even included Paul Whiteman who launched his career as a leader in 1918 and would later be identified with a mammoth organization. Fred Waring's first venture was a six man string group which he called "Waring's Banjatrazz" and got its start about 1916.

By 1920 quite a number of those who were to be important names were becoming successfully established. King Oliver was one with a group he called his Olympia Band, started in 1916 in New Orleans and brought into Chicago in 1918 where they became the Creole Jazz Band. Paul Specht had also started in 1916 and it was that same year Ted Lewis decided to become a bandleader after already having made a name for himself as a vaudeville attraction. Jan Garber came out of World War I service to organize a four piece dance orchestra in 1918 and Meyer Davis, who would become the world's largest supplier of music to top society had started in 1915. George Olsen, the pride of the Pacific Northwest, had his first band working regularly in Portland, Oregon, at least as early as 1917 and was soon to move on from there to bigger things.

So it was that when Hickman arrived in New York in 1919 he found a lot of activity and other bands well established there. Some were the future big names and some were popular local attractions whose fame would be more fleeting. Sam Lanin was just starting a long engagement at the Roseland Ballroom and Earle Fuller had a band called "Rector's Novelty Orchestra" which he kept booked solidly. There was Johnny Hamp's "Kentucky Serenaders", and Ed Kirkeby, who in addi-

15

tion to having an orchestra he called his "Melody Men" sold musical instruments and booked other orchestras. Vaudevillian Ted Lewis had by then become well known as a bandleader and Meyer Davis had his multiple band empire well organized, a forerunner of the band agencies which would come a few years later.

Joe Kayser was the leader of one of these Davis units but, tiring of working for someone else, he struck out on his own about 1921 with a five-piece band under his own name. Seeking something different from his colleagues, he decided to take music to the hinterlands, and set up a tour of one-nighters through the Carolinas. He, too, was a pioneer, but was not long in discovering that someone else had thought of it before him. Jan Garber, now having merged with Milton Davis to form the Garber-Davis orchestra had already hit the one-nighter trail and probably could claim to be the first one to do so with regularity. Their band ran quite a gamut in size during its existence, starting with five men and hitting a high of fifteen before Garber and Davis dissolved their partnership shortly after the mid-twenties.

This, however, is moving a little ahead of the story. Sometime in the early twenties another important trend began. Dancing started to move out of the Masonic Temples, Elks Clubs, and community halls into ballrooms built especially for that purpose. The dance business was beginning to become a big business. In addition to the ballrooms, most of the country's leading hotels now found it profitable to provide dancing, and rooms devoted entirely to that purpose began to be a standard hotel attraction. As such places grew in number, so did the number of orchestras available to play in them.

New York and its bright lights was the magnet which attracted all of them during those early years. There, in addition to top hotel spots, were Broadway shows and the possibility of being lucky enough to become part of one of them. Even more important was the opportunity to record, for with the exception of some limited activity in Chicago all of the recording was being done around the New York area.

The West Coast continued to be the starting place for several of those who were New York-bound, with Paul Whiteman probably the first to follow Art Hickman in that direction. As a bandleader, he, too, was initially of San Francisco origin having organized his first group there for an en-

LAWRENCE WELK AD — Prior to his leaving the farm to lead his own musical group, Welk built a local reputation as an accordionist appearing with other organizations. —*Photo courtesy of Lawrence Welk.*

gagement at the Fairmont Hotel in 1918. That band included at least two who would be with him for years and well known in their own right: banjoist Mike Pingatore and trumpet player Henry Busse. The story as told by some is that the band when originally formed was actually Busse's. However, Busse, not long over from Germany, had such an accent that he could not make announcements fluently and violinist Whiteman was asked to become the front man. Whether or not there is truth in this story the band enjoyed a successful engagement at the Fairmont followed with a short stay at a Santa Barbara hotel and a longer session at the Alexandria in Los Angeles. Then they took leave of California and moved eastward where the Whiteman name quickly blossomed into national prominence.

16

LAWRENCE WELK'S ORCHESTRA — Just after the mid-20s. — *Photo courtesy of Lawrence Welk.*

THE SCRANTON SIRENS — 1921, at which time Russ Morgan was on trombone and Jimmy Dorsey can be seen on saxophone. — *Photo courtesy of Russ Morgan.*

RAY MILLER'S ORCHESTRA — Also was filled with top-flight musicians, among them Frankie Trumbauer and Miff Mole when this picture was taken in New York, 1923. — *Photo courtesy of Ward Archer.*

Not much later George Olsen followed Whiteman's example and also transferred to the East Coast. So, too, did another well-known Pacific Coast favorite, Abe Lyman, who had been one of Hickman's earliest successors on the Cocoanut Grove bandstand where he enjoyed great popularity and a long stay. Unlike the other two, Lyman would return to continue making Los Angeles the base of his operations.

Old-timers who first heard these West Coast groups when they invaded eastern territory recall that they brought with them a special musical bounce which was new to eastern audiences and was well received.

In his early days Whiteman called his orchestra "The Californians" and there followed a procession of leaders who temporarily used the same name. Included in this group were Abe Lyman, Max Fisher, and even Ben Pollack who came out from Chi-

cago to form a band in Los Angeles in 1925 for an extended run at the Venice Ballroom after which he took them back to the Midwest. The Pollack band included a couple of ambitious sidemen named Glenn Miller and Benny Goodman, both of whom had come to the Coast to join him.

Other orchestras identified themselves with names which also indicated California origin. "California's Own Sons" was the trademark used by Tom Gerun who was a product of the San Francisco-Bay Area. The background of the "California Ramblers" involves a conflict of information as to whether or not they came from that state. Some sources maintain that Arthur Hand organized them on the West Coast but took them immediately to New York via Atlantic City. Other stories indicate this band was put together in New York by Ed Kirkeby for a Brooklyn engagement, then turned over to Hand with the name of the group coming later when they moved into "The California Ramblers Inn" about 1924. There is no quarrel about the musicianship of the group which included at various times most of the top rated instrumentalists of the day.

The California Collegians became famous in a slightly different manner. Starting out in Laguna Beach in 1923 as a dance band, they soon developed novelty routines which launched them on the vaudeville circuit and took them into New York about 1926. Back on the Coast for an engagement a couple of years later, they signed up a handsome saxophonist by the name of Fred MacMurray who at the time was trying to crash into the movies. Joining the Collegians proved to be his big break. He returned to New York for a place in George White's Scandals followed by "Three's a Crowd" and "Roberta". The band continued as a top vaudeville attraction but the attention MacMurray received got him his first movie role.

Some of those who stayed on in California proved that tag lines of geographical nature were not necessary to success. Without one, Earl Burtnett was able to establish himself firmly at the Los Angeles Biltmore and Vincent Rose did equally well at the Montmarte Cafe. They did, however, take the name of the places where they played as did Herb Wiedoeft who finally took his "Cinderella Roof Orchestra" east with quite an imposing list of sidemen, including his saxophone playing brother, Rudy.

But California had no corner on all the talent to come out of the West. From the shadow of the Wasatch Mountains came a cornet player who would not only make a name for himself, but stay around a long time to enjoy it. Loring Nichols, soon to be better known as "Red" left his home town of Ogden, Utah, about 1921 to take his first dance band job in Piqua, Ohio, when he was a

PAUL SPECHT AND HIS ORCHESTRA — 1922 in New York. The band had a lot of great talent, including Arthur Schutt, Chauncey Morehouse, Don Lindley, and Russ Morgan. — *Photo courtesy of Russ Morgan.*

BEN BERNIE AND HIS ORCHESTRA — Taken in the mid-20s.

KAY KYSER branches out from the North Carolina Campus, 1926. — *Photo courtesy of Harry Thomas.*

JOYLAND CASINO
Lexington, Ky.
A. M. JAMES, Mgr.

Presents

Kay Kyser

And His

ORCHESTRA

FROM THE UNIVERSITY OF
NORTH CAROLINA

3—Weeks—3

Commencing

Monday, September 10th

DANCING NIGHTLY EXCEPT SUNDAYS

Admission 25c—Park Plan Dancing

MAL HALLETT AND HIS ORCHESTRA — The pride of the Boston area.

ROGER WOLFE KAHN — A popular orchestra leader in the New York area in the late 20s. — *Photo courtesy of Anson Weeks.*

JEAN GOLDKETTE'S ORCHESTRA
VICTOR RECORDING ARTISTS

The All-Star JEAN GOLDKETTE ORCHESTRA of 1926 included Joe Venuti, Don Murray, Tommy and Jimmy Dorsey, and Bix Beiderbecke, who did not show up for the picture date. — *Photo courtesy of Jean Goldkette.*

Immortal BIX BEIDERBECKE enjoys a laugh with Don Murray, left, and an unidentified friend.

young man of 17. Playing dance music was by no means a new experience for him. For years he had been playing week-end dances with his father's group, made up of the Nichols family and featuring Red on cornet. The fifty cents to a dollar per night which they each received for these dates gave little indication of what music would do for Red a few short years later.

He returned to Ogden for a brief visit after a few months with the Ohio band and made "top billing" appearances with a local orchestra. Then he was off to the East Coast to join "The Syncopating Five", winding up in Atlantic City in 1923 where they became known as the "Royal Palms Orchestra". Soon Johnny Johnson gave him a chance to head up his own band at New York's Pelham Heath Inn, and the famous "Five Pennies" were launched. The balance of the twenties saw Nichols alternately leading his own band and working as a sideman with such bands as the California Ramblers, Sam Lanin, Vincent Lopez, Ross Gorman, George Olsen, and Paul Whiteman. But few could equal his activity on records during this period for he was busy on as many as a dozen labels, gave his band an equal number of recording names and constantly used musicians on these sessions who would later make the labels a virtual "Who's Who" of music of that era.

While all this was taking place, I was a kid growing up on a farm in Southern Nebraska. In the Spring of 1925 the farm was sold and the family moved into town to pursue other occupations. One of the big events in our life about this time was the purchase of our first radio set. Under the guise of doing homework, I used to sit up until midnight to catch Coon-Sanders and the Kansas City Night Hawks beamed in from station WDAF and the Muehlbach Hotel.

A few miles away from our home town was an amusement park operated by the Senter Brothers and which, not very surprisingly, was called Senter Park. Long before I should have been allowed out so late, I used to sneak away to this amusement spot on dance nights. The attraction was not an interest in dancing, but rather the traveling bands which appeared there.

There were a lot of good territory bands working the area with regularity. Some of them are long-forgotten, but I well remember that out of Omaha there came a number of fine Negro bands, including Ted Adams, Hunter's Serenaders, Art Bronson, and slightly later Red Perkins who became the area's hottest attraction by the end of the twenties. All of these played Senter Park regularly and on one big occasion the Senter Brothers even brought in a well-known relative from Denver, Colorado, Boyd Senter and his orchestra. This was the band in which Glenn Miller got his start, although he had left it prior to this engagement. However, there was a popular territory band in that section of the country billed as "Glenn Miller and His Seven Aces" and who right then may have been better known than the other Glenn Miller the nation would later come to love.

From Senter Park we graduated to nearby Hastings where promoter Lib Phillips was bringing in a constant parade of bigger attractions. Most of the top white bands who came through Nebraska appeared at Phillips' dance spot. Up from Kansas City he occasionally brought in such great Negro bands as George E. Lee, Benny Moten, and Walter Page's Blue Devils. Fletcher Henderson, out of New York on a Midwestern tour, appeared there for a one-night stand with only a small percentage of his audience aware they were hearing one of the all-time greats. It was also here in the late twenties that we began to see dance posters graced with the trademark "Presented by M.C.A.". Few, if any of us, paid much attention at the time to what those three letters stood for, but we accepted it as an indication that any orchestra so identified was from the big time.

Meanwhile, another Midwestern farm boy who was to make his love for playing dance music a very profitable career had moved into town. At Strasburg, North Dakota, an accordion player named Lawrence Welk left the farm to form a dance band of six men, billing them as the "Biggest Little Band in America". Before long they had built up a wide following in the Dakotas, which was broadened when Station WNAX in Yankton began to feature their music sometime late in 1925. By 1928 they had become known well enough to try for bigger things and moved to Pittsburgh, Pennsylvania, from which point they worked the ballrooms throughout the East.

But every section of the country had its own territory favorites. Some of them gained acclaim on a wider scope, but many of them remained local operators. In order to stimulate sales of sheet music, publishers were in the habit of giving it a "local touch" by featuring pictures of these dance bands on copies distributed in their area of influence. For those not able to gain access to the limited radio facilities of the early and mid-twenties, or big enough to get on records, this sheet music coverage was most welcome and represented their only medium for publicity.

The State of Pennsylvania turned out a wealth of fine musicians who became famous, and was the starting place for a lot of great bands. Fred Waring, raised in his father's music store in Harrisburg doubtless did the most to publicize the state although he actually became well known in Detroit. Paul Specht did not start his first band there, but he did headquarter in the state for several years and used a lot of well-known Pennsylvania musicians. Ted Weem's first orchestra was organized in Philadelphia in 1923 although he soon moved on to Chicago attracted by a greater opportunity to get into radio.

Among the favorite sons the coal-mining section of Pennsylvania produced were Russ Morgan and the Dorsey boys, Jimmy and Tommy. The paths of these three would cross several times before they would become famous with their own individual organizations. The manner in which the Dorseys are listed here is in terms of their age sequence. In the years that followed, Tommy's success would always overshadow that of his good-natured older brother. They made their first attempt at having a band of their own in 1922 while they were still teen-aged kids, but after the job for which it had been organized folded, they gave up the venture. During the next several years they would show up as sidemen in most of the top bands of the period.

Usually it was Jimmy who joined up first, but he would soon find a place for brother Tommy. One of the hottest bands in the Pennsylvania area in the early twenties was the "Scranton Sirens" in and out of which moved a long list of all-stars. Jimmy signed on with them, but there was no place for Tommy at that point since the trombone chair was being held down by Russ Morgan. Somewhat later Morgan left and Tommy immediately came in to replace him.

ISHAM JONES AND HIS ORCHESTRA — Had become famous by the mid-20s. —*Photo courtesy of Chuck Brandon.*

Probably it was the strict discipline of the Dorseys' father and his insistence that they put in long hours of practice which developed the musical ability that in later years would earn for them the title of "The Fabulous Dorseys". It was something else, though, that in the early years earned for them from their fellow musicians the title of "The Battling Dorseys". A lot of stories are told about their continual disagreements which erupted into violence at the drop of a hat and one of these comes from Red Nichols with whom they worked in the California Ramblers shortly after leaving the Scranton Sirens.

Strangely enough, the argument on the night in question was over the same thing which would be credited with the breakup of the famous Dorsey Brothers Band in the mid-thirties. Following the completion of a number, Tommy, from the brass section in the rear protested to Jimmy seated directly in front of him as follows:

"Hey, big brother, weren't you playing that one a little too fast?"

Jimmy turned around and gave him an angry look as he said:

"Why don't you mind your own damned business and play that trombone?"

The band resumed playing and finished out the set. As they prepared for an intermission, Jimmy carefully placed his saxophone on his stand in front of him. Meanwhile, Tommy got up from his own chair, walked around to the front of the bandstand, and without a word laid Jimmy's saxophone on the floor where he proceeded to jump up and down on it. Two minutes later they were out behind the place pummelling one another all over the alley with the efforts of the entire band required to separate them.

When Russ Morgan left the Scranton Sirens, he joined up with the already famous Paul Specht orchestra, and stayed with that group for the next several years. From there he moved into the Jean Goldkette band in Detroit where he again spent a lot of time, leaving Goldkette to become musical director of a local radio station for a brief period before he returned to the band business as a sideman and arranger for Ted FioRito and other important leaders.

During the mid-twenties, the State of Florida had a real estate boom under way, and this created a sizable market for dance music, both directly and indirectly. Blue Steele was one of those who became quite famous as part of this, and the op-

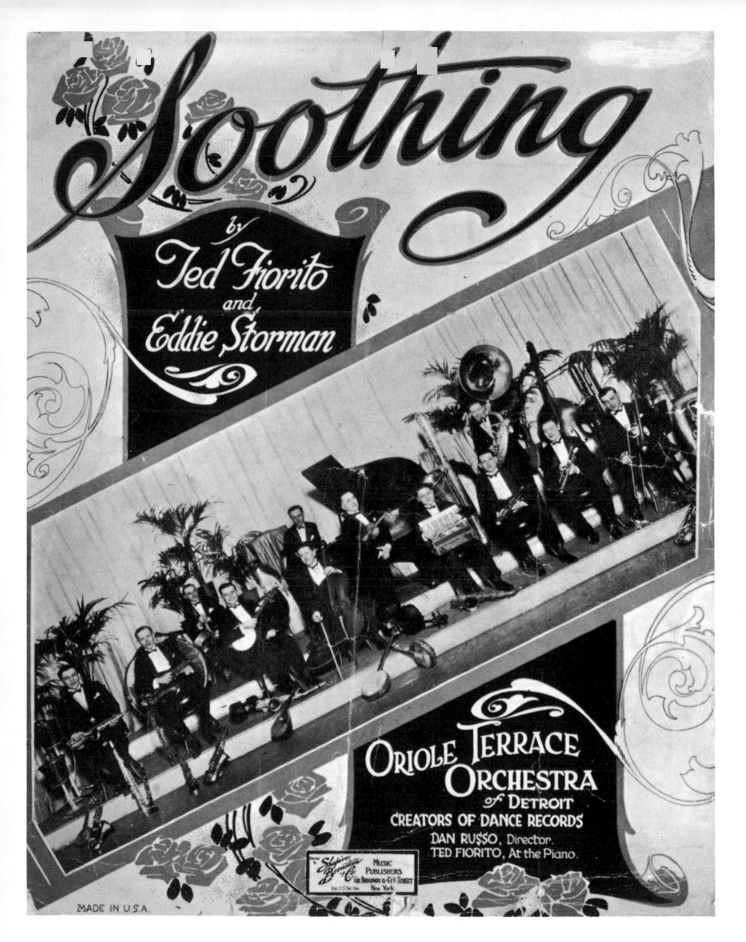

The Dan Russo-Ted FioRito Oriole Terrace Orchestra, featured on the sheet music of one of FioRito's compositions.

portunity which it gave him to be heard regularly on radio. The Garber-Davis band also cashed in on it, and spent an extended period of time in that area. Another popular musical organization with a strong southern following about that time was George McCullough and his "Georgians" who also participated in the Florida prosperity.

The many resort areas and amusement centers of the East Coast offered a ready market for dance orchestras. Atlantic City was the first stop for a great many bands before they invaded New York. This was the route taken by Paul Whiteman and most of the others who came in from the West Coast, with some of the Chicago and Detroit bands taking a similar path to Broadway. But bookings in that city were not limited to those just breaking into the big time. The Ray Miller band was already well known when it appeared there as the biggest attraction of the 1924 season, moving later in the year into New York's Hippodrome and then the Arcadia Ballroom. Miller's organization of thirteen men, in addition to himself, was larger than most white bands of that date, and included such stars as Frankie Trumbauer and Miff Mole. His first group had been a six piece combination called the "Black and White Melody Boys", and which had been featured in a New York musical production.

By the mid-twenties the band business in the New York area was flourishing with a multitude of dance locations and an equal number of top bands. Those who had been operating successfully when Hickman arrived in 1919 were still there and doing very well. However, they were now sharing the limelight with a lot of others who had become prominent.

Whiteman was already firmly entrenched in the New York scene and George Olsen was doing nearly as well. So, too, was Vincent Lopez who had given up studying for the priesthood in favor of a musical career about 1917 or 1918. Ben Bernie, after breaking up a vaudeville act with Phil Baker to become a bandleader in 1921, was a major contender and by making the most of his vaudeville experience would soon be one of the most popular "front" men in the business. Other popular New York leaders were Bert Lown, Emil Coleman, Freddie Rich, George Hall, and Roger Wolfe Kahn.

While most of these were in music for a livelihood, this was not necessarily the case with Roger Wolfe Kahn. He could afford to be in it as a hobby, since his father was Otto Kahn, millionaire

CHARLIE STRAIGHT — A big attraction in Chicago during the mid-20s. — *Photo courtesy of Karl Kramer.*

steel magnate and art collector. Roger put together his first band when he was 17 years of age. That he was not without musical talent is evidenced by the fact that he composed several tunes which were near hits and did the entire score for a Broadway musical.

However, money was not the major objective and some of the names in his band in the midtwenties and just a little later were from the ranks of New York's top sidemen. He was reputed to have formed one group of top-flight musicians, rehearsed them for six weeks on full pay, and then disbanded them without ever playing a single job.

He loved to play golf, but only if he could have a high-stake bet going on the outcome. Red Nichols and he were great friends and he used to entice Red onto the golf course with regularity, taking

26

him for a $100.00 wager each round. Red finally gave up trying to beat him and swore he was giving up the game forever.

Sometime later Red and his wife were moving across town to a new apartment. With everything in the front room ready to be picked up by the movers, Mrs. Nichols went into the back bedroom for a double check, where she discovered Red's golf clubs in the closet. Thinking he had forgotten them, she carried them out to be loaded onto the van.

A few minutes later she was in the back bedroom again and was somewhat startled to see a set of golf clubs leaning against the wall. While she was sure she had carried them out earlier, she proceeded to do so again.

Fifteen minutes later she made another trip to the bedroom closet and this time she refused to believe her own eyes. There against the closet wall she saw once again a complete set of golf clubs.

Leaving them there, she cornered Red in the front room and said:

"I must be losing my mind, I know I've carried your golf clubs out here twice, but they're still back there in that closet."

"Don't worry about a thing, honey, you're all right, but those golf clubs have cost me all the money they're going to. I've decided it's cheaper to leave them right here and I never want to see them again."

Washington, D.C. made its contribution to the business by providing a training ground for Duke Ellington. Born there about the turn of the century he began to study piano at the age of seven and worked with local dance groups while in high school. His first group was called "The Washingtonians" and it was with at least part of this original group that he moved into New York's Kentucky Club in 1923, and then to the Cotton Club in 1927 after a four-year run. Now he was able to

The BEN POLLACK ORCHESTRA included Benny Goodman and Glenn Miller when this picture was shot in Chicago, 1927. — *Photo courtesy of Gil Rodin.*

At left CHARLIE DOERNBERGER AND HIS ORCHESTRA — Million Dollar Pier, Atlantic City, 1927. Doernberger was a Whiteman graduate. — *Photo courtesy of Paul Weirick.*

Below, left, JAN GARBER — 1926. This 15-piece band was substantially larger than most other white bands in the mid-20s. — *Photo courtesy of Paul Weirick.*

At right, a youthful LOUIS ARMSTRONG, the exact date not known. — *Photo courtesy of Joe Rushton.*

compete for top honors with the Fletcher Henderson band which had been making a name for itself at the Roseland Ballroom since 1924 and Carroll Dickerson, who came into the Savoy Ballroom from Chicago about 1926.

Sedate Boston was not to be left out and had its own important names including Jimmy Gallagher and his Checker Inn orchestra. Better known, however, would become Mal Hallett and Leo Reisman. Hallett's starting date is not known, but he was well entrenched in the business by the early twenties. So, too, was Reisman, who had first tried his hand at having an orchestra when he was in grammar school. Hallett was one of the earliest to lean heavily on novelty numbers. Reisman throughout a long career would cater to the dancers and his group would later be described as a "society" band, even though during the late twenties he would be the author of a trade magazine column on jazz.

A lot of the early "names" first became prominent in Detroit. Fred Waring spent a lot of his early years there prior to the advent of his big "Pennsylvanians" band. Paul Specht adopted Detroit as headquarters about 1919, and there pioneered in dance band radio broadcasts. After these had made him famous he alternated his activity between that city and the New York-Philadelphia area, finally moving permanently into New York about 1925 or 1926. A European tour which was not too successful apparently dampened his interest in leading a band, and he gradually turned to operating a booking office. This finally ended in the complete breakup of the band which included at various times some great all-star musicians and such future leaders as Russ Morgan, Charlie Spivak, Orville Knapp and Artie Shaw.

Many of the Specht sidemen returned to Detroit to join up with Jean Goldkette, who had taken over the Graystone Ballroom and had become the city's top purveyor of dance music. Goldkette, who had come to the United States from France in 1910 while still a teenager, was really a concert pianist. But it was his ambition to have a dance band under his name and the success of his ballroom venture made this possible. He spared no expense to get the best men available and a long list of all-stars worked intermittently for him, several of whom he eventually put in front of bands billed as Jean Goldkette units in other Detroit locations.

His was a multiple-band operation in the pattern so well established by Meyer Davis in New York. But one particular unit was his real love, and the one which he liked to call "The Jean Goldkette Orchestra". At one time its line-up included both Tommy and Jimmy Dorsey, Joe Venuti, Don Murray, Frankie Trumbauer, and Bix Beiderbecke. Russ Morgan had also worked with this unit prior to Tommy Dorsey. Musically, it was one of the greatest organizations of the twenties and the only one which the highly rated Fletcher Henderson band considered its equal. With it, Goldkette invaded New York for an engagement at the Roseland Ballroom, where the New York musicians flocked to hear first-hand the orchestra whose reputation had preceded it. Soon after this, the group, still rated by many as the greatest band of all time, was broken up with most of its stars going to Whiteman. The heavy payroll had been so great that Goldkette was never able to break even on it, although many blamed the situation on poor management.

Goldkette pretty much let the band run itself, as he had so many things going at one time. He was kept busy managing the ballroom and booking the many other orchestras he was handling. These included McKinney's Cotton Pickers and the Orange Blossom Band, the latter emerging not long after as the Casa Loma Orchestra. At a time when it appeared that he had a virtual band empire put together, Goldkette suddenly disbanded the whole thing. Years later he explained this action to me as being the result of irritation over the problems of handling temperamental artists and the fact that he completely underestimated the success that was within his grasp.

Detroit also gave the Danny Russo-Ted FioRito orchestra its early fame at a place called the Oriole Terrace, which was an old theater converted into a nightclub. Prior to this engagement they had been enjoying mediocre success in Chicago under the name of the Oriole Orchestra, and landed the job of opening the Detroit Club because the owner had liked their style. From that time (about 1922) until they split up as co-leaders, they continued to be known as the Oriole Terrace Orchestra, although they had given up Detroit as a headquarters point and returned to Chicago.

Russo's fame never spread far beyond the Middle West but FioRito was destined for bigger things. By the mid-twenties he was already recognized as one of the country's most prolific song-writers. This kind of popularity coupled with a pleasing personality made it easy for him to find success as a bandleader when he went his own way to eventually enjoy a reputation as one of the country's top names.

Cleveland's contribution to the band business was quite substantial, although its development of big attractions may not have begun as early as some of the other cities. During the early twenties, one of its better known orchestras was Austin Wylie's which played at the Golden Pheasant for several years. It was also in Cleveland that Guy Lombardo began to enjoy a measure of success in the states and some years later it would be the starting place for Sammy Kaye. Kay Kyser was another who spent a great deal of time in that area, although his real starting point was North Carolina.

But the city of Chicago was the only one which could really compete with New York as a band building area, and there are many music people who rate it as having been the more important of the two. It moved into that position in the early twenties and maintained it well into the mid-thirties. Some of the bands it built were developed there, others were attracted from outside areas to adopt it as a headquarters city. By 1925, Chicago had a good share of these.

Jules Stein and Billy Goodheart had started a new venture in 1924 which would later be the world's largest band agency. In late 1925 they were able to announce to trade journals that under their M.C.A. banner successful tours had been completed by the bands of Ted Weems, Carl Fenton, Benny Krueger, and Isham Jones. By the end of the next year they had signed most of the important white Chicago bands, and this now included the Coon-Sanders orchestra which had moved in from Kansas City. It also included Wayne King who took over the Aragon Ballroom about 1927 and Charlie Straight who had a ten piece band playing a style which he later described as being the forerunner of "Swing".

Straight's activities in front of the band were apparently not as sensational as his music since most operators who booked him described him as a "dead-pan" and "lackadaisical" leader. Complaints constantly filtered back to M.C.A. on this score until one night when they booked him for a private function given by a wealthy society matron. The next day she phoned the office to tell them how pleased she had been with the band,

and particularly with Straight himself, who was described as the most animated leader she had seen, constantly moving around the bandstand to inspire the best from his men. Words of praise were passed along to Straight by an M.C.A. official who could not resist asking this question:

"What was there about this society date that had you so excited, Charlie?"

Straight's reply bowled the agent over:

"To tell you the truth, I was wearing a new pair of shoes, and they were so damned tight I just couldn't stand still."

The Benson Orchestra was very popular around Chicago at that time and another big favorite was Don Bestor. Benny Meroff was already well known, and Paul Asche was a leading attraction in the theaters. Art Kassell was at the Midway Gardens where he had formed his first band in 1924. The Russo-FioRito Orchestra had returned to Chicago from Detroit and it was their band which opened the Aragon Ballroom for the first time in 1926. Ben Pollack had migrated back to his hometown from the West Coast for engagements at the Blackhawk Restaurant and the Southmore Hotel in 1927, but then moved on to New York in 1928.

Lombardo arrived on the Chicago scene towards the end of 1927, having signed up with M.C.A., who prevailed upon Al Quodbach to book the still relatively unknown "Royal Canadians" into his Granada Cafe. Here they eventually hit pay dirt although it was not much in evidence during their first month or so.

Finally, in order to compete with the Blackhawk Restaurant where the Coon-Sanders Band was aired nightly, a radio wire was put into the Granada. During the next two years, both the Cafe and Lombardo were made famous. In late 1929, Lombardo gave in to repeated offers from the Hotel Roosevelt Grill in New York and began the music business' longest engagement. He was replaced at the Granada by Paul Whiteman.

At the time he went to New York, Lombardo's tag line "The Sweetest Music This Side of Heaven" was known from Coast to Coast. It was almost a foregone conclusion that someone would have a little fun with a billing of that type and they did. The Benny Moten Band working out of Kansas City took the opposite stand and began billing itself as "The Hottest Band This Side of Hades".

Lombardo's home had originally been Ontario, Canada, and not long after he left there another musical group from the same area made a similar move. This was the orchestra of Freddie Large who in addition to being a friend of the Lombardo family played a fairly identical style of music. Large and his boys were having some difficulty getting under way in the States, but luckily about the time the going got really tough they ran into Jan Garber. At the time, Jan was still associated with Milton Davis and the Garber-Davis band was headquartering in Atlanta. Although they had been a big attraction in the South, Garber was anxious to dissolve the partnership and form a new band in the Midwest. He worked out a deal with Large, taking over his band intact, and was soon a strong competitor in the Chicago area where he eventually became a national attraction.

Although many of them may have originated elsewhere, there were probably more Negro bands steadily employed around Chicago during the span of the twenties than in any other American city. Among the earliest to establish themselves firmly were Charles Elgar and King Oliver, both of whom billed themselves at various times as "The Creole Jazz Band". Carroll Dickerson was well known by 1924, as were Jimmy Wade's Syncopators in which organization Eddie South was featured on violin. Others included Doc Cooke and his Doctors of Syncopation, Erskine Tate, "The Alabamians" out of which group came Cab Calloway to front "The Missourians", and Earle (Fatha) Hines was leading his own band at the Grand Terrace by 1928. It was also in Chicago about 1927 that Louis Armstrong had the first band under his own name, playing for awhile at the Sunset Cafe.

Although some of these were small groups originally, many of the Negro bands of this period were substantially larger in personnel than the average white orchestra.

The potency of Chicago grew steadily in the last half of the twenties. Doubtless the beginning of Music Corporation of America in that city was a strong factor in attracting bands to the area and contributed to the build-up which they received there. Prior to this time, a great number of the leaders of importance had really been small booking offices themselves, with multiple units working under their names.

The Edgar Benson Agency had been the most active forerunner to M.C.A. in the Chicago area. Both Paul Specht and Goldkette had operated in this manner in Detroit, and Specht later moved into New York to open an office there. In that city, the practice was even more prevalent with Meyer

Davis, George Olsen, Ben Bernie, Harry Yerkes and Vincent Lopez all having several groups working simultaneously around the city.

Old-timers tell about seeing Rudy Vallee with saxophone under his arm making the rounds of these offices seeking work in 1927. Vallee himself enlarges this story to tell how in some cases he also carried his small portable phonograph to play some recordings made in England where he had worked during 1924 and 1925.

But Vallee didn't go on looking for work very long. In January of 1928 he formed an orchestra of his own, named them the "Connecticut Yankees", and booked them into the "Heigh Ho Club" on East 53rd Street. Soon with the help of orchestra leader Bert Lown he convinced Station WABC that they should pick up his music from the Club. His style caught on quickly and although he did not have the biggest band around he soon became the music world's biggest attraction. His popularity resulted in America's first demonstration of mass hysteria over a personality, a phenomenon to be repeated intermittently in later years with other stars of radio, records and television.

Years later, reviewing his long career in retrospect, Rudy made it clear he considered himself to have been a radio personality rather than a bandleader. This was certainly true, for the band behind him became a backdrop as his popularity increased. But it was as a bandleader that he got his start and few would deny that he made a worthwhile contribution to the business. Along with his idol, Rudy Wiedoeft, he did a great deal to advance the popularity of the saxophone.

It was also his success which did much to make vocalists an accepted and necessary feature of the dance orchestra, and his ingenuity which made their work easier. Sound systems for public address had not yet come into usage except in a few locations so it was necessary to depend on a megaphone for any voice amplification. Vallee developed one of his own, a special wide bell type which gave the voice greatly improved volume. The effect which he obtained with it was so impressive that he put it on the market for use by other singers who were quick to recognize its advantages and buy it. A good number of the contemporary male vocalists not only adopted the megaphone he had designed, but did their best to imitate his singing style.

Vallee very quickly became a controversial figure, with the public dividing itself into one group

which professed to hate him and the other which idolized him. Few of either actually knew him. Doubtless a great percentage of the "anti-Vallee" factions were expressing the jealousies so often felt for one who attains outstanding success. None could have been further wrong than those who disparaged his rapid climb into the spotlight and labelled it a lucky accident.

Few people in any phase of show business ever had Vallee's ability to appraise his own talents, or for that matter, his own limitations. Timing may have given him an assist, but only in a minor way. Little that developed was not the result of his careful planning, strong determination, and the recognition of opportunities when they presented themselves.

One of the controversies which developed involved Rudy and Will Osborne, and soon had the public, at least in the New York area, lining up on one side or the other. The newspapers had a field day. An awful lot of people suspected that the whole thing might be a well-contrived publicity stunt, but in his book "My Time Is Your Time" published in 1962, Rudy makes reference to it, insisting that if it was for publicity he had no part in arranging it, and that Osborne probably benefited from it much more than Vallee. By the time Rudy's book was released, the mild mannered and likeable Osborne had retired from bandleading

At left RUDY VALLEE who became one of the nation's first radio personalities. — *Photo courtesy of Rudy Vallee.*

Above, Vallee's CONNECTICUT YANKEES just before their Heigh-Ho Club engagement catapulted them to success. — *Photo courtesy of Rudy Vallee.*

At right, VALLEE and his famous megaphone — *Courtesy Rudy Vallee.*

BERT LOWN — Popular New York leader who played a big part in Vallee's success. — *Photo courtesy of Red Nichols.*

and was entertainment director for Harvey's Nightclub at Lake Tahoe. When queried on the subject, he merely smiled and said "No comment".

The incident occurred in 1929 when Vallee took his then sensational Connecticut Yankees to the West Coast to make his first movie. Osborne's band, with Vallee's full approval, was brought into the Club where the "Connecticut Yankees" had been playing, to fill in until the picture commitment was taken care of. The assignment also included doing a commercial radio show from the spot for Herbert's Blue-White Diamonds.

Instrumentally, Will Osborne was a drummer, but although not much has been made of it previously, he was also a vocalist. Coincidentally or otherwise, his singing style also closely resembled Vallee's and with access to almost unlimited air time he began to get a lot of recognition. Newspapers, knowing a good thing when they had it, soon began to pose the question of which one was imitating the other and which had really been the first crooner. Vallee had a clear title to this dis-

tinction, although Osborne was the first to be a bandleader, having started in 1924 in a small New York club. Prior to the Vallee hassle, he was quite popular in the New York area, but now became known Coast to Coast. The feud eventually wore itself out and was forgotten by the public, if not by the participants.

As the dance band business became more firmly established, the size of units grew larger than those of the early twenties when five piece bands were common and prevalent. Although it was with this size group that a great many of them started, they added men as they became more successful until nine or ten men became average for the bigger names by about 1925.

A majority of the bands of that early period used no arrangements of any kind, but instead memorized the sheet music. Paul Whiteman is generally credited with being the first white leader to use completely arranged orchestrations to fit the instrumentation of his band and Fletcher Henderson was the pioneer Negro leader in the use of

RUDY WIEDOEFT — One of the best-known saxophonists of the '20s. — *Photo courtesy of Anson Weeks.*

Announcing Rudy **Wiedoeft** MODEL Holton Saxophones

THE world's greatest saxophones, designed in collaboration with Rudy Wiedoeft, the world's premier saxophonist. Built by Frank Holton & Company, Elkhorn, Wis.

DICK LUCKIE'S ORCHESTRA — About 1925 or 1926. A good example of the part costumes played during that period. Headquarters, Chicago. — *Photo courtesy of Elmer Eberhardt.*

written parts. The effects thus obtained soon caused the rest to follow suit, eventually making the arranger one of the most important members of the orchestra. Most of Whiteman's arrangements were the work of <u>Ferde Grofé</u> while Henderson did his own.

A surprising number of the well-known leaders of the twenties could not read music themselves. This created no particular difficulty as long as they stuck to dance engagements, but soon after the middle of the decade theaters began to use bands as stage attractions. The bill on these programs always included other acts who had special music for their accompaniment which left little margin for error. Playing these shows developed some complicated and amusing situations for the leader who did not know what those spots on the arrangement in front of him meant.

The truth of the matter was that a great many of these leaders were simply "front men" who did not really direct the band but merely beat time to it. The trick was to surround themselves with capable musicians who could play simultaneously in tempo, regardless of what the leader did. Quite often the attempt to outguess what the maestro's signals meant resulted in a difference of opinion as to when they were ready to start a number or how long the final note was to be held.

One very famous leader was notorious for his inability to give a recognizable downbeat to get the band under way. Because of his popularity he was in demand as a stage attraction and loved to introduce the numbers on the program. Unfortunately, he never did it twice in the same way. One night as he was in the middle of such an announcement, he glanced down at the lapel of his tuxedo and discovered some dust had settled there. Being a neat individual he made a quick pass at it with his right hand, intending to brush it off. The band mistaking this gesture for the downbeat, began playing, cutting him off in the middle of telling the audience what they were about to hear.

As ten men became the size of the average group, the instrumentation used also became fairly

Art Landry and his Call of the North Woods Orchestra. — *Photo courtesy of Dr. Keith Bryant.*

Al Katz and His Kittens — Million Dollar Pier, 1926. — *Photo courtesy of Al Katz.*

standard. It was usually three saxophones, two trumpets, one trombone, a piano, drums, bass, and a banjo. The banjo was king as a rhythm instrument, with very few using the guitar until the end of the twenties. The tuba was used almost exclusively as a bass instrument and it was not until later that the string bass took its place. Violins began to disappear from most bands, with the exception of the larger groups, although many of the leaders were violinists themselves.

The saxophone had now become one of the most important instruments in the dance orchestra. However, this was not accomplished without a struggle, as was indicated by some of the humor of the period, with even some of the manufacturers who made the instrument having their share of fun out of it. The following bit of humor was contributed by the Selmer Instrument Company's publication "Wit and Halfwit" in the fall of 1927:

"A musician approached a banker for a donation of $5.00 to help bury a deceased saxophone player.

"The banker replied, 'Here's $25.00. Why don't we bury five of them?' "

Even the Boston *Post* could not refrain from getting into the act with this little gem:

"The only music typically American is that made by the mockingbird, the saxophone and the cash register."

It was common practice for the bands of that era to adopt the use of "gimmicks" of all sorts to attract popular attention, but these did very little to enhance the quality of the musical product. Funny costumes were the order of the day. As aviation increased in popularity its influence was clearly noticeable in some of the band uniforms. I recall one Midwestern group who wore white flying coveralls and pilot helmets, and at least two more who were outfitted in flight jackets and field officers' boots. Ted Lewis was a great one for decking his men out in clown suits and the first Ray Miller orchestra was similarly attired.

As early as 1924, a novelty band billed as "Hen Youngman and His Original Swanee Syncopators" played the popular boardwalk spots at Coney Island. The group consisted of a violin, drums, piano, saxophone, trombone, cornet, and a vocalist. They featured singing, dancing, and comedy routines and soon became an East Coast sensation. Later Youngman became one of the country's top vaudeville comedians.

The name of Youngman's group was typical of those used by many musical organizations all through the twenties. Some of them indicated the locale from which they originated, others gave some clue to their style, and some added little beyond a catchy sound. For awhile, Lawrence Welk identified his group as the "Hotsy Totsy Orchestra", and Art Landry's was the "Call of the North Orchestra". There was a "Dok Eisenbourg and his Sinfonians", and it was only natural that Al Katzenberger would bill himself as "Al Katz and His Kittens". There was also a "Cliff Jackson and His Krazy Kats", and from out of the South came the "Atlanta Footwarmers".

The ballroom operators, to stimulate interest in the spot and also the bands who appeared there, introduced all sorts of promotional ideas. One of those quite prevalent was the booking of two dance bands on a single evening and then billing the occasion as a battle dance. The bands either alternated on the stand or in the case of the larger spots, two bandstands were provided, one at either end of the dance floor. Constant music was maintained with each band taking a half hour on and a half hour off. Some of these developed into real contests, with the band receiving the most applause and acclaim from the dancers being declared the winner although just what they were the winner of was not always clear. This type of promotion reached its zenith during the last half of the 1920s. Practically every prominent band participated at one time or another, but some of the most lively contests featured Fletcher Henderson, McKinney's Cotton Pickers, and the great Negro bands of the Chicago area.

For the band struggling to make a name for itself, there were many obstacles to overcome. In the early days of the business it was quite difficult for any leader to enjoy a reputation extending beyond the locality in which he started and the result was that there were many so-called "territory bands". Many factors contributed to this situation, communication perhaps being the greatest, since in general it was very poor. Radio in the early twenties was still in its infancy and the networks had not yet been formed. The problems of group travel were enormous and it was a long way from one coast to the other. The highways of the day were not conducive to long distance travel, nor were the automobiles equal to it. As the practice of "one-nighters" grew, many leaders found it impossible to keep engagements as close as 150 miles apart when bad weather made the dirt roads impassable or their transportation broke down.

As the strength of the unions developed, individual locals established regulations aimed at discouraging traveling bands from invading their territory. For years, agencies booking outside organizations into Chicago could not get permission to do so unless they simultaneously arranged an out-of-town tour or location for a Chicago band. In Detroit, the situation was even rougher, with a few instances of physical violence inflicted on outsiders attempting to move in. Eventually these problems worked themselves out as it became apparent the business could not expand under such restrictions.

But sticking to the big cities to avoid adverse travel conditions was no guarantee of job security, especially for the smaller groups. This was the era of the "Noble Experiment" when prohibition, dating from mid-1920, supposedly made it impossible to buy a drink with alcoholic content. Yet speakeasies were everywhere and on these the smaller musical groups depended for employment. Raids came with unpredictable regularity and it was not uncommon for the place where a group had been working one night to be padlocked by the authorities when they showed up the following evening.

Most frequently raids on these places would be made while they were in operation, and while the evening's work for the band was in progress. Depending on the size of the place, it was not always easy for the enforcement officers to identify the operator of the establishment, so consequently everyone present was considered a suspect. If at all possible, the musicians beat a hasty retreat, often being forced to leave their instruments behind.

When there was no access to an exit not blocked by the law, other methods of avoiding arrest were attempted. If not on the bandstand at the time, they got there as quickly as possible in the hope that this would establish the obvious fact that they were simply employed by the management. Usually, however, they were still subjected to complete grilling before they were permitted to go free.

No doubt there was justification for this since it often developed that the band had more members during the raid than it had a few minutes earlier. Among the often repeated stories of speakeasy operators in the New York area is one about

The great FLETCHER HENDERSON — Late 1920s. — *Photo courtesy of Red Nichols.*

a character known as Max the Waiter, who periodically operated a place on Fifty-first Street. One night when it was raided, Max jumped on the bandstand with the musicians and grabbed a clarinet, the only thing not already in the possession of someone else. The agents handling the raid apparently were not so easily fooled for they asked each member of the band to identify himself and the instrument he played. This might have been all right had not one of them decided he would like to hear them each play a solo. When it came time for Max to take his turn, he could produce nothing but a hideous squawk and was soon on his way out of the place wearing handcuffs.

But the effect of prohibition on the music business took even more sinister form. As the underworld became better organized for rum-running and bootlegging, it was not content simply to be the supplier. It operated many of the top nightclubs in all of the major Midwestern cities and New York.

To attract thirsty customers, members of the underworld wanted the best talent available. Not only did they want it, but they had the money to buy it. On the face of it, this would seem to add up to an ideal situation, but many leaders discov-

38

At right, RED NICHOLS and GLENN MILLER, Mrs. Nichols and Mrs. Miller at a New Jersey amusement park, 1929. — *Photo courtesy of Red Nichols.*

Below, LEO REISMAN — Egyptian Room, Hotel Brunswick, Boston, Mass., in the late 1920s. — *Photo courtesy of Leo Reisman.*

ered it wasn't necessarily that way, and often it was the biggest names who encountered the most difficulty.

Whoever said "Nothing succeeds like success" was apparently never faced with attempting to terminate a successful engagement in a club owned by a top gangster. The period covered by the initial contract often turned out to mean nothing at all. When the time came to move on to the next location, the word might come down from the top that they were being "held over" indefinitely. Usually no negotiations regarding financial return were involved, but instead they were reminded that a displeased underworld lord sometimes expressed his unhappiness in an unorthodox fashion.

A great many stories are told of such incidents. One involves a leader who became a top attraction during the twenties and who still is as this is written, but who has asked to be left nameless here. At the time of his brush with the underworld he had been playing in one of Capone's Chicago clubs for a couple of years, but wanted to move out to take a New York engagement. When the time came to make the move he was given the word that he was staying on, and stay on he did, month after month. Finally, in desperation, he decided on a maneuver whereby his regular musicians moved out one at a time, replaced by new faces. Eventually he was fronting an entirely new band and one night, he too failed to show up for work. He reassembled his band in New York and opened there, but it was a long time before he ventured out alone without a bodyguard.

Before Capone attained success in his own right in his chosen profession, he took some of his basic training as a bouncer in a New York spot, the Harvard Club. One of Red Nichols' favorite stories involves his good friend, Miff Mole, and an incident which occurred when Miff was playing trombone with the Memphis Five at this club. Capone, it seems, didn't particularly care for trombone music and was not bashful about saying so. One night when Miff returned to the bandstand after an intermission, he found a neat bullet hole in the bell of his trombone. No one was talking, but the consensus was that Capone had taken this means of making his opinion known.

THE TED WEEMS ORCHESTRA — Chicago, 1929. — *Photo courtesy of Joe Rushton.*

Above, GUY LOMBARDO AND HIS ROYAL CANADIANS — 1929. — *Photo courtesy of Guy Lombardo.*

At left, handsome bandleader BUDDY ROGERS chats with West Coast leader Jess Stafford, 1929. — *Photo courtesy of Bill Stafford.*

However, not all of the music critics of the twenties expressed themselves quite this emphatically. Some of the short reviews given dance bands of the day were literary gems in terms of the description given the band's style and activities. In the November, 1926 issue of a magazine called *Melody* the following items appeared in the Chicago news section:

"Elmer Kaiser and his Radio Melody Masters have in their capable hands, terpsichorean destiny of the Riverview Park Ballroom."

"The peregrinations of Al Short and his boys have surely made nomads, figuratively speaking, of Chicago audiences, much to their delight and appreciation. They are currently appearing at the Capital."

"Benny Meroff and his band of twenty-five pepsters recently opened the costly Mark Brothers' Granada Theater on the North Side. Meroff is an overnight success in his line and the talk of the town."

The issue of *Melody* which included the foregoing reviews also included another very interesting news story. This announced a new dance sensation called "The Gigolo", instructed the reader to pronounce it "Jeeg-o-lo", and identified it as a recent importation from Paris. It went on to say that this new dance, along with the "Black Bottom", "Valencia", and some others were being hailed as the successors to the "Charleston". The story let it be known that in France the word "Gigolo" was a word to describe "dancing man who leases his service as a dancer to the highest bidder". It concluded with the comment that while the dance might catch on in America, the profession

HAL KEMP AND HIS ORCHESTRA — 1929. Note John Scott Trotter, Skinnay Ennis, Saxie Dowell. — *Courtesy of Coliseum Ballroom, Davenport, Iowa.*

for which it would be named would never appeal to the American male.

The ten year period which ended on New Year's Eve, 1929, is usually referred to under one of two titles, "The Roaring Twenties", or "The Jazz Age". But, the word jazz during this period held a somewhat different meaning for the general public than in later years. This very broad line between "Jazz" and "Commercial" had not yet been drawn. Music magazines published during the twenties and still available, indicate quite clearly that every group which played popular dance music described itself as a jazz band and was so accepted.

Once again, *Melody* is the source of an example. Some of the country's more staunch and staid citizens did not look too favorably upon this dance music which people called jazz, and publicly expressed their dislike. Among them was Henry Ford, who in 1927 was widely quoted as having a very low opinion of jazz music, feeling that it contributed to the delinquency of the younger generation. In the issue of *Melody* referred to, he was taken to task at some length by Leo Reisman who stated that as one of the country's better known jazz bandleaders himself, he simply could not keep silent on the subject. He suggested to Mr. Ford that jazz music was no more an influence for immorality than was the automobile which Ford was producing. He went on to suggest that anyone who doubted this should take a few nighttime trips down some of the country's lovers' lanes and then try to estimate how many Ford automobiles were similarly parked in the darkness of back roads all over the United States on any given evening.

The jazz critics of a few short years later would not have permitted the Reisman musical style to wear the label of "jazz band", but in 1927 the era of the super-critic had not yet arrived. The bandleader looked out from his bandstand and saw an audience which came there not to criticize but to have a good time, and regardless of his musical style he might well have some of the future jazz greats in the band behind him. During the course of the evening, these artists played dance music to fit the mood of the crowd and as the leader wanted it played. Playing strictly for their own amusement was reserved for the after-hour jam sessions.

Ted Lewis, who would later be classed as one of the most commercial leaders in the business, employed a long list of musical greats. Several of them also got their early starts with the Jan Garber-Milton Davis Band, and some still-available reviews of this orchestra during its years in the South indicated it was rated one of the area's best white jazz bands. Equally well stocked with talent was Art Kassel's first orchestra in which Benny Goodman worked briefly and which included Bud Freeman and Muggsy Spanier. Goodman also spent some time with Ted Lewis. However, it might be worth noting that if Goodman actually worked with all the leaders who made such a claim in later years, he must have been the busiest sideman in existence.

The twenties, like the years which followed, had its share of organizations described as "a musician's band". To many, the Ben Bernie Orchestra of the late twenties deserved this title, and it was also given to Isham Jones. Slightly earlier, Ray Miller's Orchestra was rated by fellow musicians as one of the greatest, and the California Ramblers were consistently considered deserving of a place in the same league.

During the span of the decade, four white bands stand out above the rest as having supplied the training ground for those who would be the big name leaders of the future. It was Paul Specht who had the strongest line-up during the early years. A little later it became Jean Goldkette, Ben Pollack, and Paul Whiteman. Migration from one to the other had no consistent pattern except that most of the musicians eventually ended up with Whiteman. Pollack is generally credited with discovering most of them, and the best talent from all four took time out along the line to record with Red Nichols and one of his many all-star groups.

During the same period, there were an equal number of Negro bands who played their part in shaping future trends, as well as participating in the current picture. Perhaps there were even more, although many of those popular in the twenties did not survive into the thirties, at least not under the same name. Ellington was a sensation by the end of the twenties, but few would deny that Fletcher Henderson was the most dominant Negro leader of the decade, and the one who left his mark most indelibly written. At one time or another, most of the future big Negro names. had been regularly employed by him. But this was not his biggest contribution. He was well ahead of his day in the use of original arrangements and the style which he called "Big Band Jazz" was to show

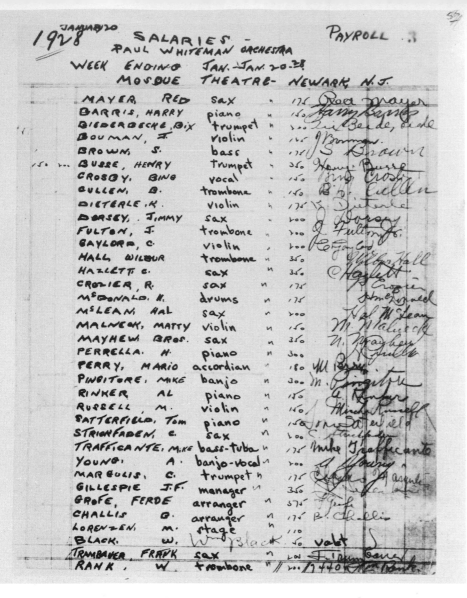

MAYER, RED	sax	"	175
BARRIS, HARRY	piano	"	150
BIEDERBECKE, BIX	trumpet	"	300
BOUMAN, J.	violin	"	145
BROWN, S.	bass	"	175
BUSSE, HENRY	trumpet	"	350
CROSBY, BING	vocal	"	150
CULLEN, B.	trombone	"	150
DIETERLE, K.	violin	"	175
DORSEY, JIMMY	sax	"	300
FULTON, J.	trombone	"	300
GAYLORD, C.	violin	"	300
HALL, WILBUR	trombone	"	350
HAZLETT, C.	sax	"	350
CROZIER, R.	sax	"	175
McDONALD, H.	drums	"	175
McLEAN, HAL	sax	"	300
MALNECK, MATTY	violin	"	150
MAYHEW BROS.	sax	"	350
PERRELLA, H.	piano	"	300
PERRY, MARIO	accordian	"	180
PINGITORE, MIKE	banjo	"	300
RINKER, AL	piano	"	150
RUSSELL, M.	violin	"	150
SATTERFIELD, TOM	piano	"	150
STRICKFADEN, C.	sax	"	300
TRAFFICANTE, MIKE	bass-tuba	"	175
YOUNG, A.	banjo-vocal	"	300
MARGULIS, C.	trumpet	"	175
GILLESPIE, J.F.	manager	"	350
GROFE, FERDE	arranger	"	375
CHALLIS, B.	arranger	"	175
LORENZEN, M.	stage	"	110
BLACK, W.			50 valet
TRUMBAUER, FRANK	sax	"	300
RANK, W.	trombone	"	300

At right, VARIETY cover features Whiteman band at beginning of 1928. — *Photo courtesy of Variety.*

At left, this reproduction of Whiteman's payroll in January, 1928, clearly indicates how well he took care of his employees. — *Photo courtesy of Bob Archer, Wall Street Journal.*

up as the basis for the style of the powerhouse "swing bands" of the thirties.

Without question, however, the most dominant leader of the period was Paul Whiteman, and America acknowledged this fact by giving him the title of "The King of Jazz". Writers of a later date might challenge the right of his music to wear the jazz label, but they could not minimize the position he occupied at the end of the twenties. He had become a national institution and even the toast of the European continent.

Numerically, his was by now the biggest organization in the business. Featured on *Variety's* cover for the January 4, 1928 issue with individual photos of the members, the total was 34 of the top talents in the musical world, including "The Rhythm Boys" made up of Bing Crosby, Harry Barris, and Al Rinker. Not only was this the biggest band in existence, but also the best paid. Whiteman made money for himself and all those who associated with him, and it was his influence on the industry which set the pattern for the upgrading of the salaries of all musicians.

An aggregation of this size needed special facilities for proper presentation, and so the late twenties found Whiteman, who had started out in the dance field, moving towards concentration on concert and stage appearances.

Regardless of its brand of humor and just how its music should best be described, this was a fabulous era. Call it the "Roaring Twenties" or the "Jazz Age" or any other title which seems more descriptive, but it still remains the period during which those people who were in it laid the firm foundation that later was to build the dance band business into one of the largest forms of live American entertainment.

22ND ANNIVERSARY NUMBER

VARIETY

PRICE
25
CENTS

Published Weekly at 154 West 46th St., New York, N. Y., by Variety, Inc. Annual subscription, $10. Single copies, 25 cents.
Entered as second class matter December 22, 1905, at the Post Office at New York, N. Y., under the act of March 3, 1879.

VOL. LXXXIX   **NEW YORK CITY, WEDNESDAY, JANUARY 4, 1928**   NO. 12

HARRY BARRIS   BIX BEIDERBECKE   JOHN BOUMAN   BOYCE CULLEN   RUBE CROZIER   KURT DIETERLE   TOM DORSEY

JAMES DORSEY   JOHN FULTON   CHARLES GAYLORD   WILBUR HALL   CHESTER HAZLETT   HAL McLEAN   MATT MALNECK

ROBERT MAYHEW   BING CROSBY   MICHAEL PINGITORE   HENRY BUSSE   HAROLD McDONALD   JACK MAYHEW   NYE MAYHEW

HARRY PERRELLA   MARIO PERRY   AL RINKER   FERDIE GROFE   MISCHA RUSSELL   TOM SATTERFIELD   CHARLES RICKFADEN

FRANK TRUMBAUER   AUSTIN YOUNG   BILL CHALLIS   STEVE BROWN

MICHAEL TRAFFICANTE   CHARLES MARGULIS

HAPPY NEW YEAR
TO YOU

AND THIRTY-FOUR REASONS
WHY IT SHOULD BE A
HAPPY NEW YEAR FOR ME

AND HIS
GREATER ORCHESTRA

FRED WARING'S ORCHESTRA — In the early 1930s. Vocal group is the famous Lane Sisters. — *Photo courtesy of Muzzy Marcellino.*

After the Depression Came Prosperity

THE BAND BUSINESS would really come into its own during the ten year span which made up the thirties. Its maturity would bring prosperity to many who had been on the verge of attaining it during the twenties and who would now share it with the twenties' top names who were still actively enjoying it.

But the strong upward surge of the decade would really come from the impetus given by young new leaders who, compared to their predecessors, could be called a new breed.

The majority of the new bandleaders who would gain prominence during the thirties differed in that they were accomplished and sometimes great instrumentalists rather than just "front men". These were the featured and talented sidemen who worked for the big names of the previous decade. There would be exceptions, of course, including the phenomenal success of Kay Kyser. Even such sports figures as Buddy Baer tried their hand at fronting dance orchestras.

If the 1930s were to be the Golden Age of the dance bands, there was little evidence of it as the period started. The country was just entering the Big Depression which would grow much worse before it would get better.

Like all other segments of the nation's business, the entertainment industry was hard-hit. The band business was no exception and it affected different units in various ways. To some bands that had been growing in size, it meant once more reducing personnel to six or seven men. In this manner they were able to keep going, but their hardships were many.

Guarantees for engagements were progressively reduced or completely eliminated. In many cases when given, they meant very little, for if the evening were not a financial success the promoter simply couldn't pay off. A great many of the bands, particularly local territory groups, faced up to reality by operating without asking guarantees, but taking instead 70% of the evening's gate receipts.

The Andy Kirk Band, working out of Kansas City, is said to have taken engagements up to 100 miles away for a guarantee for his whole band, including transportation, as low as $50.00 per evening. Yet Kirk at that time was already developing into quite a Midwestern name. If bands of this caliber were forced to accept guarantees so low in order to keep busy, it does not take much imagination to surmise that lesser names were offered even less inducement, as was definitely the case.

My own memory of that period includes some time spent playing with a small band of eight, sometimes nine, men in central Nebraska. The leader of the outfit was a drummer named Lloyd Heinz, who had worked with several well-known orchestras along the East Coast. Because of his last name someone had affectionately nicknamed him "Pickle" Heinz, and it was only one step further for jokesters to speak of the band as "Pickle Heinz and his All-Pickled Orchestra". Needless to say, there were some occasions when the title could not be disputed.

To say that our guarantees were less than 50 dollars would be gross understatement. Guarantees indeed! We had trouble getting 50% of a sometimes fast count box office take. A top admission price would be fifty or seventy-five cents, and this was the rare occasion; in most instances the charge was twenty-five cents for a whole evening's dancing. The all-time low came one stormy Saturday night in northern Kansas when we drove ninety miles to the job, played four hours, and split up the pay-off at ninety cents each for the evening's work after expenses were deducted.

Not all of the jobs were quite that bad, however, and there was seldom one that didn't have its compensations in laughs. Musically, we were doubtless a long way from great, but we usually received enough response from the crowd to make us feel that we earned our money. Consequently, none of us were prepared for the surprise we got one night in a western Nebraska town when a brick came crashing through the window onto the bandstand, bounced once, and went through the head of the bass drum. We never got to meet the party who hurled it, but if it was intended as an expression of criticism, the point was clearly made.

More hospitable were the citizens of our home town when we occasionally played there. During one such event the banjo player's wife was sitting proudly on the bandstand beside him enjoying any reflected glory which might exist. Meanwhile, he had been fortifying himself with an occasional drink and had a pint flask of wine in his inside coat pocket. Just as we finished a lively fox trot, and the applause gave way to silence, the cork from his flask let go with a loud report, and after propelling itself some twenty feet into the air, landed in the middle of the floor in front of the bandstand.

Midnight to dawn dances were quite popular in the Middle West at that time, particularly on the eve of a holiday. One July 4th we had such a date in a town in central Kansas. It was a hot muggy night and everyone was celebrating but the band, a situation which hardly seemed fair to us and which we decided to correct at intermission time. Straws were drawn to see who would go in search of a bottle of liquor, and I was elected. Liquor was illegal, we were in a strange town, and the intermission would be only fifteen minutes long.

With a time schedule like that, I decided nothing but the direct approach would make it possible to find what I wanted. There was a restaurant directly across the street from the ballroom, and I dashed over, entered the place, and walked directly up to the white jacketed proprietor behind the cigar counter. There was nothing subtle about my introduction — "I'm with the orchestra across the street and I'd like to find a bootlegger." "So would I young man," he said, as he pulled back his jacket to reveal a big star, "I'm a deputy sheriff."

In spite of the generally bad conditions of the time, the deserving bands somehow kept going and continued to build strength. As is so often the case, adversity seemed to make them more determined. The chances are probably good, however, that a lot of people who became important later stayed in music at this time because there wasn't much else they could find to do anyway.

But for those lucky enough to be steadily employed with a going name band, the income was considerably better than the average of other jobs and in some cases by the standards of the day could be termed excellent. Living costs were low for traveling groups. You could get a room for a dollar and usually eat three meals for about the same amount. Gasoline could be had for as little as a dollar for eight gallons, although you weren't always sure what you were getting.

The glamour of the business was doubtless a strong factor in inspiring many of these people to be in a dance orchestra. Interest in dancing was high, even though money was scarce. When young people could raise the price of a dance admission, that's where they went, and they idolized people who were in the big bands, particularly those who were also on radio.

The picture had changed considerably since the early twenties. Then it had been records on which an orchestra relied for its major, if not only, source of build-up. Now it was radio which was the chief medium by which a band became big. Before the end of the thirties, records would again assume their importance, but now they were in a slump with sales at an all-time low.

The scene of activity also changed as the West Coast began to increase in importance. Part of this was traceable to radio opportunities. Expansion of the networks and the big sponsored shows resulted in many of them originating from the West. The motion picture industry was also beckoning to name bands, and several of those who had made their reputations elsewhere now adopted Los Angeles as headquarters.

Ted FioRito was one of the early ones to make the western move. He had become a big attraction in the Chicago area where he and Danny Russo had shared billing as the FioRito-Russo orchestra. About 1928 he left Russo to go on his own. A reputation from a multitude of hit songs of his own composition made it easy for him to become nationally known with radio time from Chicago's Aragon Ballroom also contributing.

Although it was a movie which brought the FioRito band West, for the next several years he spent a lot of time in the Los Angeles Cocoanut Grove and the San Francisco Bay Area's St. Francis Hotel with occasional time out for cross-country tours.

The West Coast had its own bands which were either already in the national spotlight or fast moving in that direction. Perhaps the one which had been there longest was Abe Lyman's which

GUS ARNHEIM AND HIS ORCHESTRA — on lawn of Ambassador Hotel, 1931. At his right is Jimmie Grier who would soon leave to form his own band. — *Photo courtesy of Jimmie Grier.*

RED PERKINS — Pride of the Cornbelt in the early 1930s. — *Photo courtesy of Eddie Sheffort.*

Ted FioRito's orchestra was well on its way when this 1934 picture was made. Vocal group is "The Debutantes". Directly behind Ted is Muzzy Marcellino. — *Photo courtesy of Muzzy Marcellino.*

Jimmie Grier's First Orchestra — 1932. Vocalists on the stand include Loyce Whiteman and Harry Barris. — *Photo courtesy of Jimmie Grier.*

GRIFF WILLIAMS' FIRST ORCHESTRA — October, 1933. Vocalist is Cora Lee Scott. — *Photo courtesy of Virginia Lauc.*

THE LAUGHNER-HARRIS ORCHESTRA — At the St. Francis Hotel, 1931, with the Harris personality clearly the big attraction. Violinist at right is Muzzy Marcellino. — *Photo courtesy of Muzzy Marcellino.*

PHIL HARRIS takes his own band into the Cocoanut Grove, 1932. — *Photo courtesy of J. T. Ferguson.*

HERMAN WALDMAN — The pride of Texas on roof of Peabody Hotel, Memphis, 1934. — *Photo courtesy of Herman Waldman.*

had been around since the early twenties. From out of his organization had come Gus Arnheim who got his build-up in virtually the same spots where Lyman had gotten his, and eventually he became as well known. He, too, developed some talented people who graduated into the business on their own and became well-known leaders.

Jimmie Grier was one of these, and before too many years after his 1932 start he fairly well dominated the Hollywood musical scene playing regularly at the Biltmore Bowl, recording, arranging for motion pictures, and had a place on two or three major radio shows. Grier never became as big as he might have if personal problems had not caused him to fade from the scene earlier than need be, but some of his early recordings played back in later years indicate that as an arranger he was ahead of his time.

Grier always enjoyed telling a story about his days with Arnheim where, in addition to playing saxophone he had done practically all the arranging. Arnheim was quite a versatile songwriter and called upon Grier to do the arranging for all of his compositions along with the other tunes the band played. His fee at the time for each arrangement was $25.00, a figure which Arnheim constantly told him was too much.

One day Arnheim brought him a new song which he wanted whipped into shape for its introduction at the Cocoanut Grove where they were appearing. Once again the subject of the arranging cost was raised and probably because he was tired of hearing it repeated, Grier made the following suggestion:

"All right, Gus, I'll make you a deal on this one. Instead of the usual $25.00, I'll turn out the arrangement for 5% of any royalties that it earns for you. How's that?"

Arnheim's acceptance was instantaneous.

"I'll take you up on that before you change your mind. I've been paying you more money than I'm making myself."

The song they were discussing was "SWEET AND LOVELY". Within a few months it became one of the biggest hits in the country and at the end of the first year Grier's earnings on the five per cent basis amounted to slightly over twelve hundred dollars. If Arnheim ever again objected to paying twenty-five dollars as a regular arrangement fee, he didn't mention it to Jimmie.

Meanwhile, San Francisco, birthplace of the Hickman and Whiteman bands continued to make its contribution to the business with one after another organization which got its start there going on to greater things. One of the biggest of these in the early thirties was Anson Weeks who, after starting in Sacramento, took his band into the Mark Hopkins Hotel in 1927 and stayed there for seven years.

Patrons dancing past the Weeks' bandstand during 1931 could look up and see future leaders, Xavier Cugat, Griff Williams, Jimmy Walsh, and Bob Crosby who at that time was holding down his first singing job. Other important vocalists who worked with Anson at one time or another included Carl Ravazza, Ben Gage, Tony Martin, Dale Evans, June Knight, and Kay Saint Germaine. Before the mid-thirties Weeks moved out of the Mark Hopkins, and with the reputation built during this long engagement had no difficulty in moving on to Chicago and New York where in the latter city he enjoyed a long run at the St. Regis Hotel. Other Bay Area leaders readily acknowledged that it had been Anson who taught them how to play music in danceable tempo.

Down the hill from the Mark Hopkins, the St. Francis was doing its own job of name building. In the early thirties it was the Lofner-Harris Orchestra with its co-leaders, pianist Carol Lofner and drummer Phil Harris. Lofner usually directed the band but Harris was unquestionably the star attraction. With his drums up in the front row, he alternated between singing across them and just charming the audience with his smile. Some stories even insist that he had a telephone on the stand beside his drums so that he might take calls from his many girl friends while he worked.

Sometime in 1932, they left San Francisco for a tour, shortly after dissolved their partnership and went their separate ways. Harris made Los Angeles his headquarters, moved into the Cocoanut Grove for a long stay and before too long had become one of the biggest names in radio as well as the dance field.

Following Lofner-Harris, the St. Francis Hotel was the scene for the launching of another California band which would eventually enjoy great popularity. Dick Jurgens, a Sacramento boy who had not been voted the lad most likely to enjoy a successful musical career, was its leader. Jurgens had been playing the summer seasons at Lake Tahoe and while there was signed by Music Corporation of America who got them the St. Francis booking. Lou Quadling was induced to come over from the Kay Kyser Orchestra to do the arranging. Ronnie Kemper was already with the group and it stayed approximately twelve months on its first booking. They were brought back about a year later for a longer stay during which time Eddy Howard joined up to play guitar. This was the nucleus of the band that would make Jurgens a big favorite in the Chicago and Midwestern area a few years later.

And who could overlook Horace Heidt who got his start in Oakland's Athens Club about 1927, joined the Fanchon-Marco vaudeville circuit in 1929 and eventually became one of the most commercially successful leaders in the business?

Not destined for such long-lived popularity was another band which started on the West Coast even though its leader was to become nationally known in other fields. This band was fronted by Ted Mack, a saxophone player, who by the mid-thirties had become a regular part of the Major Bowes Amateur Hour on radio and when the Major died several years later would carry on the show himself.

No individual area had a monopoly on developing talent for it was appearing from everywhere. The State of Texas introduced many big musical names and one of its favorite leaders of this period was Herman Waldman. He played the hotels in Dallas, New Orleans and Memphis, and a circuit of one-nighters throughout the South and Southwest. His band included some excellent talent and it was with Waldman that Harry James had one of his earliest jobs.

Anson Weeks tells an interesting story about a tour he made to Texas in the early thirties. While they were playing a one-nighter in Port Arthur, a tall distinguished looking gentleman in the audience kept coming over to the bandstand at every intermission. Each time he asked the same question: Couldn't his boy who was waiting on the sidelines with his trumpet sit in with the band? Anson kept stalling him until the next intermission, hoping he would forget about it or stop pressing the issue. But such was not the case and finally the man was told that union regulations would not permit it.

DICK JURGENS — first big break, a 1934 booking into the St. Francis Hotel. — *Photo courtesy of Ronnie Kemper.*

ANSON WEEKS ORCHESTRA — Mark Hopkins Hotel, 1931. You'll recognize Xavier Cugat and Bob Crosby in the front row, Griff Williams at the piano in back row. — *Photo courtesy of Anson Weeks.*

GEORGE OLSEN — Mid-1930s. — *Photo courtesy of Muzzy Marcellino.*

After a big build-up at Chicago's Trianon Ballroom, JAN GARBER makes his first West Coast trip in 1934 to play Catalina Island's Avalon Ballroom. — *Photo courtesy of Crescent Photo Shop, Avalon, Catalina Island.*

Whether he believed this or not, the gentleman apparently accepted it as being a point which further discussion would not change, but as he turned to walk away he gave Anson this bit of information.

"My kid is a darn good trumpet player and you're going to be hearing a lot about him."

The gentleman from Texas couldn't have been more right for he was Harry James' father.

A lot of Kansas City's fine Negro bands had moved out to other centers of greater activity or were in the process of doing so. This was also true of the Coon-Sanders Band, which as the Kansas City Night Hawks had received enough attention on radio to make Chicago's Blackhawk Restaurant want them. A long stay there, including consistent air time, got them a New York offer in the early thirties. During their stay at the Hotel New Yorker Carlton Coon passed away in 1932 and Joe Sanders attempted to carry on with the band. Somehow he never attained the same degree of success which the Night Hawks had enjoyed before Coon's death.

Chicago became a major band-building center during the twenties and continued to enjoy this position during the thirties. The Blackhawk was one of the leading spots in this band build-up and it was here that Hal Kemp, Kay Kyser, and later in the thirties Bob Crosby, became big names. The Aragon and Trianon Ballrooms owned by the Karzas Brothers made an even longer list famous, but in the early thirties it was Wayne King at the Aragon and Ian Garber at the Trianon.

Most of Chicago's leading hotels were now featuring and heavily promoting bands. Ben Bernie had moved from top New York spots to the Sherman's College Inn about 1930 and made it his home for the next several years. This was where both George Olsen and Buddy Rogers spent much time, and where Frankie Masters became well known shortly after the mid-thirties. The Drake's Gold Coast Room was a constant user of the bigger names as were the Stevens, Palmer House, Congress, Morrison and Edgewater. It was at the Drake that Horace Heidt built a great deal of his fame after leaving the West Coast about 1929 on a vaudeville circuit which included a successful engagement at New York's Palace Theater.

The 1933 World's Fair brought a lot of people to Chicago increasing the amount of work for the bands already there, plus attracting a few more to the area to share the temporary boom.

But New York was still the "main stem" and the place where the most action could be found.

The New York hotel scene was very active and had a great many more hotels than Chicago which featured bands. Lombardo was dug in at the Roosevelt for what would probably go down in history as the longest engagement in the music business. Over at the Taft George Hall had been holding down the bandstand for several years and would eventually be followed by Vincent Lopez. The Astor and Pennsylvania competed briskly for top honors as band-building locations, and there were at least a half dozen others of almost equal importance.

Ben Pollack was still around New York, first at the Park Central and then at the Silver Slipper, a Gotham supper club. His band included many of the best musicians of the day, and was the place where they got their first breaks. It was during his Park Central stay that Jack Teagarden joined Pollack and became such a part of the band that its style came to reflect his musical personality.

Like Goodman, there were countless stories about how Teagarden came to New York, with whom he first worked, etc. Out of all of them it appears he arrived in New York in 1927 from Texas with the Doc Ross Band. Here Al King hired him for a Dixieland unit in the Elizabeth Bryce Show and he next worked with Eddie Edwards before joining Pollack. From Pollack he moved on for a brief session with Mal Hallett and then joined Paul Whiteman with whom he would stay until he formed his own band in the early forties.

The big city was full of good dance bands including Meyer Davis, Emil Coleman, Al Kavelin, Paul Tremayne, and Leo Reisman who had moved in from Boston. No small attraction of that period was Larry Funk and his "Band of 1000 Melodies" and handsome Bernie Cummins was another favorite of the area, particularly with the hotel and cafe society groups.

Future big names were getting their starts as leaders, such as Eddy Duchin who took off on his own after years of playing piano with Leo Reisman. Although he first opened at Ross-Renton Farms in New Jersey, he was not long in making it to the Waldorf-Astoria where he became almost a permanent fixture. Even Russ Columbo had a band for a brief period, and Freddy Martin was becoming well established after starting at the Bossert Hotel in Brooklyn with a six piece band in 1931. Martin had previously worked with vari-

MEYER DAVIS — Monarch of the society band business, 1933. Pianist back in far corner is Claude Thornhill. — *Photo courtesy of Meyer Davis.*

FREDDY MARTIN'S ORCHESTRA was two years old when this photo was made on the Marine Roof of Brooklyn's Bossert Hotel in 1933. — *Photo courtesy of Freddy Martin.*

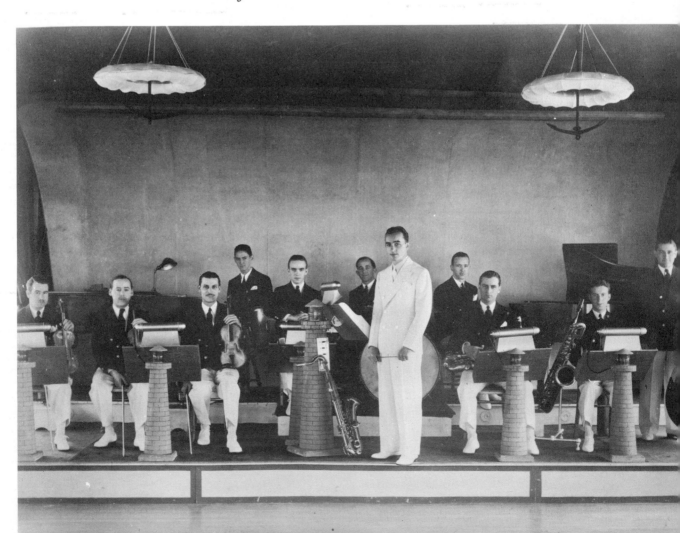

BERNIE CUMMINS — A favorite in the New York area for many years. — *Photo courtesy of M.C.A.*

THE CALIFORNIA COLLEGIANS were still intact in the 1930s, with Fred Mac-Murray, at right, a featured saxophonist. — *Photo courtesy of Lou Wood, trombonist in band.*

ous organizations including Arnold Johnson's, but it was the encouragement from his good friend, Guy Lombardo, which launched him as a leader.

Don Redman's band, made up primarily of ex-Fletcher Henderson men, was one of the most progressive and perhaps most imitated bands around New York at that time. Cab Calloway was already hi-de-ho-ing over at the Savoy, while Duke Ellington was still doing big business at the Cotton Club but would soon be leaving for Europe to be replaced at the Cotton Club by Calloway.

From out of the Goldkette Band had come the Casa Loma Orchestra which moved into New York from Detroit for a long stay at the Essex House. In those days it was a cooperative organization first fronted by Mel Jensen while Glen Gray played in the saxophone section. It was not until early 1937 that Gray moved up front and the band became identified with his name.

The first attempt at having a band of their own had been made by Jimmy and Tommy Dorsey in 1922 but was short-lived. The second venture, and the one which would launch them on their way to ultimate success was begun in early 1934. However, in spite of their having been featured instrumentalists with almost every top leader in the business their names at the outset meant little to the public and lacked box office appeal.

The nucleus around which the band had been built was Glenn Miller, guitarist Roc Hillman, tenor sax man Skeets Herfurt, and trombonist Don Matteson. These four had come into New York from Denver in a group, bringing with them vocalist Kay Weber. The move had been Miller's idea and it was he who made the deal with the Dorsey boys. In the months ahead it would also be Miller who would function as the go-between for the brothers in an attempt to maintain peace and keep the band together.

Because of their limited name power, they cast about for something which would give the necessary hypo. Both the brothers were friendly with Bing Crosby, having worked with him in the Whiteman Orchestra. Bing was by this time a big name on radio, records, and in motion pictures, and it was decided that the next best thing to having him was to get his brother, Bob, who was at the time singing with Anson Weeks.

Whether the deal was made through Bing or a direct contact, Bob came into the band to do the male vocal chores, although there was a while when the rest of the group wondered if he'd stay.

He had the magic Crosby name, but in that stage of his career lacked the tone quality which developed later. To perfectionist Tommy, he was singing flat, and he was not reticent about telling him so. During a rehearsal for an auto show, he kept Crosby at the microphone for half an hour doing one number over and over in an attempt to get the tone inflection he thought the song required. Suddenly the Dorsey temper let go and he hurled his trombone javelin style over Crosby's head onto the auditorium floor and stomped out of the place. Nobody knew where he went, but he didn't show up again until the engagement was over.

On the road the Dorsey Brothers Band usually enjoyed pulling practical jokes on one another, dreaming up anything just for the sake of a laugh. Their travel was by bus and finally someone started a game of minor pilferage each time they stopped at a restaurant for lunch or made a rest stop for a coke. This rapidly became a contest to see who could display the greatest prize when the bus got rolling again. On one of these stops, band manager Eddie MacHarg decided to top them all and proceeded to do so. When the bus was once again under way, he waited until everyone had displayed his loot, then he said:

"While you guys were lifting chewing gum and candy bars, I put myself in business. Take a look at this peanut vending machine. From now on you guys can buy your peanuts from me."

The laughter and kidding which this announcement produced lasted for several miles and then was suddenly interrupted by a police siren's wail. They pulled the bus over to the roadside and got out to face a state policeman who demanded to know whose band it was and whether or not one of them had stolen a peanut machine.

MacHarg assumed the responsibility for answering all questions, and the ingenuity with which he did so proved beyond doubt his right to be a manager. Noting that the names of the Dorseys produced no response from the officer, he decided to try others which might. In addition to Bob Crosby, whose name should ring a bell, the band included a bass player named Jim Taft who bore a strong resemblance to Charles Lindbergh.

"Officer," said MacHarg, "I'd like you to meet some of our band and I think you'll agree they're all a good clean bunch of guys. First, I'd like to introduce Bing Crosby's brother, Bob — and this fellow is a brother of Charles

THE DUKE ELLINGTON BAND of the 1930s was a thrilling thing to listen to. — *Photo courtesy of Joe Rushton.*

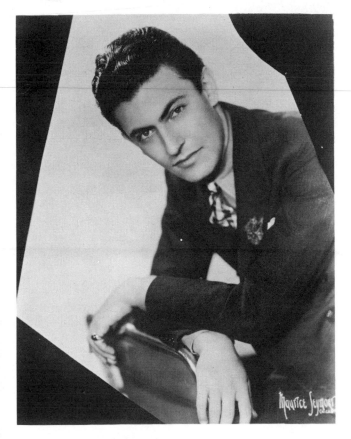

EDDIE DUCHIN who started his first band in 1931. — *Photo courtesy of Freddy Martin.*

CAB CALLOWAY — the king of Hi-De-Ho and professor of jive, a language which he helped originate. — *Photo courtesy of Elmer Eberhardt.*

SAMMY KAYE — At the Cleveland Trianon, 1933. — *Photo courtesy of Tony Briglia.*

Lindbergh. If you have kids, you might want autographs, we'd be happy to oblige.

"Now about that peanut machine — I'm the band manager and I'm sure you wouldn't suspect me. If anyone else in the group took it, it would only have been for a laugh. Let me look on the bus and it it's there I'd appreciate your returning it for us."

A few minutes later, the state patrolman was headed in one direction with the peanut machine and his autographs while the band bus rolled off in the other. Everyone was still laughing, but Mac-Harg was out of the peanut business for good.

The Dorsey Brothers Orchestra made it to Broadway and the Palais Royale in the fall of 1934, staying until early 1935. Then after a tour of the hinterlands, they returned in May for a date at New Rochelle's Glen Island Casino. It was here that they broke up to form two bands and go their separate ways. The split was the result of another on-the-stand clash between the brothers. Perhaps if Glenn Miller had been around to pacify them it would not have occurred, but he had tired of the role of peacemaker some months earlier and left them to go with Ray Noble. Tommy took over the Joe Haymes Orchestra while Jimmy continued on

with an augmented version of the original Dorsey Brothers' group.

But prior to this other events of importance were occurring. In 1933, something took place which would do much to make the demand for music greater. The long awaited repeal of Prohibition finally became a reality shortly after President Roosevelt took office. Light wines and beer were made legal first, with hard liquor available on a legal basis early in 1934. The former speakeasies now became respectable nightclubs. Hotels which had previously experienced difficulty in underwriting top talent suddenly had a profitable revenue which permitted them to do so. Every phase of the entertainment business was given a healthy shot in the arm and the band business was the first to benefit since it was the backbone around which every show was built.

Although the repeal of Prohibition had tremendous effects on the music business, it is debatable whether it did more for it than another event which took place in 1934. Certainly from the standpoint of musical history, the second event was the greater. A new band attained success that year — one which was to change the whole course of popular American music.

It was in July that Benny Goodman, after several years of playing with most of the big names in the country such as Ben Pollack, Ted Lewis, Paul Whiteman, Red Nichols, and others, starting a band of his own played his first job at Billy Rose's Music Hall. He had long been rated one of the best musicians in the business, and had some very definite ideas as to what was wrong with most of the dance music being played and what ought to be done about it. He felt that it needed to be given more life, and with his own group set about to accomplish this.

It was no easy task, as he was to learn before success finally came his way. Among the early spots played by the band was the Roosevelt Grill in New York where they followed the monarch of all sweet bands, Guy Lombardo. When the Goodman brass section cut loose, the management of the spot was frantic. Needless to say, they were not held over and what happened here was typical of most of their early engagements. At least as far as hotel jobs went, the band was consistently criticized for being too loud.

Heading out of New York on an extended tour, their reception continued to be disappointing. Most of their engagements turned out to be little more than rehearsals since there were not many cash customers around for either dancing or listening. Reaching Denver they played the city's popular Elitch's Gardens, facing stiff competition at the other top Denver spot, Lakeside Park, where the Kay Kyser Band was appearing. Kyser had not yet attained the peak of popularity which would soon come his way, but even so he was too much for the Goodman band. He had the crowds, but the fame of the Goodman style had already spread among professional musicians, and one of Kyser's problems was to keep his own men from sneaking down the street to listen to Goodman instead of working at their own jobs.

When they reached the Palomar Ballroom in Los Angeles, the tide suddenly turned. The audience went wild over the Goodman style, and so did the amusement trade journals in advising the world that something important had just happened.

Few people will disagree that the rise of the Goodman band was the greatest single event that ever took place in the whole history of American popular dance music. To begin with, it provided a

THE CASA LOMA ORCHESTRA with Mel Jensen fronting, Glen Gray playing in the sax section. This photo made at Lido Venice in Boston, 1930. — *Photo courtesy of Dave Jacobs.*

JIMMY DORSEY'S BAND in this 1936 picture included Freddy Slack, Bobby Byrne, Bob Eberly, Roc Hillman, and Ray McKinley. — *Photo courtesy of Roc Hillman.*

The WILL OSBORNE ORCHESTRA, 1934. — *Photo courtesy of Will Osborne.*

THE DORSEY BROTHERS ORCHESTRA, 1934. The girl is Kay Weber, Glenn Miller stands at Jimmy's left and down front are Roc Hillman, Skeets Herfurt, and Ray McKinley.— *Photo courtesy of Roc Hillman.*

Popular leader OZZIE NELSON and vocalist HARRIET HILLIARD (Mrs. Nelson). — *Photo courtesy Maury Foladare. Picture made about 1934.*

65

ISHAM JONES AND HIS ORCHESTRA, about 1934. —
If you look closely you'll spot Woody Herman in
the sax section, Walt Yoder on bass. — *Photo courtesy of Walt Yoder.*

Two Whiteman graduates, BING CROSBY and
HENRY BUSSE get together on the Paramount lot.
— *Photo courtesy of Gus Angelo.*

At right, BENNY GOODMAN makes his first return
to the Palomar following the triumphant 1935
engagement which made him the toast of the
nation.

66

strong upsurge of interest in dancing and in music at a time it was sorely needed. His innovations and success opened up entirely new horizons for dance bands, and paved the way for many others to rise to fame never before visualized. The style which he made famous had its roots in Fletcher Henderson's arrangements, but it was the Goodman touch that planted it firmly in the musical history books. Goodman did something else for the business as well as establishing a style which would be widely imitated. It was he who first broke the color barrier to bring top Negro talent into the great white bands, first by using Fletcher Henderson as an arranger, and later by featuring instrumentally such great artists as Mary Lou Williams and Lionel Hampton.

Just who created the term "swing" by which Goodman's music became identified is not quite clear, but soon every band in the dance field was either "swing" or "sweet" with some who compromised with both and were a little of each.

Goodman's success was the spark which touched off what would later be described as "the big band era". In reality, his band of the thirties was not really big in number of men, which totalled only twelve. Most of those who would follow him into the spotlight he created would be larger.

As the trend towards larger groups gained momentum it soon included many who had long been identified as small bands. Best known of these was Red Nichols who by 1935 had augmented his "Five Pennies" to a full sized band of ten men, and not too much later was using thirteen. Along with many other big names, he carried a featured male vocalist and for quite some time featured a girls' trio.

Many Paul Whiteman graduates were now active as leaders with trumpeter Henry Busse among

DINING · DANCING AND ENTERTAINMENT CENTER OF THE WEST

THE PALOMAR

VERMONT AT THIRD

PROGRAM — WEEK OF JUNE 29th

Attend The
FAREWELL PARTY
For
ISHAM JONES'
Orchestra
TUESDAY EVENING, JUNE 30th
then . . . . . the OPENING of "America's
Greatest Swing Band"

Benny Goodman
AND HIS ORCHESTRA
● The Same Noted Hot Rhythm
Group that made "Swing" music
famous during the past year—the
musical stars of the "Elgin Revue,"
the "Let's Dance" and the "Camel
Caravan" programs, and other popular National Radio Broadcasts

Returns to the Palomar on

Wednesday, July 1, 1936
FEATURED WITH THE BAND WILL BE:
HELEN WARD GENE KRUPPA
"America's Premier "The World's Greatest
Orchestra Bluestress" Drummer'

**BENNY
GOODMAN**

HERBIE KAY'S ORCHESTRA — Chicago, 1936, vocalist, Dorothy Lamour. Kay's band was very popular all during the 1930s and early 1940s. — *Photo courtesy of Charles "Bud" Dant.*

LES BROWN and the "Duke Blue Devils" on the stand — DON KRAMER on drums. This was the first band fronted by Brown and had the usual "ups and downs" before becoming a permanent part of the musical world. — *Photo courtesy of Don Kramer.*

the more successful. Those who worked with Busse described him as a mild-mannered individual who seldom let anything upset him. He consistently declined to accept dates which were any great distance apart. In addition to disliking the pressure of too rigid a schedule he loved to take time out en route to wander into roadside pastures to hunt prairie dogs and other small game with a 22 caliber rifle.

Shortly prior to the breakup of the Dorsey Brothers Band in early 1935, Glenn Miller had left them, partially because of their constant quarrelling. He soon became busy helping Ray Noble organize his first American orchestra and doing his arranging chores. Noble had come to the United States alone after several successful years as a leader in England. However, he was not permitted to bring English musicians because of England's long-standing ban against American musicians, and against which a counter-ban had been imposed in this country.

The ban was put to test in the same year (1935) when another English leader, Jack Hylton, came to the States bringing his band with him. The furor which resulted included a threat of a $100,000.00 suit initiated by Paul Specht and some strong comments on the part of Music Corporation of America's Jules Stein. Eventually Hylton gave up and returned to England.

The high public interest in dancing during the last half of the thirties was conducive to the start of a lot of new organizations and they made their appearances in a steady stream. Most of them were able to make a place for themselves, and many went on to great fame and fortune.

The Bob Crosby Band made its appearance in 1935. Actually, this was not a new band at all, it just had a new leader. The previous year Ben Pollack had taken a tour to the West Coast with an organization including such top musicians as Gil Rodin, Matty Matlock, Nappy LaMare, Ray Bauduc, Yank Lawson, Charlie Spivak and Gil Bowers. While on the Coast something happened and the band parted company with Pollack, who remained in California while the band returned to New York.

For a while they kept the group intact, working and recording under various names and for a short time worked a Broadway show under the direction of Red Nichols. Determined to keep going they decided that a name leader was necessary if they were to be successful. Bob Crosby had been sing-

ing with the Dorsey Brothers, but they had now broken up. Cork O'Keefe, of the Rockwell-O'Keefe Agency, set up a meeting for the band and Crosby to get together, and over a drugstore sandwich a deal was made for Crosby to come into the group as its leader. After much rehearsal time they played their first date at the Roseland Ballroom, then took off on a series of one-nighters for additional experience.

While this was happening, another band was also getting itself a new leader. Isham Jones had decided it was time for him to retire, and as had been the case with the Pollack men there was a strong desire to stay together and remain active. Woody Herman had been playing sax in the band for several years and it was he who took over the job as front man.

Both the new Herman Band and the Bob Crosby organizations were cooperative or corporation bands, with each member owning stock and sharing in the profits.

The first Russ Morgan Orchestra came into existence in 1935 after Russ had spent years of grooming in the nation's top musical organizations,

JACK HYLTON with friend RED NICHOLS. Hylton's attempt to bring his own band from England created quite a controversy. — *Photo courtesy of Red Nichols.*

Vincent Lopez — Gold Coast Room, Drake Hotel, Chicago, November 6, 1937. — *Photo courtesy of Ernie Mathias.*

Russ Morgan's First Orchestra, 1935. — *Photo courtesy of Russ Morgan.*

The inspiration for "RIPPLING RHYTHM" came to Shep Fields while sipping a soda.

Rippling Rhythms

by

SHEP FIELDS

and his

Orchestra

HAL DERWIN

CLARE NUNN

SHEP FIELDS AND HIS "RIPPLING RHYTHM" — 1936, the year his unusual style caught on and made him a national attraction. — *Photo courtesy of St. Francis Hotel, San Francisco.*

TOMMY DORSEY moved into the top brackets in 1937. This picture was made in 1939. — *Photo courtesy of Dave Jacobs.*

ORVILLE KNAPP whose career was cut short by a tragic mishap. — *Photo courtesy of Freddy Martin.*

This was the start of Kay Kyser's great success – at the Blackhawk restaurant in Chicago, about 1937. — *Photo courtesy of Harry Thomas.*

both as a sideman and arranger. His last job was with Freddy Martin in New York and it was there that "music in the Morgan manner" was born.

Tragedy overtook one of the new leaders before he had time to really get under way. In July, 1936, Orville Knapp, a former saxophonist with Coon-Sanders, was killed in the crash of a small plane while he was practicing take-offs and landings. His "Music of Tomorrow" had been styled somewhat ahead of the times, but a little later was copied by several others. Shortly after Knapp's death, George Olsen took over the orchestra almost in its entirety, adopting much of its style and the "Music of Tomorrow" trademark. Leighton Noble, who had been the Knapp vocalist, started his own organization and astounded everyone in the trade by getting his initial booking at Frank Dailey's Meadowbrook. It had been in Olsen's Band that Noble had gotten some of his early experience before working with Knapp.

The struggle for recognition had many approaches, with attempts to develop unusual styles producing some sounds never written in the music books. Shep Fields parlayed a straw, a fish bowl full of water, and a few bubbles into something he called "Rippling Rhythm". Standing in front of a microphone, he blew bubbles through the straw to get the sound effect he wanted. Publicity releases maintained he had gotten the "inspiration" for this sound while drinking a bottle of Coke. The Coca-Cola people remained strangely silent, but other bandleaders were quoted as suspecting there was something besides Coke in the bottle at the time. Shep didn't seem to care, however. His "Rippling Rhythm" sold a lot of records for him, including one entitled "Plenty of Money and You". This all took place about 1936 and by the end of that year there was doubtless "plenty of money" in the Fields bank account.

While Fields' "Rippling Rhythm" was being criticized by musicians there were other popular musical styles which were being subjected to the same thing by a minority segment of the general public. The new musical style which had been identified as "Swing" was being given the same treatment by the "longhair" critics as had been heaped on the so-called "Jazz bands" of the 1920s. In fact, their theme was much the same as that of their predecessors ten years earlier. They looked upon this music as an evil influence on the health and minds of both the public and the musicians.

Luckily their effect was no greater than those who criticized Shep Fields.

It was in 1937 that Kay Kyser found his success formula after almost ten years of trying. He had been knocking at the door for some time, having moved into Chicago's Blackhawk Restaurant through the influence of his good friend, Hal Kemp. His style of introducing numbers with a "Singing song title" had already become a well-known trademark. At the Blackhawk he originated an off-night specialty which he called "Kyser's College of Musical Knowledge". An audience participation program with small prizes awarded, it caught on like wildfire and was soon picked up as a local radio feature by Station WGN. When the American Tobacco Company took it over as a network show, Kyser became a national sensation within a few months. He made little claim to being a great musician, but as a showman he certainly knew his way around.

Tommy Dorsey also moved to the top in 1937. When the two brothers broke up in 1935, Tommy took over the Joe Haymes Orchestra in Detroit rather than organize a completely new group. They had been doing very well under Dorsey's leadership and needed nothing but that little extra nudge to put them over. It came in the form of a big record followed in quick succession by several others. The mythical title of "Band of the Year" was his without question as the year ended. *1937*

Shortly after Tommy moved into top name status, an amusing incident resulted when his path and that of a fellow Pennsylvanian, Russ Morgan, crossed once again. It happened in the Spring of 1938 and was the result of both leaders being booked for an important Eastern college prom.

Several days prior to the engagement Morgan called Dorsey long distance, reminding him of the date, and explaining that his reason for calling was to find out in advance which band would open the program.

Tommy's reply was right to the point.

"Well, Russ, at the present time I am a bigger name than you are, so I guess you should lead off."

"Fine, Tommy, that's okay with me," said Russ, as the telephone conversation was terminated.

Dorsey should have known Morgan better than to believe he would accept that kind of comment without attempting to turn the tables. On the

RED NICHOLS with his
big band — Virginia
Beach, 1939. — *Photo
courtesy Red Nichols.*

Below, the great BEN-
NY GOODMAN band,
1936. — *Photo cour-
tesy of Harry James.*

PAUL WHITEMAN — September 1938. The signatures on the photo will clearly indicate that Whiteman still had an all-star organization. — *Photo courtesy of Paul Whiteman.*

ORRIN TUCKER who struck pay dirt in 1939. — *Photo courtesy of M.C.A.*

The date of this ARTIE SHAW picture is not definite, probably late 1930s. — *Photo courtesy of Arsene Studio, New York City.*

night of the prom, Russ Morgan sent the band in early, telling them to start on time under the direction of George Hill. After approximately fifteen minutes of their opening half-hour stint had been played, Russ came to the doorway dressed in a white suit and carrying his trombone over his arm. Meanwhile, the Dorsey Band was on the stand at the other end of the ballroom, preparing to take over when Morgan's Band quit playing.

Morgan's entrance was the signal for Hill to halt the band in the middle of the number. Russ walked across the floor, through the crowd of dancers and mounted the bandstand. The band immediately broke into the Morgan theme "Does Your Heart Beat For Me". No sooner was this completed when Russ followed it with "Marie", "Song of India", and "Chicago", big record hits which had brought about Dorsey's success the previous year, and played them exactly as the Dorsey arrangement was written. Following these, he signed off the half hour with Tommy's well-

known theme song "I'm Getting Sentimental Over You" and then made this announcement:

"Ladies and gentlemen, I would now like to introduce to you the world's greatest trombone player, my good friend, Tommy Dorsey."

While this was taking place, Dorsey was standing at the other end of the room, shaking his fist.

In 1938, Artie Shaw walked off with the "Band of the Year" honors. Shaw was no newcomer to the business, he had worked as a sideman with a long list of well-known leaders, including Paul Specht. Few people had his determination to succeed. In a book which he authored some years later, he pictured himself as a mediocre musician who forced himself through long hours of practice to become proficient. Contemporary musicians who worked with him during those early years dispute this, rating him instead as a man with great talent. When he started his own band about 1936, he had a rough time keeping it afloat, although he surrounded himself with some top men, including several future leaders. Among these was Jerry Gray who did most of the band's arrangements. It was Gray's arrangement of "Begin the Beguine" which, when placed on wax, became the hit record needed to move them into the top ranks. This made Shaw the second big time clarinet playing leader, and many of his records of that era indicate his awareness of the other, Benny Goodman. The arrangements of several of these were note for note duplication.

By this time some of the Goodman sidemen were ready to try their own hand at leading a band. Gene Krupa was the first to make the move, cutting out to form his own group in the Spring of 1938. Harry James followed in less than a year to become his own boss, for the first time, in early 1939.

Apparently both of them had Goodman's blessing when they made the move, and it was rumored that in the case of James he also had Goodman's financial support. He quickly assembled a lot of top talent, including vocalist Connie Haines and a then unknown male singer, by the name of Frank Sinatra, who had no intention of remaining unknown. Sinatra immediately attracted attention as a promising comer and before many months one of those who became interested was Tommy Dorsey. James at the time was struggling to keep the band afloat and considering Dorsey's offer an opportunity for Sinatra, gave him his release. In future years, the two would look back and kid one another about the contract which never was completed.

Handsome Orrin Tucker in 1939 moved up to be a top contender with the help of Wee Bonnie Baker whose rendition of a tricky little tune called "Oh, Johnny" made them both famous. It was also the year when Larry Clinton's "My Reverie" put the ex-Casa Loma arranger solidly in the big time with his own orchestra, where he remained for many years.

Now the second of the two great bands who were to have the greatest all-time influence on the dance band business came into its own. It is extremely difficult to find anything to say about Glenn Miller which has not been written over and over, but 1939 was his year and he well deserved the success which he attained. Like Goodman, the style which he created would live on and on and be imitated by a great many people. Starting his first band in 1937, few leaders were ever better

HARRY JAMES' ORCHESTRA — his first band in Atlantic City, 1939. Frank Sinatra, often kidded about his thinness, appears to outweigh James here. On James' right is great female vocalist, CONNIE HAINES. — *Photo courtesy of Harry James.*

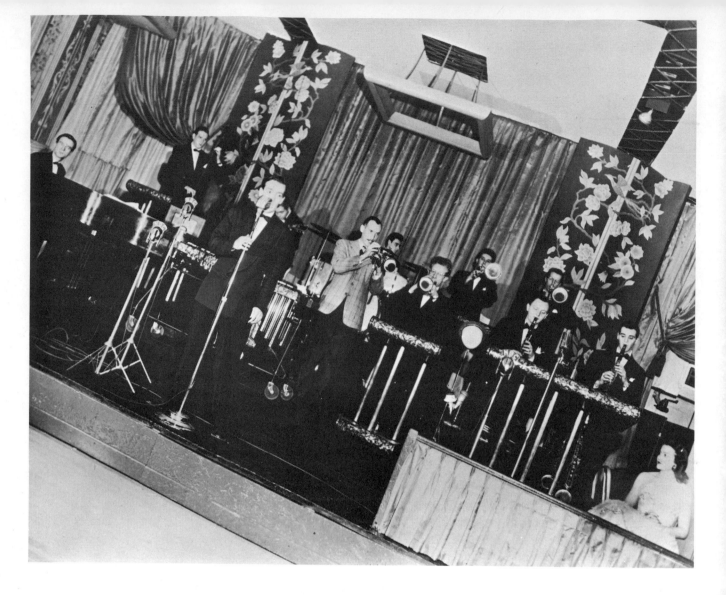

LARRY CLINTON's start as a bandleader followed years of arranging for the Casa Loma Orchestra. — *Photo courtesy of Arsene Studio, New York City.*

Headlines from *Billboard, 1939.* — *Photo courtesy of Billboard magazine.*

Trumpeter James To Take Out Band

NEW YORK, Jan., 1939.—Harry James, Benny Goodman's star trumpet pupil, is staking it out in the ork world in his own right, band being sponsored by Williard (MCA) Alexander and Goodman ... but they won't start him on the top, booking James in smaller locations for schooling.

Frank Sinatra Joins James Ork as Singer

NEW YORK, July, 1939.—Frank Sinatra, cousin of maestro Ray, this week joined Harry James at the Roseland Ballroom, New York, as vocalist. Young Sinatra is a Hoboken boy.

CHARLIE BARNET — on bandstand of Palomar Ballroom, Los Angeles, October, 1939. — *Photo courtesy of Gil Harris.*

musically equipped to do so. He had been a top musician and arranger since the early twenties, working in the bands of Boyd Senter, Abe Lyman, Ben Pollack, Paul Ashe, Red Nichols, Smith Ballou, the Dorsey Brothers, and Ray Noble. Some portion of the success enjoyed by all these leaders was the result of Miller's arranging. All of the arrangements for Ray Noble's first band were done by Miller and it was during this period that he is said to have started, mentally at least, developing the style which he was finally able to make a reality with his own orchestra.

The band signed with the Tommy Rockwell Agency in January of 1937 and after playing some break-in dates and cutting a few records, went on the road. Seymour Weiss, owner of the Roosevelt Hotel in New Orleans, still takes pride in the fact that it was he who gave this struggling band its first major hotel job. He booked them in for two weeks, but kept them on for two months.

Success was not yet to be theirs, and would not come for some time. Having sunk most of his capital into the venture without having it start to pay off, Miller became discouraged and put the whole band on notice on New Year's Eve. Some months later he was once again able to get the type of support which would justify his starting up once

more, and after screening a lot of top talent and signing up the best of them, he did so. Still nothing much happened, and by June of 1938, Glenn was once again so discouraged with the situation that he had almost decided to disband permanently. Then a few breaks started to develop for them. The first of these was at the Paradise Restaurant in New York. From there they went into Frank Dailey's Meadowbrook and things started looking even brighter. The big payoff finally came at Glen Island Casino and from that point the band never looked back.

To a great degree the manner of Miller's ultimate success closely paralleled Tommy Dorsey's. He insisted on having top instrumentalists and also made use of talented vocalists. Like Dorsey, his big break was the result of a hit record. His "In the Mood" did the trick in the summer of 1939 and was followed by others in a virtual stream. Also, like Dorsey, it was a cigarette sponsor who put him on commercial radio making his "Moonlight Serenade" theme song known coast to coast.

Miller was a musical perfectionist and as such was considered a hard taskmaster by many. Yet when success came people in the trade were unanimous in saying it couldn't have happened to a nicer guy.

BUDDY ROGERS' ORCHESTRA — late 1930s. Rogers' success as a bandleader was greatly enhanced by his extensive motion picture work. — *Photo courtesy of Gene's Photo and Rock Shop, Avalon, Catalina Island.*

THE GLENN MILLER ORCHESTRA — late 1939 or early 1940. — *Photo courtesy of Wilbur Schartz.*

BOB CROSBY'S ORCHESTRA — about 1940. A lot of top talent including Jess Stacey, Ray Bauduc, Nappy LaMare, Gil Rodin, Billy Butterfield, and the vocalist? — a young girl named Doris Day. —*Photo courtesy of Max Herman, Local 47, A. F. of M.*

JIMMY DORSEY ORCHESTRA — featuring Bob Eberly and Helen O'Connell in Panther Room of the Sherman Hotel, Chicago 1940. — *Photo courtesy of Rod Hillman.*

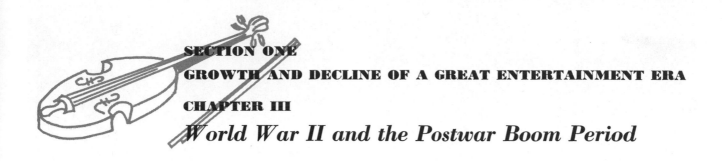

World War II and the Postwar Boom Period

As 1940 GOT UNDER WAY, the world of popular music appeared bright and prosperous in all of its segments.

Record sales were good and getting better, commercial radio was showing an increased interest in dance bands, locations and one-nighters were plentiful. It looked as though anyone who had the desire and ability to organize a group with talent and a distinguishing style could do so and find success waiting for him.

Downbeat, at that time one of the most popular music trade magazines, carried in each issue a department titled "Where the Bands Are Playing". Leaders had only to provide them with an itinerary to be included. Numerically, the listing of name, semi-name, and local favorites averaged in the neighborhood of eight hundred organizations.

The line-up of big names remained pretty much the same although quite a number of those who had started during the thirties were showing signs of momentum which would place them among the top contenders. Moving up fast were Woody Herman, Jimmy Dorsey, Bob Crosby, Sammy Kaye, Gene Krupa, Dick Jurgens, Jan Savitt, and Charlie Barnet. With the exception of Sammy Kaye, all of these leaned towards the swing side with Crosby featuring a Dixieland group within his larger band. Kaye had already started his "So You Want to Lead a Band" feature and it was paying off big at the box office.

Benny Goodman took himself out of competition early in 1940 for what became almost a year of rest after a throat ailment had hospitalized him. This left Tommy Dorsey and Glenn Miller vying for top honors and in the greatest demand. Artie Shaw, who had disbanded in the fall of '39 labelling the whole business a "racket" forgot the things he didn't like about it and came back, soon to become more active than ever.

Among the new entries that year, Vaughn Monroe and Charlie Spivak were looked on as sure winners. Spivak had years of experience in the nation's best musical organizations behind him and his start was financed by Glenn Miller. Monroe, although not around for so long, had been working in the Boston area with Jack Marshard's units, and was backed by them. Big things were also expected of Lionel Hampton who had decided it was time to go it on his own when Goodman's disbanding put him and other Goodman sidemen out of work.

There were other events deserving of notice in passing. Freddy Martin found the key to overdue success by adapting the classics to popular dance tempo. Jan Garber celebrated twenty years as a bandleader with all of his contemporaries who had access to air time, paying tribute to him in special broadcasts. Ace trombonist, Jack Jenney, started a big band of his own for a while, but when the venture proved unsuccessful went back with Artie Shaw after Shaw's reorganization. The perennial funnyman of the band business, Joe Venuti, stopped clowning and really started to get serious about being a bandleader. Gray Gordon took his "Tic-Toc Rhythm" into New York's Edison Hotel for a four week stand early in the year and then stayed on for thirty. Quite a human interest story got heavy coverage when Bobby Byrne was stricken with acute appendicitis during an engagement at the Strand Theater and all the other bandleaders in the New York area quickly arranged to take turns fronting his orchestra in his absence.

One of the year's biggest song hits was "I'll Never Smile Again" and this, too, involved a great human interest story. It was written by Ruth Lowe who had been the pianist with Ina Ray Hutton's highly popular all-girl orchestra. Miss Lowe left the band to become the bride of Harold Cohen, a Chicago music publisher. A few short weeks after their marriage, Cohen passed away and in-

DICK JURGENS' BAND — Chicago's Aragon Ballroom, about 1940. Ronnie Kemper at piano, Eddy Howard on guitar. — *Courtesy Ronnie Kemper.*

spired by her grief Miss Lowe composed the song. Contributing greatly to its success was the record made by Tommy Dorsey with the vocals expertly rendered by Frank Sinatra and the Pied Pipers.

As the summer wore along, some of the bright outlook began to be tinged with uneasy apprehension. There was a war going on in Europe and as Hitler marched roughshod over smaller nations with increasing success, the ranks of Americans who thought it must eventually involve us grew steadily larger. To develop a semblance of preparedness a draft bill was passed which provided for a year's military service by the young men of the nation not exempt because of dependents or essential occupations. In mid-October the musicians within the age group answered a summons to register for the draft and did so with a firm conviction that selective service boards were not likely to consider their jobs necessary to the defense effort. In addition to holding what would likely be classed non-essential occupations, they were particularly vulnerable since a large percentage of them were under thirty-five.

Just before the year's end, the music world and its followers were shocked and saddened by the sudden death of popular Hal Kemp, killed in an auto accident at Madera, California. At the time he was en route from the Cocoanut Grove in Los Angeles to an engagement at the Hotel Mark Hopkins in San Francisco.

True to the tradition of show business, the band opened without him at the Mark Hopkins. Guest leaders appeared on the stand with them until some decision could be made as to the future of the group. Ex-Kemp men, Skinnay Ennis and John Scott Trotter were among those who jumped into the breach immediately. Music Corporation of America toyed for a time with the idea of turning the band over to football star Tommy Harmon who was on the Coast at the time to appear in the annual East-West game. Although Harmon had never been identified with music he was a big

LIONEL HAMPTON above at right. — *Photo courtesy of Associated Booking Co.*

GRIFF WILLIAMS above, and his orchestra were a big hit in Chicago's Stevens Hotel in the early 1940s. — *Photo courtesy of M.C.A.*

JOE REICHMAN and his orchestra were popular in the nation's top hotels.

85

Ray Noble's Orchestra, above. — *Photo courtesy of Gene's Photo & Rock Shop, Avalon, Catalina Island.*

After years with Dick Jurgens and Horace Heidt, Ronnie Kemper, below, tries it on his own. — *Photo courtesy of Ronnie Kemper.*

RAY HERBECK — One of the Midwest's most popular leaders during the 1940s. — *Photo courtesy of Anson Weeks.*

Below, an early picture of STAN KENTON's fast-rising band. — *Photo courtesy of Capitol Records.*

HORACE HEIDT was at the peak of his bandleading career when this picture was made in the early 1940s. Frankie Carle was the featured pianist and the group includes Ronnie Kemper, Art Carney, Ollie O'Toole, and Fred Lowery.

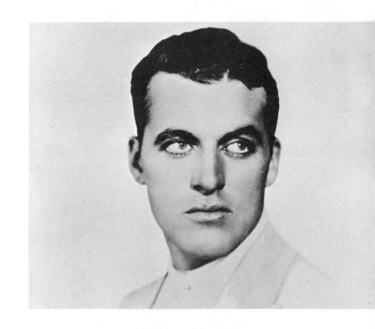

ART JARRETT — right, took over the Kemp band following Bob Allen's leadership. — *Photo courtesy of Joe Rushton.*

THE HAL KEMP BAND — about 1940. Vocalists are Janet Blair, Bob Allen. Allen took over band briefly after Kemp's death. — *Photo courtesy of R.C.A. Victor.*

PHIL HARRIS and ALICE
FAYE who were married in
1941. — *Photo courtesy of
Eddie MacHarg.*

attraction and the idea of his fronting a band was not without precedent. There had been other instances of agencies putting non-musical names in front of dance orchestras, including heavyweight Buddy Baer, although this was a short-lived venture. In the case of Harmon it did not work out and vocalist Bob Allen became the front man until the orchestra was finally taken over by Art Jarrett several months later. For the next several years the distinctive Kemp style was to have many imitators.

The opening of the Hollywood Palladium in the Fall of 1940 was one of the year's most publicized events and Tommy Dorsey was brought out to open it. He was followed by a string of other top names, all happy to be identified with the plush dance spots. The new ballroom not only filled the West Coast gap created by the Palomar's burning a year before, but quickly became one of the nation's top dancing locations. Its own natural glamour was greatly enhanced during its early years by the cream of Hollywood's talent which made it a regular gathering place.

It was from the Palladium's bandstand that Stan Kenton was launched into national prominence. Kenton's new band had been building a heavy local following at nearby Balboa all during the summer of 1941. The Palladium management's policy of booking nothing but top names had not been broken until now but they relaxed it to bring Kenton in for a November booking on an experimental basis. He astounded everyone by practically breaking all previously existing house records.

Kenton was a showman as well as a musician. On opening night, he waited near the main entrance while the band took the stand for their first number. When they were all in place, Stan let go with a loud shout, ran across the floor through the crowd which had already formed, and leaped onto the bandstand. As his feet touched the floor, he gave a down-beat which sent the band into his theme "Artistry in Rhythm". The crowd loved it and a new star was born. Kenton followed his Palladium run by moving into New York's Roseland Ballroom and then, firmly established, found himself sought after by the other top operators and promoters across the nation.

By the time World War II suddenly dragged us into it in late 1941, Jimmy Dorsey, by virtue of a series of big records, had moved up to join the group at the top and breath the same rarefied air previously reserved for his brother Tommy and a few others. Harry James was threatening to follow

Jack Teagarden — Photo at right shows "Big Jackson" who was on the road with a full-sized band of all-star musicians during the early and mid-1940s. — *Photo courtesy of M.C.A.*

Death claims Bunny Berigan in June, 1942. — *Photo courtesy of Lawrence Welk.*

Harry Owens and his Royal Hawaiians in a U.S.O. appearance in June, 1942. — *Photo courtesy of Ronnie Kemper.*

BUNNY BERIGAN

Bernard (Bunny) Berigan, 33, orchestra leader and trumpet player, died June 2 at Polyclinic Hospital, New York, which he entered the previous day suffering from an intestinal ailment. He was stricken May 31 at the Van Cortlandt Hotel, New York, where he made his home.

A native of Fox Lake, Wis., Berigan earned his living playing violin and trumpet from the time he was 14. He attended University of Wisconsin and while there taught trumpet and played in dance bands after school hours. Since his graduation he appeared as featured soloist with the Hal Kemp, Rudy Vallee, Tommy Dorsey, Abe Lyman, Paul Whiteman and Benny Goodman bands.

Berigan made three attempts to organize a band of his own. His last try met with success. Since starting his own orchestra he played trumpet in nearly every number and directed the band at the same time. His best known recording, which became his theme song, was *I Can't Get Started With You.*

Berigan first became ill last April 20 while on tour. He was confined to Allegheny General Hospital, Pittsburgh, until May 8, at which time he was discharged and warned not to play his trumpet. However, wishing to keep his band at the peak of its popularity, he insisted upon playing the instrument. It is said that this hastened his final collapse.

In compliance with Berigan's wish, band will be kept intact under his name. Mrs. Donna Berigan, his widow, will maintain his financial interest in it. Vido Musso, sax player in the band, will be the leader.

Besides his wife, he leaves two daughters, Patricia and Joyce; his mother and a brother.

Funeral services were conducted June 3 at St. Malachy's Church, New York. Buried at Fox Lake.

him into the winner's circle by the same route when his "You Made Me Love You" became the nation's biggest hit.

Pearl Harbor found the music business no better prepared for it than anyone else. In the first few weeks that followed, pandemonium reigned. One-nighters were cancelled by blackouts, with the bands on the stand ready to play. News bulletins interrupted remote broadcasts with such regularity that programming was impossible. In addition, the shock of the sudden attack left few people in the mood for night-clubbing and dancing. Business in spots featuring music dropped off to virtually nothing.

One leader found himself in the middle of the war right from the first shot. Billy MacDonald had opened an engagement in Honolulu late in the fall and was still there on December 7th. Like the rest of Pearl Harbor's citizens, he and his band members were awakened by the falling bombs on Sunday morning and when the action was over, they all pitched in to help clean up and care for the wounded. It was several months before they were able to get back to the States, and some of them found draft calls waiting for them when they arrived.

The initial daze which came with our precipitation into war was quickly shaken off by the music business as the nation mobilized. Its members lost no time in seeking means to make a contribution to the war effort. Many sidemen and a substantial number of leaders immediately volunteered for active service. Others waited to be called in the normal course of events, meanwhile working in other ways to participate. Almost en masse, they moved into the field of morale building with over two hundred bands making themselves available for U.S.O. shows. Kay Kyser was a leader in this program, announcing very early in the war months that all of his engagements for the duration would be played in army camps or from naval stations.

Although the war's beginning had plunged the band people into gloom about the future business outlook, this feeling was short-lived. It soon became evident that an entertainment boom was getting under way. As the country's mobilization was stepped up, the biggest spending spree in history was touched off. Defense industries working at top production capacity put a great deal of money into circulation and this money was in the hands of people who were in a mood to spend it. Military personnel on leave also needed amusement, and before long there were Army and Navy bases everywhere. Hotels, nightclubs and ballrooms, did turn-away business, and one-nighters began to establish grosses never dreamed of previously.

Not everything was milk and honey, however. Wartime restrictions were immediately put into effect, most of which would last for the duration. First to directly affect all amusements was a midnight curfew at which hour all dancing must be terminated and all liquor service brought to a

Lawrence Welk in Chicago about 1942. — *Photo courtesy of Lawrence Welk.*

The Coast Guard Band directed by Lt. J. G. Rudy Vallee and assisted by Chief Petty Officer Jimmie Grier, in 1943. — *Photo courtesy of Rudy Vallee.*

Capt. Glenn Miller and his Service Band, below, in the Yale Bowl just prior to going overseas. — *Photo courtesy of Don Haynes.*

CHARLIE SPIVAK and vocalist IRENE DAY, above, during War Bond Drive, Times Square, 1944. Appearances such as this were a daily occurence for all the important leaders. — *Photo courtesy of Charlie Spivak.*

FRANKIE CARLE with his orchestra, at right, playing for soldiers at Ellington Field, Texas. — *Photo courtesy of Frankie Carle.*

93

halt. This meant, in most cases, that musicians must go to work an hour earlier. Going along with the basic theme and wanting to make sure that his group was patriotically identified, Jimmy Petrillo decreed that all broadcasts and public performances by musicians must be concluded with the rendition of the National Anthem.

In the early Fall of 1942, gasoline and tire rationing became a reality, necessitating the presentation of proof that driving was essential to the war effort in order to get more than a basic gasoline ration or purchase a tire. Although much of their time was involved in appearances for morale-building purposes, dance bands received little favorable consideration by most ration boards. Under such circumstances, travel by personal auto was out of the question. The chartered bus was the only solution left and all of the old equipment in the country was dragged out of mothballs for this purpose. Even in this regard, the bands were at the bottom of the list and much of the transportation equipment made available to them left the possibility of arrival on schedule a matter of extreme doubt.

The draft soon started to take its toll of sidemen and deplete the ranks of available replacements. Leaders were forced into a position where bidding against one another for competent personnel was necessary. Everyone raided everyone else, resulting in the development of some long-lasting hard feelings. Horace Heidt, never completely orthodox in his approach, kept a "help wanted" ad running constantly in *Billboard Magazine* and made a similar pitch for sidemen on his sponsored radio show. He made it clear that he was ready to pay attractive salaries and that no ceilings existed if the right people applied.

In spite of manpower shortages, the size of the bands continued to grow. In part this was due to the tempo of the times. The nation seemed to be out of the mood for soft sentimental music, but instead wanted to hear it loud, full, and on the up-beat side. Many leaders, long identified with sweet music, now switched to a swing style. Perhaps the most surprising style conversion was that of Jan Garber who made the transition in the late summer of 1942, assembling some of the greatest swing musicians available.

Patriotism was prevalent among members of the music business as it was with any other group. At the very outbreak of the war, there had been a wave of enlistments. Then, the initial white heat of indignation over the unexpected attack subsiding, they developed a more realistic appraisal of the situation and the manner in which each could best make his proper contribution. For many of the band people the decision was to get into plane or ship building, either giving up their musical activity for the duration or working at it as a sideline.

But the war was not many months old before important leaders took the initiative for some form of still more active duty. Almost the first of these to go was Artie Shaw, who first took a special U.S.O. assignment to organize bands for camp shows and then went into the Navy as a first class seaman. Orrin Tucker soon joined the same branch of the service, with a commission as Lieutenant, Junior Grade. Next to go was Eddy Duchin, who became Navy Lieutenant. Benny Goodman attempted to get into the Army but was classified 4-F because of an old back injury. Kay Kyser was similarly turned down after rumors that he was joining the Army with the rank of Major had widely circulated. Claude Thornhill went into the Navy, insisting that what he wanted was not a soft Special Services assignment, but the real thing in the form of active duty.

There were even some instances of entire bands enlisting en masse. Clyde McCoy and his orchestra were probably the first to take such a step, and they were followed not long after by Buddy Clarke, who had been a successful bandleader in the Middle West and the East.

In the late summer of 1942, Rudy Vallee enlisted in the Coast Guard, was given the rating of Chief Petty Officer, and before long became Lieutenant Vallee. His duty was to organize a band for this branch of the service, which he immediately set about doing. He was soon joined by Jimmy Grier, who became assistant bandleader and did the necessary arranging. Together they built a mammoth show unit which toured the nation playing U.S.O. shows and various fund-raising functions.

None of these made quite the same big news, however, as did Glenn Miller's enlistment which came in September. Riding along at the peak of his career, Miller had grown increasingly restless as our country got further into the action. He decided to volunteer and was inducted into the Army as Captain Glenn Miller at Omaha, Nebraska,

GLEN GRAY and the Casa Loma Band, 1943. Pee Wee Hunt in foreground. — *Courtesy Capitol Records.*

ALVINO REY's orchestra was booked solidly when this 1943 photo was made. — *Courtesy of Del Courtney.*

The "Old Smoothie," DEL COURTNEY and his orchestra, 1943 — *Photo courtesy of Del Courtney.*

PEGGY LEE with Goodman Band, at left, 1943. Like the other leaders Benny had increased the size of his orchestra during war years. — *Courtesy of Joe Rushton.*

TOMMY DORSEY's band of the mid-1940s with 19 girl violinists, indicative of the shortage of male musicians during final months of World War II. Vocalist is Stuart Foster. — *Photo courtesy of Dave Jacobs.*

on October 1, 1942. His last job as a civilian bandleader was a theater date at the Central in Passaic, New Jersey. The sentimental tension of his final performance was too much for everyone concerned. The audience, the musicians, and Miller, all broke into tears during the closing number and Miller, along with vocalist Marion Hutton left the stage while the band's theme was closing the show. This was the end of a brilliant career as one of America's greatest bandleaders, and in giving it up to participate in the war Miller was simply proving to the world the greatness of which those close to him had long been aware.

On the breakup of the Miller Band, its musicians scattered in many directions. Those not immediately headed for service themselves had no difficulty in finding lucrative jobs in other bands. There quickly developed active competition between Jan Garber and Horace Heidt to see who could hire the most of them. Garber even had a deal consummated for the services of vocalist Ray Eberle, until a difference of opinion during rehearsals torpedoed it. Heidt was ribbed by other members of the trade for paying Tex Beneke's expenses to the West Coast to join his band at the rumored guarantee of $500.00 per week, only to see him answer his draft call about three weeks after arrival.

As the first year under wartime conditions drew to a close, it was without any regrets on the part of the band business. It had been a fateful year which would leave many lasting impressions.

In addition to the tension created by the country being at war, tragedy had struck in many forms. Several renowned music people were injured in transportation crashes. On June 2nd, death had taken popular trumpeter Bunny Berigan, veteran of the Goodman and Dorsey bands, and well-known as a leader of his own unit.

Berigan had been in ill health for some time. Hospitalized for an intestinal ailment for several weeks, he was released to go back to the band on condition he would not play his trumpet. But he could not resist the requests heaped on him by fans and continued to play despite doctors warnings. Doubtless, this hastened his death.

An attempt to keep the band going under sax man Vido Musso's leadership was made. And few people were aware that Tommy Dorsey, considered a tough guy by many who knew him, now put Berigan's name on his payroll and established a fund for his children, to which he induced others to contribute. Prior to his death, Berigan had worked for Dorsey at least twice and each time was fired because he could not comply with the discipline Tommy maintained.

In November, the whole nation was shocked by the holocaust which destroyed Boston's Cocoanut Grove, claiming hundreds of lives, including several members of the Mickey Alpert Band who were

97

The all-girl bands made a place for themselves.
— *Photo courtesy of Barney McDevitt.*

CLAUDE THORNHILL who had interrupted his bandleading career for active navy duty.
— *Photo courtesy of Freddie Large.*

playing there at the time. Alpert himself escaped by breaking out a basement window and was credited with helping save the lives of several spectators.

During the year, individual bandleaders had, as in previous years, improved their status in the business. Outstanding among these was Stan Kenton, who had gone East to New York's Roseland Ballroom in February followed by an appearance at Frank Dailey's Meadowbrook in New Jersey. Virtually unknown twelve months earlier, these appearances had been the final touch in making him a national attraction and the balance of the year had been spent in playing the other major spots around the country.

But 1942 had really been a Harry James year, all the way. Starting off in the early months with his hit record of "You Made Me Love You", he continued to gain momentum. By fall he was the hottest box office band in the business, and even earlier was able to announce the purchase of the interest in his orchestra which had been retained by Benny Goodman for his initial financial assistance. Trade journals reported the amount involved to be $25,000.00 and not too many months before the James band clicked, Goodman was rumored to be willing to sell out for $5,000.00. Harry's claim to the title of "Band of the Year" was undisputed.

Throughout the duration of the war, the heavy demand for musical entertainment continued at a very high level. One-nighter guarantees continued to climb up and up but it didn't seem to make much difference. With a minimum expenditure for publicity and advertising, the leader on most such dates went into a percentage over his guarantee, and under these circumstances the promoter as well as the leader was happy. Hotels and nightclubs could not take care of all the business which came to them and often had reservations booked weeks in advance. Food shortages complicated their problems with wartime regulations even dictating what could be served. A good steak was considered a prize but regardless of the size of the party only half of the group was permitted to order one. Such shortages drove many people into the ballrooms which served food, even though it may have been there only as a side line. Once there, they gladly paid their cover charge, gulped down their food and left, often completely ignoring the big name talent which was appearing on the bandstand while they ate.

The HARRY JAMES band grew to this size during the mid-1940s. — *Photo courtesy of Harry James.*

BANDLEADER HAL McINTYRE (right) confers with his manager Don Haynes. Both had been with Glenn Miller. — *Photo courtesy of Don Haynes.*

SKINNAY ENNIS orchestra — Tacoma 1946. Back from the service, Ennis quickly gets back into the business with a full-size band. — *Photo courtesy of Bob Hope.*

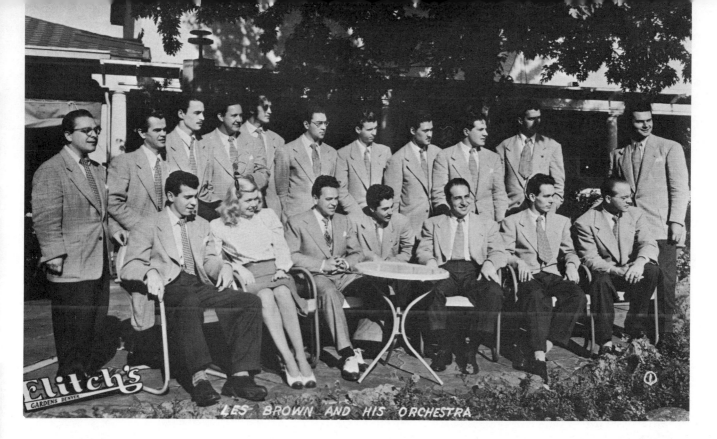

By now — 1945 — the LES BROWN band is hitting its stride. Vocalist is Doris Day. — *Photo courtesy of Evan Aiken.*

Major locations attempted to hedge against band shortages by lining them up months in advance. The leaders, plagued with ever-increasing travel hardships, were equally anxious to book in this manner. Consequently, many "for the duration" contracts were signed, although not too many of them actually remained in effect on that basis. In order to provide themselves with a permanent location, several financially able leaders purchased ballrooms themselves, among them Horace Heidt and Tommy Dorsey.

None of these adversities of the period, however, seemed able to slow down the trend towards increasing the size of the individual units. The last band fronted by Artie Shaw before his induction into the service was made up of thirty-two members. In the middle of the war years other big names were attempting to top this figure. Ironically, there was now a new incentive stimulating the big payroll. In late 1942, legislation, later modified, established a $25,000.00 annual earnings ceiling for salaried employees. Since bandleaders had already been classified as employees, they were affected by this ruling. Many of them reasoned that since they could not keep any portion of their now substantial earnings above that figure, they would use part of it to hire additional musicians. String

sections became the order of the day, with some of them larger than the previous total personnel of the bands in which they worked.

The draft had already created a shortage of musicians and this race to establish bigness further aggravated the situation. Under these competitive conditions, there just could not be enough male musicians to go around and the young ladies started to move in. Even the brass sections of several bands were graced by members of the fair sex. Woody Herman was featuring a very capable and attractive trumpet player from the Pacific Northwest named Elizabeth Rogers whose musicianship had the respect of all her male contemporaries. Because many of the girls were proficient on the violin, they became a common sight in the string sections. Towards the war's end, Tommy Dorsey's band was featuring nineteen strings, all of them girls. There were a substantial number of all-girl orchestras enjoying the success of the times, and in some cases the wives of leaders who entered the service took over their husband's chores as bandleader to keep his name alive until he could return.

The contribution to the country's morale made by the orchestra leaders and their members could never be adequately measured. U.S.O. shows went

TEX BENEKE, with the Glenn Miller library, kept the Miller band active, sponsored by Mrs. Miller. — *Photo courtesy of General Artists Corp.*

EDDY HOWARD'S was probably the outstanding individual success story of 1946. — *Courtesy of M.C.A.*

The ELIOT LAWRENCE band turned out some great music during the late 1940s and early 1950s. — *Photo courtesy of Arsene Studio, N.Y.C.*

everywhere and bands gave their services without reserve. In a fund-raising capacity they were equally active, appearing for bond rally functions wherever and whenever needed and the need continued undiminished until the end of the war finally came.

Unfortunately, that end did not come in time to bring home from military service the man who was probably America's most beloved bandleader. The story of Glenn Miller's disappearance has been written again and again, and portrayed on the screen by Jimmy Stewart in an excellent movie titled "The Glenn Miller Story". But it took the shock of the first news of "officially missing" many months to be accepted as sad realization that he was indeed a war casualty.

Miller took off from Bedford, England, on December 15, 1944 in a plane piloted by Flight Officer John Morgan. Their destination was Paris where Major Miller was to be joined by his service band to entertain troops near the front lines. Continued bad weather had delayed the units traveling intact, and resulted in Miller's finally deciding to proceed alone to arrange for their arrival. The mystery of what happened has never been solved. When the plane lifted from the runway at 1:45 P.M. on that bleak day, the fog over the English channel embraced it and its occupants forever.

Not many months later, the war dragged wearily to a close.

As the servicemen began returning from overseas, the entertainment boom continued unabated. The shortage of musicians soon became just a memory as the uniforms were put aside for civilian life with plenty of work waiting for all of them.

Leaders who had been away hastened to take up where they had left off. Quickly they recruited the necessary personnel, and after brief rehearsals most of them booked a fast break-in tour before attempting to move into a location job. The locations were plentiful, as new clubs and ballrooms mushroomed across the country. In these and in the older established spots, their fans could once more dance to such old favorites as Orrin Tucker, Alvino Rey, Bob Crosby, Jimmy Grier, Dick Jurgens, Skinnay Ennis, Claude Thornhill, Dick Stabile, and Eddy Duchin, as these and many others resumed activity.

Encouraged by the prosperous conditions of the mid-forties a rash of new bands was formed. Many of these were organized by ex-service side-men who came back determined to be their own boss. Others were headed up by featured musicians who had ridden through the war at home, but felt the time was now right to realize long-cherished ambitions to be leaders.

Ray Anthony, who had led a service band in the Pacific area during the war became one of the fastest rising of these postwar bands. Prior to this wartime experience, he had not tried his hand at leading his own band, but had learned the business well working for Glenn Miller and Jimmy Dorsey.

In addition to Anthony, there were several other ex-Miller men fronting their own crews. Early in the forties, Hal McIntyre had struck out on his own and was well-established by the war's end. Arranger Jerry Gray's orchestra was formed not much later than Anthony's and was actually his second attempt at having a band. But there was an official Glenn Miller band operating with the blessing and sponsorship of the Miller family, and this was organized in January of 1946 by Tex Beneke. Both the Beneke organization and McIntyre's were handled by old-time Miller manager, Don Haynes, who had been with Miller prior to the war, and who had gone into the Army with him where he managed the affairs of the service band.

Buddy Rich got into the action with his own unit after several years of drumming for Tommy Dorsey. The money for this venture was rumored to have come from another Dorsey alumnus, Frank Sinatra, in spite of the fact that when they both worked in the Dorsey band they periodically engaged in arguments which usually ended up with fists swinging.

The Elliot Lawrence Band, put together as a studio group at Philadelphia Station WCAU got off to a good start and was generally considered slated for big-name status in the future.

Freddy Martin lost a string of piano players in rapid succession. First to go was veteran Jack Fina who made the jump from sideman to leader in mid-1946. His replacement, Murray Arnold, soon did the same thing and his job was filled by Barclay Allen who stayed only a few months before he also formed an orchestra of his own.

There were two Ellington bands as the Duke's son, Mercer Ellington took a brief fling at bandleading. Still more surprising was the appearance of a second Lombardo band when brother Victor took off to try his wings alone, a venture which

WOODY HERMAN gives the "go man, go" sign to Red Norvo who was playing vibes in the Herman band in the mid-1940s. — *Photo courtesy of Columbia Records.*

VICTOR LOMBARDO took a brief fling at bandleading on his own. — *Photo courtesy of M.C.A.*

BUDDY RICH, out of the Dorsey band to become a leader. — *Photo courtesy of Coliseum Ballroom.*

Jack Fina's orchestra on a one-night stand sometime in late 1940s. — *Photo courtesy of Jack Fina.*

Ray Anthony's band also had a sound clearly indicating Miller's influence. — *Courtesy Barney McDevitt.*

Count Basie's great band — date not definite, probably late 1940s. — *Courtesy Arsene Studio, N. Y.*

Will Osborne Ad — this ad indicates that in the postwar years promoters were beginning to sense a desire on the part of the patrons for a more danceable product. April, 1947.

HOAGY CARMICHAEL

The "TEEN AGERS" who toured under Hoagy Carmichael's sponsorship. — *Photo courtesy of Barney McDevitt.*

HOAGY CARMICHAEL — *Photo courtesy of Dave Bixler.*

was later abandoned in favor of the comfort of working with Guy.

Even songwriter Hoagy Carmichael got into the business with a young band called "The Teenagers" which travelled and made appearances under his sponsorship and name. There were bands with double brass sections — all saxophone bands, — bands with anything which might give them that certain something to create interest necessary to put them out in front.

Unfortunately, it just didn't work out that way for most of them. Within the next few years, many of these newcomers and others who came along later were to find the going so tough that they could not continue. In some cases, they folded because the bandleader simply was not cut out to be one. It was not just the newcomers though, who were to run into trouble, for in the last few years of the forties the old-timers also began to find the road a little rough.

First indications that the big boom might be over began to appear in the early summer of 1946. Attendance figures started to decline in ballrooms, clubs, and on one night bookings. Much of the money supporting these operations had come from defense industries which were now being cut back. The mood of the spenders also underwent a change. A lot of people who had seen no reason not to spend with reckless abandon during the war now got serious about buying homes, appli-

107

JIMMY LUNCEFORD, one of the greatest of the Negro bands. —*Photo courtesy of the Golden Gate Theater.*

ances, etc., as the relaxing of material restrictions began to make these available.

Many ballrooms which had been operating on a full six-night week reduced to only four or five, and some opened only on week ends. Hotels and nightclubs underwent policy changes. Many promoters of one-nighters suspended operations completely, usually after a series of unprofitable dates on which they experienced difficulty in even taking in enough money to pay the band's guarantee.

These guarantees had grown during the war to figures never previously dreamed of. Before the war, it was a rare occasion that a one-nighter involved a guarantee of $1800.00 and only a handful of bands could command that figure. Now it was only average. Such top names as Goodman, James, Tommy Dorsey, and Artie Shaw were asking $3,000 to $4,000 and getting it. The business had been so good that the guarantee didn't actually matter since the promoter ended up making money anyway.

Hotels and ballrooms had also been paying high figures. In the first year of postwar prosperity at least two ballrooms in the Los Angeles area were bidding as much as $7500.00 for a week's work by a top-name band. Similar situations existed in many other parts of the nation as well.

By the end of 1946, it was apparent that action must be taken to cope with the band business recession which had now become a reality.

Harry James was one of the first to recognize the signs and the first to make a realistic attempt to do something about it. He reasoned that there could be no one-nighter business if the promoters were forced out of business, and no attendance if admission prices were prohibitive. To help the promoters stay in business, he reduced the guarantees he had been asking. Since this alone would not bring people into the ballrooms, he went a step farther. Into each of his contracts he wrote a clause regulating the maximum admission charge which could be made. In some cases these had risen to $4.00 plus tax per person for top name appearances. James insisted that no one charge more than $2.00 plus tax for the privilege of dancing to his music.

But James could not reverse the trend by himself and unfortunately not enough of his fellow leaders followed his example, or at least not voluntarily. There was, however, a general move to control something else which had gotten out of hand — the payroll. During the war, salaries had skyrocketed as leaders tried to outbid one another for the available sidemen. The trend to bigness had made almost every organization top-heavy with personnel but neither individual salaries nor total payroll had made much difference and had been pretty generally ignored. Despite heavy operating expenses business had been so good that everyone made money.

Now it was suddenly different. With the market diminishing rapidly, it was easy to see that the leader could not take home a profit unless he could somehow reduce his weekly output.

This they set about doing during the winter of 1946 and 1947. Usually the procedure included complete disbanding for a short time, perhaps only a few weeks or months. During this lay-off period, a fairly complete reorganization took place and when operations were resumed it would be with a substantially smaller unit. Often many of the previous sidemen would return, but at considerably reduced salaries.

All the biggest names of the day staged shake-ups of this nature. Those receiving the most publicity in the process were Tommy Dorsey, Woody Herman, Artie Shaw, Les Brown, and Harry James, but the movement included many others, and in some cases without any alteration of arrangements to fit the smaller group. When this happened, the resulting sound was usually pretty thin. An outstanding example which I particularly recall was Henry Busse's sudden reduction from 19 to 14 men during an extended stay at the Palace Hotel in San Francisco, but with the big band library remaining in use.

Other reorganizations were made with a different objective — a complete change of style. During the war years the emphasis had drifted further and further towards music for listening and most

LEIGHTON NOBLE and his orchestra on the West Coast during the late 1940s.
— *Photo courtesy of Gene's Photo & Rock Shop, Avalon, Catalina Island.*

of the newly formed organizations followed that pattern. But there were many who felt that with the war over, the popularity of the loud, big brass section bands would wane in favor of something softer and more danceable. The first to move in that direction was Jan Garber who had been fronting a large swing orchestra since 1942. He now broke this up completely and after a few months of vacationing hit the road once more with a sweet band closely resembling that with which he had been identified prior to the war.

Many others followed Garber's example and as the remaining years of the forties unfolded it was the dispensers of smoother melodies who appeared to suffer least from the recession.

A limited number of the larger bands still kept busy but usually underwent periodic reorganization. The Kenton Band, which had come into being early in the decade, made itself a place among these and in the late forties was probably the biggest in terms of personnel. Kenton, too, had his troubles, including at least one nervous breakdown and made frequent announcements of pending retirement. By this time he had moved so far in the direction of "progressive jazz" that he preferred not to be booked at all for dances but tried to limit his engagements to jazz concerts.

Among the white bands competing with Kenton for "big-band jazz" honors were Woody Herman, Gene Krupa and Charlie Barnet. Herman, winner of all the trade journal popularity polls in 1946 appeared to be doing all right, but suddenly disbanded in 1947 to resume some months later. Krupa had disbanded in 1943, then joined Tommy Dorsey for two years, returning to bandleading at the war's end. His new crew was too large to support under the conditions which faced him and he finally reduced its size, changing at the same time his musical programming to include more encouragement for those strictly interested in dancing.

The Negro leaders resisted more stubbornly the temptation to reduce manpower or to make alterations in style. Lionel Hampton's driving aggregation of 20 had joined Basie, Ellington and Lunceford in the front ranks during the mid-forties. Eventually he had to make a concession to the trend with the addition of a limited number of arrangements aimed toward the sweet side. Lunceford's great band was broken up in late 1947 following his sudden death while on tour in the Pacific Northwest.

Vaughn Monroe became one of the most successful bandleaders of the postwar period when he finally reached the top in 1945 after years of struggling. Monroe's vocal effort, often the target of columnists and disc jockeys, played a big part in the band's success although he consistently maintained a first-class musical organization behind him.

Eddy Howard wrote the big success story of 1946 with the first of many hit records. Howard was no newcomer to the business having spent several years with Dick Jurgens prior to launching his own career as a leader in 1942. In addition to the reputation he had gained with Jurgens he was well known as the composer of at least a half-dozen popular songs. His musical style was definitely on the smooth side with some of the Jurgens influence apparent.

Russ Morgan's turn began to appear imminent during the early months of 1948. Perhaps he was overdue since he had been around with his own band since 1935, always giving the top names a run for their money. As 1948 faded into 1949 it was apparent he had something big developing with at least two of his records riding high on the rating charts, one of them a composition of his own. In the first few months of 1949 these became even bigger and were followed by others. Suddenly he was in demand for more personal appearances than he could make and had one of the biggest band attractions in the business at the end of the decade. The "old coal miner" from Pennsylvania had finally struck a vein of gold and he was making the most if it.

Aside from these, the last half of the 1940s did not produce any really great events within the orchestra world. Business continued to be reasonably good for established names, but no one was optimistic about the trend of the times. Important locations continued to drop live music or in some cases to close down entirely. Disc jockeys were replacing remote radio pickups, which had been of great importance as band-building mediums. Worse still, the jockeys were playing fewer and fewer band records, and even the recording companies appeared to be playing down dance bands. They were aggravated by the second of Petrillo's recording strikes, both of which occurred within a ten year span.

As 1950 approached, the old-timers who had found the band business a highly lucrative field were growing extremely pessimistic as to its future.

This picture of RUSS MORGAN'S ORCHESTRA was made in 1945. Morgan had his biggest year in 1949. — *Photo courtesy of Russ Morgan.*

JAN GARBER clowns with former Casa Loma vocalist Kenny Sargent as ex-Casa Loma drummer Tony Briglia faces mike. Memphis, 1948. — *Photo courtesy of Ernie Mathias.*

Jimmy Dorsey's orchestra of the early 1950s.

The big band of Ray Anthony, shown here in 1948, was a top condender through the mid-50s. — *Both photos courtesy of Barney McDevitt.*

The Decline of the 'Fifties

THE TEN YEAR PERIOD comprising the 1950s was one of steady decline of the dance band business from its once top position as a form of live entertainment to a situation where only a few of its former great names could prosper.

The progress of that decline was relentless despite periodic optimistic declarations of impending prosperity and booms which never quite materialized, even though the period did produce its individual new success stories.

That the business was not in a healthy condition was apparent to anyone who took a close look in the early months of 1950 and considered problems which had been developing for some time. Since 1946 the total market for bands had been in a continuous downward trend — now many established leaders with years of experience behind them were finding the going extremely rough, and several began to drop out. New bands were finding it next to impossible to get started.

True it was that not everyone began to feel the pinch simultaneously. For some, business had never been better. Russ Morgan, a veteran campaigner of many seasons, had just enjoyed his biggest year. Another old-timer, Jimmy Dorsey was discovering new life which might once more move him to the top of the list. Many others still prospered with the formats which brought them success in the pre-war years.

But the casualty rate among those who ventured into the business in the postwar years had been high. Only a limited few had been able to establish themselves firmly enough to be national attractions. Included in this group, and with the most promise for the future, were Ray Anthony, Tex Beneke, Jerry Gray, and Elliot Lawrence.

The mortality rate had not been quite so high among those who styled their music more for the hotels and supper clubs and for the ballrooms. While not all of them had reached coast-to-coast

prominence, many were firmly established attractions regionally. Piano playing maestros seemed to be faring particularly well. Launched during the mid-forties and now well entrenched were Frankie Carle, Carmen Cavallero, and Jack Fina, all able to book the top hotels on either coast and through the South and the Middle West.

Among the bigger bands the Buddy Rich aggregation had looked like a sure winner at the time of its organization shortly after the war. He had years of experience behind him, a name made well known as a featured attraction with Tommy Dorsey and financing by Frank Sinatra. The band's earliest bookings had included the nation's best locations. Now it had been broken up and Rich, along with others, was pointing out that if the business were going to survive it must produce new names.

Not just the musicians, but every segment of the music business was deeply concerned over the conditions and trends.

Downbeat magazine in its early 1950 issues explored the problem from many angles. Although generally inclined to give its blessing to the strictly jazz and swing bands rather than those more commercially styled, it now pointed out that the band business was basically one of providing dance music. It suggested that a lot of the people in the business should get back to playing music which was danceable if they hoped to survive the recession which was fast gaining momentum.

The magazine did not content itself with this analysis, but took positive action of its own to help fight the slump. The newly formed orchestra of Roy Stevens was selected as a test band to determine whether a good danceable organization, properly launched, could catch the public's fancy and succeed. Without actually sponsoring Stevens, the publicity they gave him was doubtless instrumental in his landing a booking at Frank Dailey's Meadowbrook for the band's debut. The resulting

JERRY GRAY's orchestra on Palladium bandstand. — *Courtesy of Barney McDevitt.*

contract for him to stay on for three months was interpreted as a possible pending revival of dance orchestra interest.

The recording companies, despite their discouraging experience with two long strikes during the forties also cooperated in the attempt to restimulate dancing. RCA-Victor produced and released a series of records styled "Here Come the Dance Bands Again". Other major labels soon followed their example, particularly Capitol who launched a heavy promotion of their own dance-styled artists.

Victor was active in another way for it had a test band of its own going. In the Spring of 1950 Ralph Flanagan's Band took to the road for its first series of locations and one-nighters. This organization had been formed in the Victor Studios in 1949. According to trade talk at the time, Victor put Flanagan in the business because they were determined to prove to some of their more "difficult to deal with" artists that they could create stars themselves. Flanagan's first records had been released with heavy build-up in the Fall of 1949 and

produced gratifying results. Quite literally they made him a "name band leader" before he ever played his first job.

As his 1950 tour got under way, the rest of the music world sat back to watch with keen interest. It soon became evident that this approach might be a new way to build a band, or at least it was working for Flanagan. By the end of the year he was well on his way to becoming America's Number One Band, a title which he claimed by the end of 1951.

This route quickly became the blueprint for others to follow. Victor repeated it themselves some months later with Buddy Morrow, although without the same degree of success. During 1951 the new band of Ralph Marterie tried it the same way with heavy build-up from Mercury Records before booking engagements in October. The next year the Billy May Band tried it with Capitol supplying the promotion through records. Like Morrow, neither Marterie nor May were able to parlay it into success approaching Flanagan's.

Meanwhile, the ballroom operators were pursuing efforts of their own to improve the still-sagging dance business. During the late forties, they had formed a trade association called "National Ballroom Operators of America". The group was now meeting annually to discuss and handle problems peculiar to their segment of the entertainment industry. One of their prime targets was the revision of the wartime cabaret tax which they steadfastly maintained should not apply to ballrooms whose feature attraction was dancing. Eventually they won their battle, but it took several years to attain victory.

With so many different people working towards building the business, it would seem it could do nothing but improve. Indeed, when the total annual gross incomes of some of its leaders were published in early 1952, the impression could have been easily gotten that there was nothing in any way wrong with it.

Because of his position at the time as the hottest new band in the field, Ralph Flanagan's total business was given widespread coverage in trade journals such as *Variety* and *Billboard*. These stories indicated that during 1951 the new maestro had racked up a very impressive $600,000.00, give or take a little. His handlers were now claiming for him the somewhat nebulous title of "America's Number One Band", but if grosses were the determining yardstick, he had not yet made it. The same sources which had published Flanagan's take indicated that at least two old perennials had topped him. Lombardo had grossed approximately $850,000. and Sammy Kaye had barely missed the $900,000. mark.

A breakdown of the revenue sources proved interesting and revealing. Kaye had a successful publishing firm and his book of poems in addition to other more normal sources of income. Substantial earnings from radio and television had been made by all three. The personal appearance income of both Flanagan and Kaye was heaviest in the one-nighter column. Theaters, which ten years before would have been very lucrative engage-

FRANKIE CARLE got going with his own band in 1944 and was well established by the early 1950s. — *Photo courtesy of Frankie Carle.*

The RALPH FLANAGAN band in action. — *Photo courtesy of Arsene Studio, N. Y. C.*

BUDDY MORROW whose orchestra Victor hoped to build into the top brackets along with Flanagan. — *Photo courtesy of G.A.C.*

BILLY MAY, who soon tired of the trials of leading a big band. — *Photo courtesy of G.A.C.*

RALPH MARTERIE was one of the new bands moving up rapidly as a result of heavy build-up by Mercury Records. May 1952. — *Photo courtesy of Mercury Records.*

SONNY DUNHAM's orchestra. Dunham had been the featured trumpet on many Glen Gray records prior to his first band venture in 1940. — *Photo courtesy of Arsene Studio, N. Y. C.*

ments, had virtually lost all importance. The Kaye and Flanagan Bands showed theater earnings of less than $40,000.00, a figure similar to a two week stage appearance during the mid-forties.

Spurred on by the lure of this kind of money and ignoring the fact that it was not a true barometer of the total picture, a whole new crop of bands appeared. During the Fall of '51 and Spring of '52, at least ten organizations got under way fronted by Sy Oliver, Buddy Morrow, Lee Castle, Don Terry, King Guion, Shorty Rogers, Maynard Ferguson, Buddy Rich, Sonny Dunham, and Neal Hefti. Without exception these men were top musicians. For many of them it was at least the second bandleading venture, but few of them would be able to make the grade.

Somewhat later in the year another "new sound" band made its appearance, for a time creating quite a stir. If advance planning could insure success, the Sauter-Finegan Orchestra should have been a cinch. Its co-leaders Bill Finegan and Eddie Sauter, both outstanding arrangers, had spent two years or more getting ready for the move, including many recording sessions. Billing it as a creative band which would provide both dance and "mood" music, they hoped to duplicate the success pattern recently established by Flanagan, Ray Anthony and Billy May. Moderate success was enjoyed for a while, but the venture was ultimately abandoned after a few years.

Territory bands now began to get additional activity as Midwestern operators found it increasingly difficult to make a profit after paying name-band guarantees. These "semi-names" began to dominate the ballroom picture in that area, and soon moved into the hotels as well throughout the Midwest, South and Southwest. Riding the crest of this trend were Chuck Foster, Ray Pearl, Leo Pieper, Paul Neighbors, Teddy Phillips, Jimmy Palmer, Tommy Reed and Tiny Hill.

It was becoming increasingly difficult to get name orchestras to make swings to the West Coast at all. Even the many who headquartered there were finding it necessary to spend most of their time elsewhere in order to keep busy. The Coast picture had already declined further than that in the Midwest and East. Many locations had suspended operations entirely, or were reluctant to pay top money, and the once lucrative Coastwise one-nighter market had dropped to little or nothing by the beginning of 1953.

The Dorseys made the biggest news of that year with their announcement in the early spring months that they would reunite. This marked the end of nearly twenty years of always aggressive, sometimes violent, competition between Tommy and Jimmy. Speculation as to whether they would resume equal billing as the Dorsey Brothers kept their friends inside and outside the trade occupied for a while as each of them fulfilled his own individual commitments prior to the merger. The question was answered when the new band took to the road in early summer billed "The Tommy Dorsey Orchestra Featuring Jimmy Dorsey". Listeners out front quickly identified the arrangements as being largely Tommy's, and it would appear little had changed from the old days of the early thirties except their ability to work together. Tommy was still the driving force and Jimmy the mild-mannered "nice guy" older brother. The new band continued as a top contender until the tragic death of both brothers a few years later within a few months of one another.

Harry James was still one of the top names around, and another merger of sorts occurred when he signed discouraged bandleader Buddy Rich as a featured headliner at a reported salary of $35,000.00 per year. This move was generally felt to have been a good deal for each of them, guaranteeing Rich more money than he had been able to earn as a leader, and adding to the drawing power of James.

Billy May, after only a couple of years with a band of his own, tired of the traveling which it involved and retired to television and recording duties more to his liking, primarily arranging. In this case, however, the band was not broken up. Ray Anthony stepped in to take it over financially, placing Sam Donohue in front of it to be its new leader as it continued on the road.

Anthony's own band had now moved up to challenge the position of Ralph Flanagan. But if it were new blood the business needed to perpetuate itself, the handwriting on the wall was becoming increasingly threatening. Aside from these two who were riding high, the going was becoming progressively rougher for all but a handful of the newer crop.

However, those who could be classified as newcomers had no monopoly on the trouble. The old-timers were also finding it more and more difficult

The SAUTER-FINEGAN orchestra in a concert appearance. — *Photo courtesy of Barney McDevitt.*

PAUL NEIGHBORS, who started on the West Coast about 1948, became a favorite in the Midwestern territory during the mid-1950s. — *Photo courtesy Paul Neighbors.*

TEDDY PHILLIPS at Chicago's Aragon Ballroom, mid-1950s. — *Courtesy of M.C.A.*

BIG TINY HILL on the stand at Tom Archer's ballroom in Des Moines. — *Photo courtesy of Tom Archer.*

RAY PEARL was a big territory favorite in the Midwest during the 1940s and early 1950s. He disbanded in 1956 after closing a Peabody Hotel (Memphis) engagement, blasting Union Boss Petrillo in a full page ad as the cause of his inability to continue operating as a leader.

TED HEATH, England's most popular band, makes a U. S. tour in the early 1950s. — *Photo courtesy of Charlie Higgins.*

Jimmy Palmer, one of the 1950s popular territory bands. — *Photo courtesy of Associated Booking.*

to show a profit and many of them began to limit their operations or to drop out entirely.

And so it went.

Each succeeding year one or more segments of the industry predicted a business upturn. Various attempts were made to revive the public's sagging interest. Yet the end of each year found a few less places hiring dance bands; a few less bands in operation.

By the time the second half of the decade got under way, there was little resemblance to the prosperity of the "good old days". Hotels, ballrooms, nightclubs, and theaters had been the major sources of employment throughout the prosperous years. Now a look at each category revealed an extremely discouraging picture.

Only a few hotels across the nation were still featuring name bands. One by one the rest had closed dancing rooms for "alterations" that were never completed, or brought in show business and recording star names backed musically with a "house band".

Nightclubs had almost completely deserted name bands in favor of "single attractions" or small combos.

Ballrooms were operating week ends, standing idle, or had been converted to bowling alleys. Gone were such old landmarks as Kansas City's Pla-Mor; Portland, Oregon's Jantzen Beach; and even Chicago's Trianon; while Frank Dailey's Meadowbrook was being converted to a bar. The one-nighter business had dwindled to what remained in the Middle West and East along with some semblance of former business in the Southwest.

Hardly a theater in the nation brought in a band as a stage attraction.

Start a new band? Only if you could be content to operate locally or be a territory name. The same factors which created national names fifteen and twenty years before could no longer be counted on. The old formula, while not as easy as it sounds, had still been a well-marked road map. Establish a local following; get on local radio; move into a spot which had a network remote airtime pickup; get a couple of hit records working for you.

Gradually remote pickups, both network and local, were discontinued. Now it would take the miracle of a big record to attract attention. To get this record would virtually involve a miracle. After their temporary revival of interest in the early fifties, the recording companies had again forgotten dance bands except for the re-issuing of the best things done by the big names during their peak years.

Now the post mortems began as everyone sought the answer to the question, "What happened to the big band business?"

Everyone had his individual opinion. Blame was directed at television, the disc jockeys, rock and roll music. The ballroom operators pointed at the bandleaders — said they had started playing for themselves instead of the customers. Bandleaders came back with the claim that operators had forgotten how to properly publicize their coming attractions and appearances and so should accept the blame themselves for the poor attendance figures.

The "smooth and sweet" bands blamed the "new sound" bands for teaching the public to listen rather than dance. The "new sound" leaders retorted by criticizing the other group for failure to develop anything new.

Privately a lot of the veteran leaders conceded that the musicians themselves had lost interest before the public had, and that one naturally followed the other.

Old-timers Paul Whiteman and Guy Lombardo, periodically consulted for opinions were quoted in trade journals and newspaper stories. Whiteman felt the turning point had come when bandleaders began over-featuring vocalists and vocal groups. He went on to remind that it was he who had first introduced such groups, but that he had made them sing in dance tempo. Lombardo's contention was that patrons of dance spots came there to dance and be entertained, not to listen to music intended to educate them. Both reminded that the big names who rose to the top got there by playing dance music, and that it was they who had built the business to the peak it finally reached.

Lombardo's comments could not be taken lightly by observers who looked closely at what the "fading fifties" had produced. Most of the new success stories were written by bands who, whether they swung it or played it sweet, did so in dance tempo. As they struggled to make it pay off, they found their toughest competition coming from old, long-established veterans who had a reputation for pleasing dancers, and the names of Lombardo, Sammy Kaye, Jan Garber, Wayne King, Russ Morgan, Freddy Martin, Charlie Spivak, and Lawrence Welk continued to grace the marquees which were still lighted.

Others whose popularity dated back to the heyday of the thirties such as Goodman, Shaw and

HARRY JAMES hires Buddy Rich to play drums, although in this picture it appears the reverse is true. — *Photo courtesy of "Pee Wee" Monte.*

STAN KENTON doing a concert, his favorite type of personal appearance, in the mid-1950s. — *Courtesy of Capitol Records.*

JAN GARBER was approaching his 40th anniversary as a successful leader when this 1957 photo was made in New Orleans with Leo Walker, recording star Rusty Draper, and Warren Wasescha, a song plugger from St. Louis. — *Photo courtesy of Roosevelt Hotel, New Orleans.*

FREDDY MARTIN was still at the Cocoanut Grove. — *Photo courtesy of Freddy Martin.*

125

LES ELGART and his orchestra, one of the few bands to survive the decline of the 1950s. — *Photo courtesy of Columbia Records.*

BENNY GOODMAN was active but choosing his jobs carefully. — *Photo courtesy of Columbia Records.*

LOMBARDO was completing thirty consecutive seasons at New York's Roosevelt Grill, 1959. — *Photo courtesy of Guy Lombardo.*

The "official" GLENN MILLER band was now fronted by Ray McKinley.
  — *Photo courtesy of Arsene Studio.*

Krupa were periodically active when they chose to be, but with smaller versions of their former units. For the most part, they concentrated on clubs rather than dance dates. This trend to reduce to smaller bands was somewhat general and eventually included some of those who had attained stardom with big bands early in the decade. Both Anthony and Flanagan were among those who eventually gave up almost entirely their travels with full bands in favor of club dates with a smaller group.

Many others who had long been dispensing fine dance music with small bands were continuing to enjoy success including Pee Wee Hunt of Casa Loma fame who had parlayed a couple of record hits in the late forties and early fifties into the necessary momentum. Red Nichols, who had always insisted that the basis for all good jazz was dance music, was still active the year round and in demand for both jazz and dance spots coast-to-coast.

Revival of dixieland had brought the banjo back for the first popularity it had seen since the late twenties. Now it actually took over in many of the clubs, particularly on the West Coast. In both Los Angeles and San Francisco "all banjo" bands were packing patrons into spots most of which featured group singing participation, but some that also encouraged dancing. By the early sixties, similar groups could be found in every major city across the nation with some reaching name status.

For whatever their reasons, the number of people who wanted to patronize public dancing continued to decline. So, too, did the number of dance bands in constant activity. In a sense the term "name band" virtually lost its meaning as many who had once fit that description restricted their operations to the point that they were in reality only "territory bands". Anyone who doubted that the glamour was rapidly fading away could find convincing evidence in the telephone directories. Names of leaders who had long insisted on unlisted numbers to insure privacy could now be found in the book along with everyone else.

By the time the sixties got under way, the "big band sound" was not much in evidence. It might be discovered here and there on a local basis, but few besides Harry James, Les Brown, and Count Basie were taking it on the road for national tours. The Glenn Miller name was still alive with the band sponsored by Mrs. Miller and fronted by Ray McKinley. Warren Covington was in charge of the Tommy Dorsey Band with the original instrumentation still basically intact as it continued on the road after the deaths of both Tommy and Jimmy. Most of the rest were confining their activities to regional coverage, principally the Middle West and East where population was more concentrated.

In 1959 the American Federation of Musicians belatedly initiated its own attempt to revive big band interest. Through a series of regional con-

RED NICHOLS AND HIS FIVE PENNIES, sometime during the mid-50s. — *Photo courtesy of Red Nichols.*

RAY ANTHONY'S small combo in a Las Vegas club, 1959. — *Photo courtesy of Capitol Records.*

PEE WEE HUNT (on trombone) and his orchestra had hit it big with records in the early 1950s and continued to do well with a small Dixie-styled band in the last half of the decade. — *Courtesy Capitol Records.*

CLYDE McCOY had given up his full-sized band for Dixieland. — *Photo courtesy of G.A.C.*

CLAUDE GORDON, national winner of the Union's band contest, 1959. — *Courtesy of Claude Gordon.*

COUNT BASIE and his orchestra were still delivering the big band sound at the end of the '50s. This picture was made at Columbia Studios. — *Photo courtesy of Columbia Records.*

tests climaxed by a national event, they hoped to find the nation's best new band. The winner would be given an appearance on a national television show and a six weeks' tour sponsored by the National Ballroom Operators Association. This send-off, they hoped, would give the band a launching towards success which could be kept rolling.

Claude Gordon, the entrant from the Los Angeles regional contest, was the winner of the national finals held in New York. Following the sponsored tour, he returned to the Coast and signed as his personal manager, Frank Monte, who was the manager of Harry James and had been for several years. Together they began to make long-range plans which they hoped would make Gordon a major attraction.

The contest was repeated the following year with Jackie Gleason, always a friend of the big bands, serving as honorary chairman. This time the national finals were held in Detroit where the winner was again an entry from the West Coast, Jimmie Cook from Las Vegas. He, too, was hopeful of big things to come.

Both had a multitude of well-wishers in the music world, most of whom were aware that the road up for any new band would be extremely difficult. Neither of them found the success they hoped for, although Gordon continued to be active on the West Coast after extended road tours which were not too productive. The union's contest was tried again in 1961, but the results were so discouraging that it was abandoned.

Where were all those whose names through the years had spelled box office magic?

Not all of them who were no longer active had necessarily dropped out because of waning popularity. Some had turned to other phases of the music business. Several who were active on a part-time basis could have been more so if the incentive existed. Many of them elected to work only a part of each year because beyond that point high income taxes took the major portion of what they made.

A lot of well-known leaders turned to television where they found personal satisfaction, along with financial return, as musical directors or arrangers.

131

Others were performing similar chores in recording studios. Even radio was still paying off for a few, not in the manner they had once been accustomed to, but as disc jockeys. Ted Weems, Joe Reichman, Del Courtney and a few others made new careers for themselves in this manner, taking occasional time out to resume bandleading on a limited basis. Courtney was particularly busy in both departments, having returned to his starting point in the San Francisco Bay Area where he now spun records on a daytime show and played local dance engagements at night.

For some, the business had paid off so well they simply retired when it became difficult to make money on the road.

The ranks were thinned out in another way as the final downbeat was taken by some who had retired, and others who were still at the peak of their careers. During the first fifteen years of the postwar period, death had taken a long list, including in the approximate order of their passing — Jimmy Lunceford, Jan Savitt, Eddy Duchin, Paul Specht, Phil Ohman, Isham Jones, Henry Busse, Gus Arnheim, Tommy Dorsey, Jimmy Dorsey, Abe Lyman, Griff Williams, Hal Grayson, Hal McIntyre, and Jimmie Grier.

The man with the big scythe had chosen his own time to cut them down, and without regard for the fact that several of them were still young men. The end came for Jimmy Lunceford in the summer of 1947 when a heart attack claimed him while he played a celebration in Astoria, Oregon. Jan Savitt, only 39 at the time, was a victim of a cerebral hemorrhage in October of 1948 while en route to a one-nighter in Sacramento, California. Eddy Duchin was still a very young 41 when a prolonged battle with leukemia claimed his life in 1951.

Barely more than six months separated the passing of the two famous Dorsey Brothers about whose part in the popular music scene volumes could be written. Tommy passed away in his sleep in his Connecticut home in late November of 1956. The band which had been under their co-leadership since their 1953 reunion carried on with Jimmy at the helm. But Jimmy was already a sick man, and in the Spring of 1957 he was forced to leave the band while on tour in Texas and return to New York to enter a hospital, suffering from cancer of the throat. It had been a long time since an instrumental record had enjoyed peak popularity, but as he lay in the hospital his own "So Rare" rose to the top position on all the nation's popularity charts. Old friends who dropped in to see him found him too weak to talk, but he could smile and point to the bedside radio as the disc jockeys gave his record the spins which it deserved. The end of his brilliant career came in June of 1957.

I was in Memphis, Tennessee, when death took Henry Busse in April of 1955, and when the

The banjo was back and being featured in clubs coast to coast. Among the fast-rising groups is DAVE WESLEY'S LEVEE LOUNGERS, playing top spots in Florida, Las Vegas, and the Twin Cities. (1963). — *Photo courtesy of Dave Wesley.*

HARRY JAMES' big band about 1959. — *Photo courtesy of Harry James.*

A few headlines continued to consider recovery a possibility but most of those who bothered to write on the subject at all were viewing the business in retrospect. — *Photo courtesy Los Angeles Times and St. Louis Post-Dispatch.*

An unusual photo of ELLINGTON taken in the mid-'50s. — *Courtesy Columbia Records.*

RUSS MORGAN, after 25 years of success with a 17-piece band, reduced it to 11 men in 1960 to concentrate his activity in the southern California area and stay off the road. Included in the new band were his sons, Jack and David, playing trombone and guitar respectively. — *Photo courtesy of Russ Morgan.*

news spread around the city it at first seemed like some very unfunny joke. Busse had been in town to play a one-night party for the National Undertakers Convention. This dancing party was being held in the Claridge Hotel, and during the course of the evening Bill Hendricks, Entertainment Director for the hotel and a former musician himself, noticed that Busse appeared extremely tired and periodically interrupted his fronting of the band to sit down in the background. Finally Hendricks suggested that Busse retire to his room and call the house doctor. The doctor's examination indicated that Busse had suffered a heart attack, and after cautioning him to remain quietly in bed the doctor left him for a few moments to arrange for a private nurse to remain by his side. When the nurse arrived, the famous trumpet player whose music had pleased millions was seated in a chair with his head in his hands, and efforts to revive him were futile.

It was also my privilege to participate in a morale-building effort which doubtless prolonged the life of one of these leaders, and which could not have succeeded without the cooperation of some of the top people in show business. In the Spring of 1957, while living in St. Louis, I was called to the Veteran's Hospital to visit Jimmy Grier who had been stricken with a liver ailment while visiting relatives in that city. Surgery was eventually decided upon and I stood beside his wife, Margie, in the waiting room while the surgeon told her chances of Grier leaving the hospital alive were extremely slim. Following the operation there was little evidence that he was on the road to recovery, and as I made my daily visit to see him I could not escape the feeling that the biggest problem was that he had simply lost the will to live.

During the thirties Grier had been a big name in the music world, particularly on the West Coast where he had fairly well dominated the Hollywood musical scene. His band had been the showcase for a lot of talent seeking careers in radio or motion pictures. But this was many years in the past and after several unsuccessful attempts to stage a comeback following World War II he had given up music to try his hand at real estate. Now he was convinced that few people really cared whether he lived or died, and had reconciled himself to permitting the end to come in the St. Louis hospital.

Grier was one of the old school of show business personalities who believed in spending to the hilt when he was making it. He had no enemy in the world except himself and never needed money so badly that he would not share what he had with any friend who asked.

Now he apparently lay dying and it hardly seemed fitting that the end should come in this manner.

After talking the situation over with his wife, I decided to see what might be done to let him know he was still remembered. The first move was to contact Bob Goddard, a show business columnist for the leading St. Louis newspaper, who ran a feature story on Grier's illness, including a review of his history in the music business. The reaction on the part of the hospital personnel was instantaneous. Next day when I visited him, he had been moved from a ward into a private room, and was being treated like a celebrity for the first time in several years.

In the early 1930s Grier had been featured on a radio show which was M'Ced by Walter Winchell. A wire which I dispatched to Winchell telling him of the bandleader's illness apparently resulted in his running the item in his column, for within a few days "get well" cards began to arrive at the hospital from the New York musicians. A similar wire addressed to a top executive of Music Corporation of America's Beverly Hills office resulted in many letters from West Coast music and show people, with a warm and lengthy letter from Grier's old-time friend, Bing Crosby, topping them all.

Overnight, his entire attitude changed, and his condition showed steady improvement. Six weeks later, his doctors, describing it as little short of a miracle, released him from the hospital and he returned to his West Coast home and the resumption of his real estate business. Two years later, a sudden recurrence of the ailment once again hospitalized him but this time he could not win the battle.

This was in the early summer of 1959. By this time little remained of the once-fabulous business of providing dance music, and it appeared that history was rapidly closing in on what had been one of America's brightest entertainment periods.

As these chapters are being put into final readiness for publication, it is early 1964.

The grim reaper has added several names of well-known musical personalities to his roster, taking within the last two years Jean Goldkette, Roger Wolfe Kahn, Jimmy Joy, Leo Reisman, Bert Lown, Ted Weems, Skinnay Ennis, Eddy Howard, Glen Gray, and Jack Teagarden.

Lawrence Welk, a man who never takes a drop of anything alcoholic himself, has made his "Champagne Music Makers" the nation's number one musical organization. Headquartering at Hollywood's Palladium where he plays week ends only, he periodically yields to the demand created by his television show for personal appearances, making upwards of a dozen quick tours annually, mostly for concerts. In between, he finds time to keep fit by almost daily golfing.

Always noted for his close attention to his fans, he is now credited with maintaining an active mailing list of 750,000 for whom he has a staff working the year 'round to see that each receives a Christmas card.

Perhaps as proof that hope springs eternal a new wave of optimism is stirring that a dance band renaissance is under way. Young musicians are once again trying to form bands, something which would not have been done five years ago. Peter Duchin, son of Eddy Duchin, recently successfully launched a career in his father's footsteps and is predicting that others could also make it pay. Woody Herman is riding the crest of a new-found popularity with a young band of sixteen men playing swinging dance arrangements. Several hotels and supper clubs have announced their return

to a "name band" policy, although most feature them as a show unit with minor emphasis on dancing.

The industry, having seen many previous revivals run out of gas, is skeptically holding its breath, afraid to really hope that this time it's for real.

PETER DUCHIN PLAYS PIANO AND LEADS BAND

Music, Maestro, Please---Fans of the Big Band Are Stirring

6-9-63

PETER DUCHIN follows in father's footsteps and predicts band revival. — *Photo courtesy of Los Angeles Times.*

FRANKIE CABLE's new group combined eye appeal with talent. — *Photo courtesy G.A.C.*

SI ZENTNER BRINGS BACK THE BIG BANDS!!

The Si Zentner Band is a SMASH on every date—a fresh original sound which is rejuvenating the ballroom scene...

Available for immediate bookings in your area

THE FABULOUS RECORD BREAKING OPENING OF SI ZENTNER AT THE HOLLYWOOD PALLADIUM JANUARY 23 AND 24.

SY ZENTNER, a veteran of many years with top orchestras, was fighting to establish his own big band at the end of the decade. — *Photo courtesy of Liberty Records.*

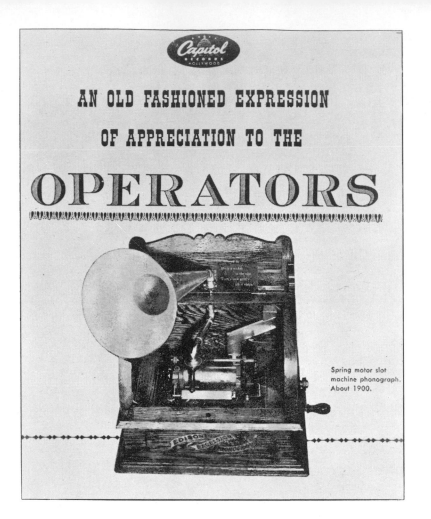

Spring motor slot machine phonograph. About 1900.

A spring-driven jukebox at turn of the century.

Typical early recording session showing pickup by mammoth horn around which musicians grouped as closely as possible. Note amplifying horn used by violinist. — *Photo courtesy of R.C.A. Victor.*

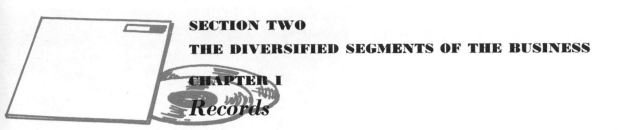

THE RECORDINGS MADE by America's popular dance orchestras provided their fans with a permanent memory of the style and accomplishments of their individual favorites. For the people who made these records they provided this and many other things as well. Discographies indicate that some of the early ones were often made only for the amusement of the musicians. This was not generally the case, however, or at least not for very long. Prior to the advent and build-up of radio, they offered virtually the only source of income other than personal appearances, and the band business was not very old before records became the biggest single medium for building a band to prominence. Except for a surrender period involving a few short years, the record industry retained its position in that regard as long as it appeared interested in doing so.

The recording industry as it is known today has come a long way from its primitive beginning. The modern record collector accepts the excellent reproduction which he gets from high-fidelity and stereo as being nothing out of the ordinary. A few of those who have been around a little longer can tell him that it was not always thus. Even now in some record shops which deal in old recordings there can be found copies of the early thick discs which were not only poor in quality, but recorded on one side only. Back in the era when these were made, the reproduction device was not called a record player, but a "talking machine" and there should be a fair number of readers who remember when it first moved into the home to replace the player piano. By winding the spring driven motor up as tightly as possible, the listener could usually get most of the way through a ten inch record before he had to rewind in order to maintain the desired number of revolutions per minute. Amplified not too adequately through a large horn came the music of Vess Ossman, the Banjo King; the voices of such artists as Josh White, Harry Lauder, Enrico Caruso, and slightly later Al Jolson, and

the never to be forgotten dialogue of the "Two Black Crows".

There might even be a few readers who recall when Edison's phonograph, invented about 1878, was still such a novelty that it was presented in public halls in concert style to audiences willing to pay $.25 to $.50 admission just to hear one for the first time. This situation existed well past the turn of the century. History indicates however, that Edison really had no thought of producing a machine for entertainment, but was actually attempting to develop a piece of office equipment used for dictation by executives. Promoters quickly saw the more commercial possibilities, and began to record something which would attract crowds to a publicized performance of the machine.

The first jukebox made its appearance in 1888, although it was not called that at the time. Before long a number of producers were in the business, offering franchises to interested people wherever they could find them. Battery driven models soon entertained patrons who listened through a tube which was an earphone of sorts, with sets having from four to a dozen of these. When all the listening tubes were busy simultaneously, on the bigger machines, it was possible for a single play to gross a total of sixty cents. The average cost of these early reproduction units was fifty dollars.

All of these models used a cylindrical type record, the only thing available at that time. Shortly before 1900 models appeared which would play five of the cylinders in rotation. Sometime before 1905 Victor and Columbia began to produce the flat disc records which gave the manufacturers of the cylindrical recording very brisk competition and eventually replaced them completely. About this same time the earphone began to be replaced with speaking horns so that larger crowds of people could be entertained simultaneously. In 1906 the Mills Novelty Company of Chicago proudly announced a new coin-operated record machine claimed in trade advertising to be the only one on the market which could play ten inch discs. Previous equipment was built for seven inch discs, the original standard size when discs began to take the market away from the old cylinders.

It was the Victor Company which developed the first practical commercial phonograph. The company was formed in 1901 by Eldridge Johnson and was originally called the Victor Talking Machine Company. Its still-famous trademark of the dog "Nipper" listening to "his master's voice" was adopted in 1906. It was destined to become the dominant name in the record business and eventually (1929) would merge with Radio Corporation of America to become RCA Victor. But along the road to that point, they were occasionally hard-pressed for survival.

Columbia, another pioneer, and actually in business prior to Victor, similarly had its ups and downs as the industry fluctuated between prosperity and depression. First called the Columbia Phonograph Company, it later became the American Recording Company. This would remain its name until many years later when, following the example of Victor, it would affiliate with the broadcasting industry and become part of the Columbia Broadcasting System.

This was the background of the record industry's beginning. By the early twenties when the dance bands started to multiply, a great deal of progress had been made in recording techniques. However, production facilities still left a lot to be desired and were not really geared to picking up a dance band properly. Musicians gathered as closely as possible in front of a large horn resembling the speaking unit of the phonograph, and by playing into this the impression was made on the wax. Instruments which could not get close enough were often not heard in the playback, and some of them could not be picked up at all. Recording studios were manned by a limited number of personnel, with the man who had the title of Engineer really facing problems in trying to produce something to the satisfaction of everyone concerned. Usually every song had to be recorded over and over before a master consistent in quality throughout the entire number could be delivered.

The home phonograph on which these records were to be played back also remained a long way from perfection. It still had to be wound up and the steel needles which were used necessitated changing after a very limited number of plays to

JOHNNY MERCER, then an executive with Capitol Records, shakes hands with one of their first and biggest artists, Stan Kenton. — *Photo courtesy of Capitol Records.*

maintain anything resembling proper tone quality, and to prevent ruining the record.

None of these things prevented the bands of the day from getting on wax at every opportunity. Paul Whiteman became a big recording artist with most of his sessions being done in Camden, New Jersey, for Victor, which was still known as the Victor Talking Machine Company, and fast becoming the strongest name in the business. Ted Weems, after starting his first band in Philadelphia in 1923, also gained early prominence in this manner on the Victor label.

But the Columbia Phonograph Company was giving Victor a strong run for the market, with

BIX BEIDERBECKE and his "Rhythm Jugglers," a 1924 all-star session at Gennett. Trombonist is Tommy Dorsey, Bix is embracing Dorsey and Don Murray. Rest of group is Paul Mertz, Tommy Gargano, and Howdy Quicksell. — *Photo courtesy of Joe Rushton.*

It was important to be identified as a "recording orchestra." Photo taken in late 1920s. — *Photo courtesy of Al Katz.*

Ken Large   DICK WHITE   Norman Donahue   Don Shoup   Fritz Heilbron   Lee Bennett

March 10, 1936   CHOS. Ford   Lew Palmer

36-1658-1

George Fortui   Jan Garber   Jerry Large   Freddie Large   Douglas Roe

A 1936 session at Decca with Jan Garber. — *Courtesy of Freddie Large.*

Many thanks to the Automatic Phonograph Operators of America for the consideration you have given our Columbia records. I am grateful for past suggestions. I would appreciate any further information regarding the type of tunes and arrangements you recommend. Write me in caro of Paramount Pictures, Hollywood,

Orrin Tucker

ORRIN TUCKER
AND HIS ORCHESTRA
featuring
BONNIE BAKER

BANDLEADER ORRIN TUCKER acknowledges that automatic phonograph operators *are* important. — *Photo courtesy of Barney McDevitt.*

FREDDY MARTIN's "Concerto" deserves the smile he's giving it. Renamed "Tonight We Love" it entrenched him firmly in the top name brackets. — *Photo courtesy of Freddy Martin.*

Brunswick following close on their heels. A lot of other labels were around with names which disappeared as the twenties rolled along, some of them simply going out of business and some being absorbed by the others. In some cases, individuals with an astute display of judgment or just plain luck, acquired some of the masters of these old companies and several years later found themselves in possession of small gold mines when the public's appetite for those early 1920 recordings began to grow.

The old acoustical method of recording was discarded and replaced with the more advanced electrical system about the mid-twenties. The new system greatly broadened the total range of the pick-up and had even greater advantages in fidelity. This touched off a real recording boom, building additional names to prominence, some of them under the name of the bandleader and some under the name of various groups. It was not uncommon

for the top musicians like Red Nichols, The Dorsey Boys, Glenn Miller, Bix Beiderbecke, Gene Krupa, Benny Goodman, and several others to be recording on as many as fifteen or twenty different labels with groups under as many names. Top pay for a recording session ran $25.00 to $27.50, and in some rare instances, the musicians actually paid for the session in order to get something on wax that they particularly wanted to cut themselves.

By 1927, the record industry had grown into a very big business and sold some 130,000,000 discs that year. Actually, though, the sale of individual discs did not usually run very high, with 25,000 being a top figure for most of those considered hits during the twenties. Many of the records made during that period sold very few at the time, but turned out to be big hits some fifteen or twenty years later when reissued. A million copy record was an almost unheard of thing, although Ted Weems' "Somebody Stole My Gal" supposedly topped that figure, and Paul Whiteman's "Linger Awhile" at approximately the same time was credited with having sold about two million.

After the mid-twenties, radio began to hit its stride, and by bringing the sound of live entertainment into the home, reduced the interest in recorded music, taking a heavy toll in record sales. Smaller stations unable to program live entertainment were broadcasting recorded music, although the announcers who spun platters had not yet been given the title of disc jockeys. In some cases the manner in which these numbers were announced gave, at least by implication, the impression that the listener was hearing a live broadcast.

In 1928, the Federal Radio Commission stepped into the picture and instructed broadcasters to identify recorded music as such when it was used, or at least desist from practices which might fool the listening public. A year later the Artists' Protective Society initiated a suit which was indicative of the stand the artists themselves intended to take in the matter. Contending that the broadcasting of phonograph records had contributed to a heavy decline in record sales, they asked that the stations playing them be forced to pay royalties to the artist whose record was thus used. Recording companies joined in supporting this action, citing Rudy Vallee and Paul Whiteman as specific examples of bandleaders whose record income had been jeopardized in this manner. Not too long after this, Fred Waring took a still firmer stand, refusing to make any records at all unless a compensation arrangement with radio broadcasters could be enforced. He maintained this position for some ten or twelve years before he once again signed a contract with a recording company.

The depression years of the early thirties caused record sales to dip sharply hitting the low point about 1932. However, in spite of the shortage of money, every college kid somehow raised enough to buy the newest form of record player, a wind-up portable unit. Sometime around 1930, something else new made its appearance in the record market, probably because of the necessity of placing recorded music in the hands of the younger generation at a low cost. This was the "hit of the week" record, a disc made of paper covered with a synthetic resin. It was recorded on one side only and first distributed in the Middle West, but it quickly penetrated the New York market as well. Its introduction involved a new idea in merchandising, for it was sold exclusively on newsstands. The producer was the Durium Products Corporation, previously unknown in the recording industry. On Thursday of each week the new "hit of the week" was released and without intending to the title had a two-fold meaning. With the needles used on record players of that period, the average life of the record was not much longer than a week if it got many plays. But at a retail price of fifteen cents, the purchaser could hardly miss, and with name artists featured at a bargain price, a lot of discs were sold. At the peak of its popularity, the "hit of the week" was reported to be selling 600,000 weekly.

Rudy Vallee, already radio's most sensational personality, made himself the idol of the sorority set by these weekly releases. In the strictly dance orchestra groove, the "hits" featured such names as Vincent Lopez, Bert Lown, Ben Pollack, Jan Garber, Ted FioRito, Harry Reser, Sam Lanin, and the Harlem Hot Chocolates directed by Duke Ellington. For a short time each record had on the unrecorded side a photograph of the artist. The initial prosperity of the venture could not be sustained, however, and in mid-1932 the label disappeared from the market.

The "hit of the week" was a passing fad which gave the business a temporary lift, but other developments of approximately the same time would have a more lasting effect. Victor, now having completed its merger with Radio Corporation of America, introduced the first record playing attachment for radio sets, and before long was producing com-

bination radio-phonographs integrated as a single unit. They also developed additional improvements in recording systems which were adopted by the entire industry.

The decline in record sales bottomed out in 1932 with the volume declining to about eight million discs, a far cry from the 130 million sales racked up just five years prior. However, from this point a gradual up-turn began. The jukebox, now greatly improved and with much greater selectivity, began to re-establish its position about 1934, and to become a very strong factor in the building of bands to prominence.

Victor and Columbia had by now taken over the lion's share of the growing retail record market. In August of 1934, Decca entered the field, headed up by three young men with a lot of record experience behind them: Jack Kapp, Milton Rack-

The dance bands dominated the record market in 1940. — *Photo courtesy of Billboard magazine.*

mil, and E. F. Stevens, Jr. They were to have a tough time of it before they made their new venture pay off in a market which up to that time had been completely dominated by Victor, Columbia and Brunswick. With a plant in Muskegan, Michigan, and another on West 54th Street in New York, they announced their intention of marketing their platters at a retail price of thirty-five cents, even though the average price of all other discs at that time was seventy-five cents.

One of the first artists they signed was Bing Crosby, an old friend of Jack Kapp. However, they quickly moved into the band field signing up Guy Lombardo, the Casa Loma Band, the Dorsey Brothers Orchestra, Ted Lewis, and Isham Jones. Before too many years, they had added many others and had a representative percentage of the strongest names in the band business on their label.

The first record released was Crosby's "I Love You Truly" and the first band release was one of Lombardo's. During the first eighteen months in business, they had an extremely hard time keeping the company afloat, with Rackmil spending a good part of his time dodging process servers who were trying to collect money. It was not until the end of 1935 or early 1936 that they had a month which showed a profit, and this came from a never to be forgotten novelty tune entitled "The Music Goes Round and Round" recorded by Mike Riley and Ed Farley. It was not long after that before they became firmly established as one of the "Big Three", along with Victor and Columbia.

Largely through the medium of the jukebox, records now became the number one builder of bands. Goodman's climb to success in 1934 could not be credited to records so much as his efforts on personal appearances, although he quickly became a very big name on wax. Almost every other leader who rose to the top during the thirties, with the exception of Kay Kyser, got there as a result of one or more hit records. Needless to say, one of the first things a new band attempted to do was land a recording contract with a major label.

During 1936, the jukeboxes were heavily loaded with Shep Fields and his Rippling Rhythm, although he did not maintain any degree of that year's success in subsequent years. 1937 saw Tommy Dorsey's recordings of "Marie" and "Song of India" make him one of the nation's biggest names. A similar success story was written in 1938 by Artie Shaw, resulting form his "Begin the Beguine". "In the Mood" made Glenn Miller the number one bandleader in 1939, with Larry Clinton also becoming a strong contender the same year through his "My Reverie". About the same time Orrin Tucker and a pint-sized vocalist by the name of Bonnie Baker hit the big time with their waxing of "Oh, Johnny".

Total record sales for 1939 were about fifty million, with something over eighty per cent of the business being done by Victor, Columbia, and Decca. At least the same percentage of the records sold featured the nation's dance bands. By this time it could not be denied that the jukebox was the best friend the bandleader had, and the manufacturers of this type of equipment were letting the world know about it by their advertising in trade magazines.

Records on the jukeboxes were making the nation's hit tunes, and from the hundreds recorded the average number built to hit status annually was quite consistent. For several years, they ground out between forty-five and fifty hits with dance orchestras featured on most of these. The only real competition to the bands was coming from such big vocal stars and groups as Bing Crosby, The Andrews Sisters, the Inkspots, Ella Fitzgerald, Connie Boswell, Dinah Shore, and the King Sisters. Eventually, a great many of these names were teamed with an important leader to share equal billing on the label. A backward glance at the "retail disc best seller" charts of that period will show the extent to which the bands dominated the market.

The early forties saw a lot of big names struggling for top position, with most of them doing quite well for themselves. Freddy Martin came through with his "Concerto", renamed "Tonight We Love", backed up with "Why Don't We Do This More Often", a musical question which he answered by continuing to do it for many years. The composers of the latter song had attended the recording session and raised some objections to it being teamed up with "Concerto" on grounds that this adaptation of a classic would never sell. Their objections changed to smiles of contentment when the record was released and it took off with "Concerto" carrying the weight to sales which topped a million copies.

With his "Amapola" and "Green Eyes" becoming big hits, Jimmy Dorsey attained equal stature

146

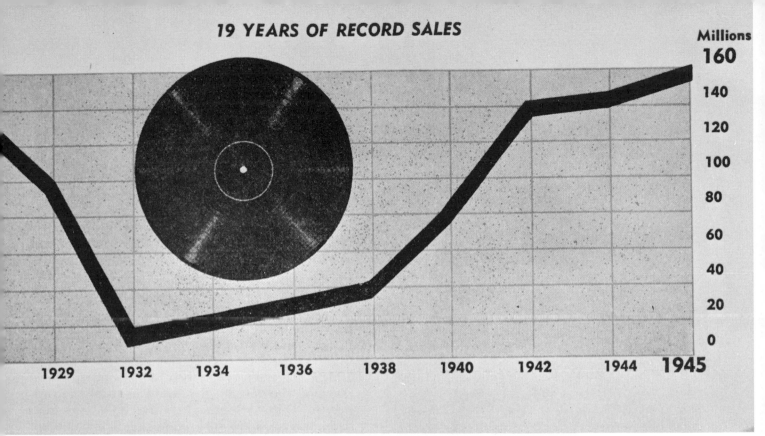

19 YEARS OF RECORD SALES

Millions
160
140
120
100
80
60
40
20
0

1929   1932   1934   1936   1938   1940   1942   1944   **1945**

This chart shows the trend of record sales over a nineteen-year
period, from 1927 through 1945. — *Photo courtesy Dave Dexter.*

with his brother Tommy in 1941, followed very
shortly by Harry James, who had been just another
bandleader until his "You Made Me Love You" became the biggest hit of early 1942. By this time
the nation had gotten into a war, and for the next
four years the band business became so big because of the demand for live entertainment that no
single medium could be said to have accounted
for the success of any individual band.

In 1942 the formation of another new company
quickly converted the "Big Three" into the "Big
Four". In April of that year, Johnny Mercer, Buddy DeSilva, and Glenn Wallichs formed Capitol
Records in Hollywood, an idea which reputedly
was born from the simple fact that Mercer felt
he was being fluffed off by some of the bigger
recording companies in his attempts to get his
compositions recorded. This company also quickly
signed up bandleaders, including the veteran Paul
Whiteman who cut their first record for them. The
newly-formed Stan Kenton band found this to be
the place to look for record success, which he
eventually found. However, it was Ella Mae Morse
and Freddy Slack who put the company's books

in the black with their release of "Cow Cow
Boogie". From that point on, Capitol was one of
the strongest factors in the recording industry, and
eventually had a sizable collection of the nation's
top bands on their label. No small share of their
initial success could be traceable to their recognition of the importance of the disc jockey with
whom they cooperated in every possible fashion.
The retail disc buyer was made quickly aware of
them also through a newsy little publication full
of items about the music world edited by Dave
Dexter, available at no cost at any record counter.

The summer of 1942 saw another event which
probably had a much greater long range effect on
the future status of bands in the recording business
than could be realized at the time. This was the
first strike against the recording industry called
by Jimmy Petrillo, heading up the American Federation of Musicians. The strike was a little difficult
to reconcile with remarks made by Petrillo a few
short months before when the war had broken out.
At that time he stated flatly that for the duration
of the war the Musicians Union would not call any
strikes of any nature. Apparently, however, he

RUSS MORGAN, 1949's biggest band on records. — *Photo courtesy of General Artists Corp.*

changed his mind and so for a period of some fifteen months, no records could be cut by A.F. of M. members. Deprived of their musical support, this made it almost impossible for vocal stars to record either. Finally, such artists as Bing Crosby and a few others found an answer by cutting records with an "a cappella background" with surprisingly good results. Eventually, the difficulties between the union and the recording companies were settled, and the musicians and record manufacturers could turn to other worries.

They did not have to look far to find trouble, for in the meantime another king-sized wartime problem hit the industry. This was the shortage of shellac which was needed for the manufacture of more crucial wartime items. In an attempt to find an answer, the major companies instigated scrap drives inviting the public to turn in all old records to the record dealers, who in turn would pass them along to a recording company to be remelted and pressed into new releases. Some of the more alert record clerks found those turned in to be great collector's items, and many of them found their

way home with these people before the recording companies could make their pickups.

At war's end when raw materials were released, new record companies began to spring up everywhere. In mid-1946 a leading trade journal published a list of all the known recording firms which totalled 197. There were predictions that the "Big Four" would quickly regain momentum enough to squeeze most of these out, and there were even times when it looked like this would occur. However, it did not come to pass although some of the small ones did fade from the scene to be replaced by others.

There was also much talk of new developments in recording techniques which would revolutionize the business. For some time there had been rumors of longer plays, although this was not the first time this subject had been publicized. Back in 1922 a magazine article had told about a British inventor who developed a device to make a record play for thirty minutes. Needless to say, at that date, this sounded very impressive compared to the average four minutes playing time of a twelve inch record. This man's invention was never heard of after the initial news release.

Now, however, each major company began to develop its version of what a longer-playing record should be, with the standard 78 rpm version giving way to one company's 45 rpm record, while the two other majors advocated larger discs turning at 33⅓ rpm. This eventually was worked out to everyone's satisfaction, but for a while the bandleaders, like everyone else, were caught in the middle. In the long run it worked to their advantage, even though collectors of old records might not have the same opinion. The value of collectors' items recorded in years gone by sunk to practically nothing as almost every important old number of the various artists was re-recorded at one of the newer speeds, most of them done from the original masters.

Records continued to be the number one springboard for building a new band, even though the hit that would accomplish it became increasingly difficult to get. During 1945, Les Brown made the top ranks with his "Sentimental Journey" and 1946 saw Eddy Howard with his "To Each His Own" doing the same thing.

In some cases it was not a new hit record or even a new band which became popular because of it. In 1947 Ted Weems had pretty well forgotten

STAN KENTON looks serious about this Capitol record-ing session. — *Photo courtesy of Capitol Records.*

PHIL HARRIS dropped his role of band-leader to score a hit with a novelty tune in late 1950. "The Thing" did a great deal for Harris but had nothing in common with the band business. — *Photo courtesy of NBC. Photo by Gerald K. Smith and Barney McDevitt.*

This billboard chart indicates the degree of Russ Morgan's success but also shows vocalists controlling more of the market than had been theirs ten years prior. — *Photo courtesy Billboard.*

April 16, 1949

Retail Record Sales
Based on reports received last three days of **Week Ending April 8**

BEST-SELLING POPULAR RETAIL RECORDS

Records listed are those selling best in the nation's retail record stores (dealers). List is based on The Billboard's weekly survey among 4,970 dealers in all sections of the country Records are listed numerically according to greatest sales. (F) Indicates tune is in a film. (M) indicates tune is in a legit musical. The B side of each record is listed in italic.

Weeks to date	Last Week	This Week	
8	1	1.	CRUISING DOWN THE RIVER ....R. Morgan Ork................ *Sunflower* ....Decca 24568—ASCAP
12	2	2.	CRUISING DOWN THE RIVER ....B. Barron Ork .... *Powder Your Face With Sunshine* ....MGM 10346—ASCAP
5	8	3.	FOREVER AND EVER......R. Morgan Ork................ *You, You, You Are the One* ....Decca 24569—BMI
20	7	4.	SO TIRED.................R. Morgan...Decca 24521—ASCAP *I Hear Music*
13	4	5.	RED ROSES FOR A BLUE LADY................V. Monroe Ork................ *Melancholy Minstrel* ....Victor 20-3319—ASCAP
5	6	6.	FOREVER AND EVER......P. Como-M. Ayers *I Don't See Me in Your Eyes Anymore* ....Victor 20-3347—BMI
13	3	7.	GALWAY BAY.............B. Crosby..Decca 24295—ASCAP *My Girl's An Irish Girl*
10	9	8.	CARELESS HANDS ....S. Kaye Ork................ *Powder Your Face With Sunshine* ....Victor 20-3321—ASCAP
15	4	9.	FAR AWAY PLACES.......B. Crosby-K. Darby Choir....... *Tarra Ta-Larra Ta-Lar* .. ..Decca 24532—ASCAP
3	18	10.	"A" YOU'RE ADORABLE...J. Stafford and G. MacRae-P. Weston Ork..Capitol 15393—ASCAP *Need You*
6	12	11.	SUNFLOWER ....R. Morgan...Decca 24568—ASCAP *Cruising Down the River*
2	22	12.	"A" YOUR ADORABLE.....P. Como-Fontane Sisters-M. Ayres Ork.....Victor 20-3381—ASCAP *When Is Sometime?*
3	22	13.	NEED YOU ....J. Stafford and G. MacRae-P. Weston Ork..Capitol 15393—ASCAP *"A" You're Adorable*

(Wesley & Marilyn Tuttle, Capitol 15423; The Highway Serenaders, Highway H-3459; B. Crosby & Crew Chiefs, Columbia 38450; J. Bradford, Victor 20-3418; G. Lombardo & His Royal Canadians, Decca 24614; Patsy Montana & D. Denny-The

WARNING! In utilizing these charts for buying purposes readers are urged to pay particular attention to information listed which shows the length of time a record has been on the chart, and whether a record's popularity has increased or decreased This information is shown in the left-hand columns under the headings: "Weeks to Date," "Last Week" and "This Week." If a record has had an unusually long run, or if its current position "this week" versus "last week" shows a sharp drop, readers should buy with caution.

Buckeroos, Victor 20-0040)

8	10	14.	RED ROSES FOR A BLUE LADY ....G. Lombardo Ork............ *Everywhere You Go* ....Decca 24549—ASCAP
5	10	15.	CARELESS HANDS ....M. Torme-S. Burke Ork........ *Always True to You in My Fashion* ....Capitol 15379—ASCAP
5	22	16.	BLUE SKIRT WALTZ......F. Yankovic and His Yanks-The Marlin Sisters .... *Charlie Was a Boxer* ....Columbia 12394-F—ASCAP

(H. Harding, Grand G-25013; R. Carroll & Carolers, Mercury 5252, L Duchow Red Raven Ork, Victor 20-3356; Socach-Habat Polka Ork, Decca 45068; V. Zembrusky, Continental C-1260; Harmony Bells Ork-J. Conway & The Wayfarers Dana 2042)

16	13	17.	POWDER YOUR FACE WITH SUNSHINE ....E. Knight-The Stardusters...... *One Sunday Afternoon* ....Decca 24530—ASCAP
14	14	18.	FAR AWAY PLACES......P. Como-H. Rene Ork.........

a record of "Heartaches" which he had made some-time around 1933 and which had been a hit at the time. He was even growing tired of leading a band and was considering retiring. There are many stories told about what happened, but the most interesting one is that a record dealer in Charlotte, North Carolina had several hundred copies of Weems' old "Heartaches" in his stock room left over from the days of its initial popularity. In an attempt to dispose of them, he prevailed upon a local disc jockey to start plugging the record and suddenly it caught fire. Every disc jockey in the nation began to play it and in a matter of a few weeks, it moved up to number one on the popularity and sales charts. It was on the Decca label that this big hit of the thirties had been released, and they were now hard-pressed to turn them out fast enough to meet the new demand. Overnight, Weems was back in the band business as a hot attraction.

At the beginning of 1948, Petrillo called a second strike against the recording companies. This one had been anticipated so bandleaders spent the last several weeks before the deadline date record-ing day and night to pile up a backlog of masters to be released over a period of months, depending on how long the strike might last. Actually, it hung on until the end of the year, but this time the foresight of the recording companies kept the pub-lic from being as aware as they had been of the strike in 1942 when the supply of new releases had been virtually cut off.

Among the leaders who recorded 'round the clock before the strike took effect was Russ Mor-gan, placing on wax everything which he, and probably Decca artists and repertoire men, could think of. Finally, they had one side left vacant, so Morgan suggested they record one of his own compositions which had been written back in the early forties, but at that time had gained little attention. This tune, "So Tired", was on its way to becoming the nation's biggest hit when the re-cording ban finally ended, and with the momen-tum from it he went on to become the number one recording artist of 1949. During the first twenty-six weeks of that year, he had an average of four, and at one time six, of the top ten records as listed by *Billboard* Magazine under "Best Selling Retail Records", "Records Most Played By Disc Jockeys", and "Records Most Played on the Jukebox". His-tory does not record any other bandleader with so many hit records going simultaneously and as this

It was big news when the Dorsey brothers re-united on records in 1953. — *Photo courtesy of Dave Jacobs.*

is written, no bandleader has topped it in the years that followed.

By 1950 the technical problems involved in a recording session had been greatly reduced by a new system which was developed in the postwar years. This involved the use of magnetic sound recording tape invented in Germany, but devel-oped and perfected in America by Minnesota Min-ing and Manufacturing Company, with others en-tering the field later. The ability to erase and re-record greatly reduced the multiple cuts previously necessary in order to produce a master which would be considered perfect enough to use for the reproduction of a saleable disc. Another important feature was the ability to splice together the best portion of two or three "takes" to produce the desired result, eliminating that portion not con-sidered up to standard.

The record business was booming now, reaching a new all-time high in dollar volume each year. The dance bands, however, were rapidly losing their dominant position in the industry to vocalists, vocal groups, and completely unknown artists, some of whom were one-record sensations. There were many indications that the major recording companies might be losing interest in dance bands, feeling that their own future could not be secure if they were dependent upon the availability of musicians in view of the two protracted recording strikes of the 1940s. Despite this concern, it was with a dance band that they first demonstrated their ability to build their own stars if they chose to do so.

Ralph Flanagan was the beneficiary of this program and the leader whose initial success was the direct result of the efforts of a recording company. He had been under contract to RCA Victor as a studio musician when they decided to make him a name bandleader. Through their heavy promotion of his early recordings, they made him a national attraction before he ever played his first personal appearance. Some of the trade talk at the time indicated they had done this as an object lesson to some of their big names who had been under contract for extended periods of time, and who were now negotiating for better renewals. Following the Flanagan build-up, they attempted to do the same thing with the bands of Bob Dewey and Buddy Morrow as replacements for Tommy Dorsey and Sammy Kaye, who had left them to sign with other labels. Moderate success was enjoyed by Morrow, but the Dewey band fell by the wayside. Other major recording companies followed Victor's example but with no success story which equalled Flanagan's.

The record people, once again with Victor leading the way, cooperated with the whole dance band industry in the early fifties in an attempt to revive public interest. However, after this program had run its course without any outstanding results, their interest appeared to drift farther and farther in other directions. Record sales continued to be generally good for top-name bands, contributing heavily to the success stories of such relatively new bands as Ray Anthony, Ralph Marterie, and Les Elgart, with old-timers like Pee Wee Hunt and Eddy Howard also having some big hits. Both Guy Lombardo and Sammy Kaye continued to be strong competitors for the record buyer's dollar and the jukebox plays.

All of this took place in the early years of the fifties. The biggest song on records during 1950 had been "Good Night Irene" with several artists cashing in on it. Popularity charts, dominated ten years previously by dance bands, were now listing fewer and fewer of them. Total record sales in 1950 found Sammy Kaye in sixth place and Lombardo in seventh. On the jukeboxes, Lombardo rated third with Kaye in the number eight spot. Gordon Jenkins had done better than either, and was the only other leader in the top ten. Jenkins actually did not belong in the category with the dance bands, however, since his was primarily a studio band.

The names that had taken over the charts included a variety of vocalists and vocal groups. Some were old-timers and some were making it for the first time. The early months of 1951 saw the trend moving even farther in that direction. Even one of the country's former bandleaders, Phil Harris, was going quite well with a not-too-musical novelty called "The Thing". The only dance band records in the top twenty-four were "Harbor Lights" done by both Sammy Kaye and Lombardo, and "Nevertheless" by Ray Anthony with "Harbor Lights" on the reverse side.

A year later, Johnny Ray's "Cry" and "Little White Cloud That Cried" were topping the list, setting off a new trend which had musicmakers shaking their heads. The only bandleaders to be found in the top thirty were Eddy Howard with his "Sin" (primarily a vocal number), Louis Armstrong with his "Kiss To Build A Dream On" and Ralph Flanagan with his "Slow Poke" backed by "Charmaine".

The position of the dance orchestras on records continued to decline during 1953 and 1954. Early in 1955 a list of the top recording artists based on their previous year's sales revealed 39th position to have been the best placement made by a dance band and it was Ralph Marterie who made it that far up the chart.

By this time, there were literally hundreds of labels in the record market. Unknown companies with unknown artists had demonstrated over and over again the ability to market a hit record. The dominance of the total disc market by "Johnny Come Latelies" had gone so far that major studios began rapidly eliminating the financial guarantees previously included in most recording contracts signed with important name bandleaders. Only a

Disc jockey AL JARVIS, originator of "Make Believe Ballroom," proves
that work can be pleasant. — *Photo courtesy of Barney McDevitt.*

few of the perennial favorites were able to retain
them, with Lombardo and Sammy Kaye topping
that list. During the lush days of record sales for
the bands, Tommy Dorsey had been guaranteed
as much as $2,000.00 per side by RCA Victor and
when he switched to the Decca label, he was reported to have received an annual guarantee of
$52,000.00 with a contract requiring not less than
fifty releases per year. Others had been almost
equally as well taken care of, with contracts which
had been virtual annuities, but now these were
gone almost completely.

In the summer of 1954, Decca celebrated its
twentieth anniversary in the business, and the entire industry paid tribute to them. Part of the
information given out by Decca at that time included a list of their artists who had enjoyed sales
of a million or more records with a single release
during those first twenty years of the company's
existence. It made interesting reading, not only
from the standpoint of the names it included, but
also because of the absence of some who had
previously been publicized as having made the
"one million club".

No one was surprised to see Bing Crosby heading the list with nineteen records which had topped
the million mark, with his "White Christmas" already having sold over ten million all by itself.

At right, the disc jockeys picked their personal favorites, both current and "all time" in *Billboard* magazine's annual poll of 1955. — *Photo courtesy of Billboard.*

MARTIN BLOCK, New York's biggest name disc jockey, visits Hollywood in June of 1950 and poses with fellow platter spinner Gene Norman and bandleader Russ Morgan. — *Photo courtesy of Hollywood Palladium.*

Even "POPS" WHITEMAN became a disc jockey for a brief period with a coast-to-coast network program. —
Photo courtesy of Freddy Martin.

Orchestra leaders named and the number of "Gold Awards" credited to them included the following:

Guy Lombardo 4
Fred Waring 1
Carmen Cavallero 1
Jimmy Dorsey 2
Woody Herman 1
Johnny Long 1
Clyde McCoy 1
Russ Morgan 1
Ted Weems 1

The previous year, the jukebox industry also celebrated an anniversary — its 65th. This was the signal for a lot of polls of jukebox operators to be taken as to which records had received the most plays in past years and in the current market. These also clearly indicated that the dance bands were no longer in the favorite positions on the nation's coin machines.

But the jukebox, credited in the early forties as being the number one band-building agency, was now running in second place in building records of any type. The creator of hits had become the disc *jockey* who had slowly taken over radio during the late forties, and now had it all to himself. Early in the 1950s, the all-night disc jockey programs became standard in every major city across the nation. This virtually killed what little

154

Disk Jockeys pick all-round favorites

BEST POP ALBUM RELEASED THIS YEAR

Position	Album	Label
1	IN THE WEE SMALL HOURS, F. Sinatra	Capitol
2	LOVE ME OR LEAVE ME, Doris Day	Columbia
3	STARRING SAMMY DAVIS JR.	Decca
4	LONESOME ECHO, J. Gleason	Capitol
5	PETE KELLY'S BLUES, M. Matlock & R. Heindorf	Columbia
6	MOOD FOR 12, P. Weston	Columbia
7	BOY MEETS GIRL	Columbia
8	SOMETHING COOL, J. Christy	Capitol
9	MUSIC, MARTINIS & MEMORIES, J. Gleason	Capitol
10	PETE KELLY'S BLUES, J. Webb	RCA Victor

ALL-TIME POP RECORD STANDARDS

Position	Record	Label
1	STARDUST, Artie Shaw	RCA Victor
2	MOONLIGHT SERENADE, Glenn Miller	RCA Victor
3	STARDUST, Glenn Miller	RCA Victor
4	TENDERLY, Rosemary Clooney	Columbia
5	IN THE MOOD, Glenn Miller	RCA Victor
6	SENTIMENTAL JOURNEY, Les Brown	Columbia
7	STRING OF PEARLS, Glenn Miller	RCA Victor
8	BEGIN THE BEGUINE, Artie Shaw	RCA Victor
9	I CAN'T GET STARTED WITH YOU, Bunny Berigan	RCA Victor
10	ON THE SUNNY SIDE OF THE STREET, Tommy Dorsey	RCA Victor
11	OPUS NO. 1, Tommy Dorsey	RCA Victor
12	SUMMIT RIDGE DRIVE, Artie Shaw	RCA Victor
13	LET'S DANCE, Benny Goodman	Columbia
14	MARIE, Tommy Dorsey	RCA Victor
15	I'VE GOT MY LOVE TO KEEP ME WARM, Les Brown	Columbia
16	STARDUST, Paul Weston	Capitol
17	MOONLIGHT IN VERMONT, Margaret Whiting	Capitol
18	DANCING IN THE DARK, Artie Shaw	RCA Victor
19	DON'T BE THAT WAY, Benny Goodman	RCA Victor
20	FRENESI, Artie Shaw	RCA Victor
21	NANCY, Frank Sinatra	Columbia
22	SEPTEMBER SONG, Stan Kenton	Capitol
23	BOOGIE WOOGIE, Tommy Dorsey	RCA Victor
24	WHITE CHRISTMAS, Bing Crosby	Decca
25	STARDUST, Bing Crosby	Decca

was left of the nighttime band remotes and left nothing but recorded music on the air. During the days of live radio, there had been platter spinners, but they usually lost their listening audience to the big name radio talent on the networks around dinnertime each evening. Now the jockeys became radio's stars.

Two of the best known pioneers in organized record programming were Al Jarvis and Martin Block. Just which of these deserves credit for originating "Make-Believe Ballroom" depends on whose opinion you ask. However, most sources agree it was Jarvis who dates his origin of the use of the title and format back to about 1935 on a Los Angeles station. Block at one time worked with him but later migrated to the East Coast where he did a program under the same title. These trail blazers were followed by hundreds of others who gained local and national prominence, with even such big name bandleaders as Paul Whiteman and Tommy Dorsey eventually taking a brief turn at a network record show.

By the early fifties, the potency of the disc jockey as a record promoter was well recognized. Most of the major record companies did everything possible to cooperate with them and make sure that the newest releases were placed in their hands. About 1954 Martin Block summed up the situation rather neatly in a trade paper interview in which he stated that the public did not determine its own preference in music, but instead was almost completely influenced to accept the music played for them by the nation's disc jockeys.

There were few people in the music business who would dispute his statement.

Because of their importance in the industry, they were constantly being looked to as a source of information and polled on various subjects. *Billboard* magazine went to them at least once a year for information on various subjects, such as which record company gave them the best service, what they looked for in a record, and the type of record they played most often. In 1951 they were polled as to the recording artists who were the most cooperative in supplying biographical material and making personal appearances on their shows. Out of the top twenty artists listed in this poll, fourteen were bandleaders. It was not, however, the recordings of these artists which were listed as having been given the most spins. The significance of this would be dependent upon whether the reader interpreted the record selec-

DUKE ELLINGTON prepares for a recording session. — *Photo courtesy of Columbia Records.*

BANDLEADER MUZZY MARCELLINO whistles his way to a new kind of hit record. — *Photo courtesy of Capitol Records.*

tions to be the result of listeners' requests, or the discretion of the disc jockey.

By the mid-fifties "Rock and Roll" which a few years before had been called "Rhythm and Blues" was dominating disc jockey programming and had cornered the hit record market. There were ominous rumblings that this was not something which had just happened. Way back in the early fifties, a few trade journals pointed with alarm to the practice of romancing disc jockeys with free gifts, meals, entertainment, etc. They asked where this would end and pointed to the fact that it seemed to be the producers of "Rhythm and Blues" records who were doing the most of it.

The subject got much additional publicity as time went along, with the climax coming in 1959. Investigation of the quiz shows on television gathered radio and the disc jockeys up in its momentum, and shook them around, too. "Payola", a word with far-reaching connotations, but actually coined many years earlier, was now in standard usage by the public in general. Yet the same public sat back and looked on with only lukewarm interest as attempts were made to prove that many of the nation's top disc jockeys had a good thing going for themselves with an under-the-table arrangement to see that the right discs were programmed. If the public reaction seemed to be a little apathetic, it may have been because many people felt that if the nation's lawmakers wanted to investigate freeloading, expensive gifts, etc., they could do a lot of sweeping up in their own backyards.

Not a great deal came of the "payola" investigation except to cast a reflection on the innocent along with those who may have been guilty. It did raise the question, however, among dance band fans as to why it would not have been as readily accessible to the bands as to other recording artists if that was the manner in which hits were made. If "payola" existed, it's just possible the stand taken by the head of the Musicians Union set the stage for it, even though his actions were probably sincerely felt to be in the best interests of his own group. At a time when he was periodically attempting to force the disc jockeys to pay for the privilege of playing a record, a multitude of ambitious but unknown talent and the people who recorded them recognized the disc jockey for the powerful sales agent he was. Petrillo's philosophy on the matter may have been technically correct, but economically unsound. In addition to the failure to recognize the importance of the disc

GLEN GRAY came out of retirement in the late 1950s to record the sounds of the great bands with all-stars from the big band era. — *Photo coutesy of Capitol Records.*

jockey, his strikes against the recording companies had doubtless discouraged them from wanting to promote band discs on recorded programs, and also inadvertently caused them to discover that the cost of turning out a disc with a smaller group was considerably less and could produce an equal return.

Those who insist on blaming the disc jockeys for killing the band business may well have overlooked the real manner in which a few of them, probably without intent, contributed to bringing it about. These were not the "Rock and Roll" exponents at all, but another group who, carried away with their own likes and dislikes in music, set themselves up as music critics. Some of them may have had the background which qualified

The Billboard
MUSIC POPULARITY CHARTS
PART IV

Retail Record Sales

Based on reports received last three days of
Week Ending September 1
1950

The Billboard TRADE SERVICE FEATURE

BEST-SELLING POP SINGLES

Records listed are those selling best in the nation's top volume retail record stores. List is based upon The Billboard's weekly survey among the 1,400 largest dealers, representing every important market area. Survey returns are weighed according to size of market area. Records listed numerically, according to greatest sales. The "B" side of each record is also listed.

POSITION
Weeks | Last | This
to date| Week | Week

10	1	1.	GOODNIGHT, IRENE.....	G. Jenkins-Weavers ..	
			Tzena, Tzena, Tzena	Dec(78)27077;	
				(45)9-27077—BMI	
14	2	2.	MONA LISA..........	Nat "King" Cole-	
			Greatest Inventor of	The Trio........	
			Them All, The	Cap(78)1010;	
				(45)F-1010—ASCAP	
7	4	3.	SIMPLE MELODY.......	Gary-Bing Crosby....	
			Sam's Song	Dec(78)27112;	
				(45)9-27112—ASCAP	
7	3	4.	SAM'S SONG..........	Gary-Bing Crosby....	
			Simple Melody	Dec(78)27112;	
				(45)9-27112—ASCAP	
11	5	5.	TZENA, TZENA, TZENA.	G. Jenkins-Weavers...	
			Goodnight, Irene	Dec(78)27077;	
				(45)9-27077—ASCAP	
13	6	6.	BONAPARTE'S RETREAT.	K. Starr	
			Someday, Sweetheart	Cap(78)936;	
				(45)F-936—BMI	
5	9	7.	CAN ANYONE EXPLAIN?.	Ames Brothers	
			Sittin' 'n' Starin' 'n'	Coral(78)60253;	
			Rockin'	(45)9-60253—ASCAP	
3	16	8.	NO OTHER LOVE.......	J. Stafford	
			Sometime	Cap(78)1053;	
				(45)F-1053—ASCAP	
11	10	9.	NOLA	L. Paul	
			Jealous	Cap(78)1014;	
				(45)F-1014—ASCAP	
13	13	10.	COUNT EVERY STAR....	H. Winterhalter	
			Flying Dutchman, The	V(78)20-3697;	
				(45)47-3221—ASCAP	
1	—	11.	OUR LADY OF FATIMA..	R. Hayes-K. Kallen...	
			Honestly, I Love You	Mercury(78)5466;	
				(45)5466X45	
3	29	12.	I'LL NEVER BE FREE...	K. Starr-Tennessee Ernie	
			Ain't Nobody's Business	Cap(78)1124;	
			But My Own	(45)F-1124—ASCAP	
18	7	13.	I WANNA BE LOVED....	Andrews Sisters-	
			I've Just Got To Get	G. Jenkins Ork.....	
			Out of the Habit	Dec(78)27007;	
				(45)9-27007—ASCAP	
10	11	14.	MONA LISA............	V. Young	
			Third Man Theme, The	Dec(78)27048;	
				(45)9-27048—ASCAP	
6	12	15.	GOODNIGHT, IRENE.....	F. Sinatra	
			My Blue Heaven	Col(78)38892;	
				(33)1-718—BMI	
2	—	15.	COUNT EVERY STAR.....	D. Haymes-A. Shaw..	
			If You Were Only Mine	Dec(78)27042;	
				(45)9-27042—ASCAP	
26	22	17.	THIRD MAN THEME, THE.	G. Lombardo	
			Cafe Mozart Waltz	Dec(78)24839;	
				(45)9-24839—ASCAP	
2	23	17.	ALL MY LOVE.........	P. Page	
			Roses Remind Me of You	Mercury(78)5455;	
				(45)5455X45—ASCAP	
2	30	19.	I'LL ALWAYS LOVE YOU.	D. Martin	
			Baby, Obey Me	Cap(78)1028;	
				(45)F-1028—ASCAP	
3	16	20.	BONAPARTE'S RETREAT.	G. Krupa	
			My Scandinavian Baby	V(78)20-3766;	

Dealer Doings

MERCHANDISING TIPS . . . Filing sheet music in alphabetical order pays off in increased sales, according to Manager E. Lynn Wilde, F...
the pote...
that pe...
asked fo...
by Shirl...
Pa., is t...
Dee, WH...
air . . .
Mich., o...
just a...
departm...
singles...
nine pr...
Each li...
33 and...
old star...
Del., tie...
by adve...
the thea...
departm...
the bes...
places t...
on the...
over.

MORE...
tle of th...
denced...
dealers...
and typ...
greatly...
a comp...
ever."—...
who say...
know w...
much to...
them, b...
Sell son...
three...
Kingsp...
cal albu...
in othe...
price w...
is becon...
Piano C...
doing a...
play an...
As more...
r.p.m...
N. C...
and 45...
store."—...
never h...
so am...
a wond...
Compar...

NEWS...
for hon...
conven...
Radio &...

On opposite page, a LES ELGART record date in progress. — *Photo courtesy of Columbia Records.*

By September 1950 the "best selling" chart had only two bands in the top 20, Guy Lombardo making the 17th spot and Gene Krupa the No. 20 spot. — *Photo courtesy of Billboard.*

them for the role, but the majority did not. None of them would have considered telling the Ford Motor Company how to build an automobile, but without hesitation they would take issue with Duke Ellington or some equally great leader over the manner in which he rendered one of his own compositions.

While this damage was being done by a limited segment of their profession, there were still a lot of top disc jockeys across the nation who remained friends of the big bands, and were conscientiously programming good music to those who took the time to tune them in. Actually, the band business was not producing much that could be called new for them to program.

In spite of this, the record business during the late fifties was not doing nearly so badly by the bandleaders as it would appear to those who listened to some disc jockeys' "Top Forty", or read the popularity charts. Those ratings reflected nothing but the current hit record market. The absence of the dance bands from the top selling popularity charts was not entirely due to outside sources, but

in some cases was partially by choice. A great many of them had elected not to compete for that market at all. Those who had been lucky enough to have records which topped the million sales mark in a single year had discovered that trying to follow such a record and maintain their position was a short cut to ulcers. They also discovered that there was more take-home pay from a record which sold three or four hundred thousand over a span of several years than from one which sold a million during a wave of popularity which ran its course in a few months. Consequently, their efforts were concentrated on the production of old standards which had already proven their popularity and would continue to sell indefinitely. Many of them were still reaping a harvest on re-issues of discs made back in the thirties, or even further back than that. Purchasers of some of the re-issues were often pleasantly surprised to find how well they came through when reproduced on modern playing equipment.

The re-issues also served to point out the many labels on which top leaders had appeared during

159

their careers. With some of them it indicated that they had been, at one time or another, under contract to almost every major company and even a few minor ones.

During the span of those careers, they had cut a lot of wax. It was not uncommon for a leader to forget he had recorded a particular number, and although it did not happen often he sometimes tripped up on discs which had been fairly big hits.

One night during the mid-fifties, I dropped in to the "Blue Room" of New Orleans' Roosevelt Hotel to see Russ Morgan who was appearing there at the time. During an intermission conversation which included Mr. Seymour Weiss, owner of the Roosevelt, Russ, and myself, the discussion switched to records and Morgan's own success in that field. One of my comments, never intended to produce the results which developed was, " . . .

"Russ, I thought one of the greatest things you did was 'Do I Worry'."

Instead of acknowledging the intended compliment, his reply took me completely by surprise:

"You must have me confused with someone else. I never made it at all."

"But, Russ," I protested mildly, "I have the disc at home and everyone who hears it says it's terrific."

"We never made a record of "Do I Worry", came back Morgan in a manner so positive I should have believed what he was saying.

But feeling just as sure myself, and still thinking he had to be kidding, I tried it once more with:

"I don't know why I should be telling you your business, but I know I have a Russ Morgan record of 'Do I Worry'."

By now he was reaching for his wallet as he challenged me:

"Just how much would you like to bet on this deal? I could use some easy money on this one."

Having just cashed a check at the desk, I had three one-hundred dollar bills in my pocket, and tossing one on the table I said:

"I'd go along with you for one of these."

"You've got a bet," said Russ, as he got up to go back to the bandstand.

Next morning I went down the street to the Decca Distributing Company and picked up the record on a small 45 rpm disc. Taking it to a neighborhood department store, I had them wrap it in

All recording was now done on magnetic sound-recording tape and Red Nichols is shown here at right in the test studio of one of the tape manufacturers. — *Photo courtesy of Minnesota Mining & Manufacturing Co.*

By 1960 not a single dance band record could be found in the top 40 indicated by disc jockeys as being most popular. — *Photo courtesy of radio station KFWB.*

FABULOUS FORTY SURVEY

FOR WEEK ENDING APRIL 2, 1960

			LAST WEEK
1.	*THEME FROM A SUMMER PLACE	Percy Faith—Columbia	1
2.	*WILD ONE	Bobby Rydell—Cameo	2
3.	*PUPPY LOVE	Paul Anka—ABC/Para	3
4.	SWEET NOTHIN'S	Brenda Lee—Decca	4
5.	CLEMENTINE	Bobby Darin—Atco	8
6.	HE'LL HAVE TO GO	Jim Reeves—RCA Victor	6
7.	*STARBRIGHT	Johnny Mathis—Columbia	12
8.	*STEP BY STEP	The Crests—Coed	20
9.	HILLY GULLY	Olympics—Arvee	5
10.	GREENFIELDS	Brothers Four—Columbia	17
11.	*FOOTSTEPS	Steve Lawrence—ABC/Para	15
12.	MONEY	Barret Strong—Anna	18
13.	BEYOND THE SEA	Bobby Darin—Atco	10
14.	WHY DO I LOVE YOU SO	Johnny Tillotson—Cadence	24
15.	I LOVE THE WAY YOU LOVE	Marv Johnson—U.A.	16
16.	HARLEM NOCTURNE	Viscounts—Madison	11
17.	*MAMA	Connie Francis—M-G-M	25
18.	*BEATNIK FLY	Johnny & Hurricanes—Warwick	9
19.	LOVE YOU SO	Ron Holden—Donna	30
20.	*HARBOR LIGHTS	Platters—Mercury	13
21.	BIG IRON	Marty Robbins—Columbia	35
22.	TEEN ANGEL	Mark Dinning—M-G-M	14
23.	WHAT IN THE WORLD'S COME OVER YOU	Jack Scott—Top Rank	7
24.	SOMEDAY	Della Reese—RCA Victor	26
25.	*THIS MAGIC MOMENT	The Drifters—Atlantic	21
26.	AM I THAT EASY TO FORGET?	Debbie Reynolds—Dot	33
27.	MR. LUCKY	Henry Mancini—RCA Victor	38
28.	*PLAYBOY'S THEME	Cy Coleman—Playboy	31
29.	*DELAWARE	Perry Como—RCA Victor	29
30.	*CHERRY PIE	Skip & Flip—Brent	New
31.	*ETERNALLY	Sarah Vaughan—Mercury	27
32.	*THAT'S THE WAY LOVE IS	Bobby Darin—Atco	28
33.	TRACY'S THEME	Spencer Ross—Columbia	22
34.	*YOU DON'T KNOW ME	Lenny Welch—Cadence	39
35.	LONELY BLUE BOY	Conway Twitty—M-G-M	34
36.	WHAT DID I DO WRONG?	The Fireflies—Ribbon	32
37.	FANNIE MAE	Buster Brown—Fire	New
38.	HAVE LOVE, WILL TRAVEL	Richard Berry—Flip	New
39.	*NIGHT	Jackie Wilson—Brunswick	New
40.	BEAUTIFUL OBSESSION	Sir Chauncey—Warner Bros.	New

a box large enough to hold a set of golf clubs and tie it with the gaudiest ribbon they could find. Enlisting the help of a bellhop, I had it delivered to his room at 11:30 a.m. when I knew he'd be having his breakfast. That evening when I returned to the hotel, there was an envelope waiting for me at the desk, and in it was Morgan's check for $100.00. In later years, we had a lot of laughs over the incident, and the check, kept as a souvenir, was never cashed.

Morgan was one of those who took to the old standards for his record income during the late fifties. Most of the other big names of the thirties and forties were similarly still available on albums in the better stores. Glen Gray, who had turned out a lot of wonderful discs for Decca during his days as leader of the Casa Loma Band, was now making the sound of all the former greats available on a series of albums done for Capitol in tribute to the leaders and the era which they represented. To those who wanted to recall a whole group of their old favorites of the swing era without changing records, these offered an opportunity to do so. There must have been a lot of those people, based on the success of his many albums produced in that vein. While Gray concentrated on reproducing the best efforts of the swing bands, Freddy

Martin turned out a similar album series in tribute to the smooth bands, and these, too, were well-received by the public.

The record counters were loaded with other "tribute" albums in addition to Gray's and Martin's, with everyone who had the remotest excuse capitalizing on former associations with such departed greats as Tommy and Jimmy Dorsey and Glenn Miller.

While most of these did quite well in the marketplace, the top bandleader on records was still Glenn Miller himself, with the records cut prior to his untimely death in 1944 still leading in sales. Statistics made public at the time the movie of his life was released in 1954 indicated that during the period from 1939 through 1944 he had earned some $500,000.00 in record royalties. In the ten year span that followed, his estate was paid almost an equal amount in additional royalties, and although later figures were not released, it was expected that the interest created by the movie would boost record royalties earned since his death to well over the million dollar figure.

The old-timers were still in the record business, but it had been a long time since records had built a new name to prominence as the leader of a dance orchestra.

161

Early broadcasting studio. — *Photo courtesy of Don Allen, N.B.C.*

The Kansas City Night Hawks, probably the first orchestra to broadcast nightly. — *Photo courtesy of Joe Moore.*

Radio Built Bands,
But Television Had Little Need for Them

"HERE COMES that band again!"

Remember that introduction? If you do, you'll recall that it was followed by a trombone sliding into the theme "Daydreams Come True At Night" and an announcer telling you that once again you were listening to the music of handsome Dick Jurgens.

Jurgens' broadcast might be originating from Catalina Island's Avalon Ballroom, the Aragon in Chicago, or one of the nation's leading hotels. While you enjoyed it in your living room or on your car radio, a happy crowd was dancing in front of the bandstand where the remote pick-up was being made.

By the time Jurgens was on the air regularly, the dance band business had come a long way from its obscure beginning to become one of America's leading sources of live entertainment. Nothing had played a bigger part than radio in bringing this about.

It was inevitable that radio and America's dance orchestras would form an alliance advantageous to both — although in the beginning radio's need for doing so was perhaps the greater. There was little or no organization to early broadcasting, and most programming was a spur of the moment thing.

As the few first stations came into existence, the deficiencies of broadcasting made little difference — the sheer novelty of hearing a voice from a distant point was enough to sustain interest. Originally, only one person at the receiving end could listen at any given time, while the rest sat around the room watching his expression and waiting impatiently for him to turn the headphones over to someone else. At the origination point, someone calling himself an announcer talked into a funny looking gadget resembling a cross between a tennis racket and the temperature gauges mounted on the radiators of the automobiles of the period.

This gadget was called an "enunciator"; sometime later it became a microphone.

Radio station KDKA in Pittsburgh, Pennsylvania is credited with being the first to inaugurate regular broadcasting and this event occurred in 1920. It was a broadcast picked up from this station which gave me my own first exposure to radio reception, picked up on a headset all the way out in central Nebraska. The program was not too exciting and consisted of thirty minutes of tuning up by a prison band.

Following KDKA, other stations quickly came into existence all across the country. They, too, initially offered little except contact with the outside world. In many of them, any amateur who had the courage to do so was permitted to walk into the studio and play, sing, or just talk over the air waves. There was no other way to fill out the scheduled hours of broadcasting.

If radio were to become important, this could not go on indefinitely, and it didn't. Some ingenious inventor found a way to do away with the headphones, replacing them with a speaker which sat on top of the set and from the side view, resembled a question mark. Some of them were, but when they worked everyone in the room could hear simultaneously. The novelty was gone — people in the room now wanted to be entertained.

To provide at least some of this entertainment, the broadcasters had to look beyond their own facilities and thus was born the remote pick-up. In general, there were two areas in which they could find something taking place in an organized fashion, or at least of a nature lending itself to broadcasting. The first of these was the sporting events, but these had limitations as to hours of availability. The other and more versatile source was the ballrooms and hotels where the dance bands were playing.

Even prior to this stage of radio, several of the nation's orchestras had been heard on the air, but with no regularity. It is generally accepted as fact that the first leader to try his hand at it was Paul Specht. His first broadcast took place in September of 1920, originating from the studio of WWM in Detroit.

But it was from the Muehlbach Hotel in Kansas City that a band was first heard nightly on the radio. The year was 1925 and the band was the Coon-Sanders Orchestra, led jointly by Carleton Coon and Joe Sanders. Listeners had to stay up late to catch them, for they came on at midnight. One night, one of the band's members wise-cracked:

"What are we doing on the air now? No one but the night hawks will be listening in."

From that moment on, they had a name which became their tag line — they were the "Kansas City Night Hawks". Old-timers will still remember the little tune with which they came on:

"When Coon and Sanders start to play,
The Night Hawk Blues you'll start to sway.
Tune right in on the radio
Write a little note and say hello.
From Coast to Coast and back again,
You can hear that syncopated band.
It's a bear,
You'll declare,
When you listen to the Night Hawk Blues;
I mean —
Listen to the Night Hawk Blues."

Just what these nightly airings could do for a band's popularity soon became evident. The Night Hawks quickly became known throughout the Middle West in the area covered by Station WDAF. Jules Stein of Music Corporation of America heard them and went down to Kansas City to see what it was all about. He was so impressed that he returned to Chicago and convinced Otto Roth of the Blackhawk Restaurant that he should hire them, an engagement which started in 1925 and lasted approximately six years. Simultaneously with their Chicago opening, broadcasting equipment was put into the place. The broadcasts which followed established the Blackhawk as a major Chicago night spot, and the Coon-Sanders Orchestra as a big name. When they finally terminated their engagement, it was to go into New York and the New Yorker Hotel.

Other leaders were quick to see the power of radio and made every effort to get on the air. Guy Lombardo was so convinced of its importance that he did his early broadcasts from Cleveland, Ohio,

without pay, even talking the station into letting him play. Once again it was Jules Stein who became interested and brought him to Chicago to work in the Granada Cafe, operated by Al Quodbach. When the first few months at the Granada resulted in only mediocre business, Quodbach finally yielded to Lombardo and Stein and agreed to bring in a radio wire. The cost was $75.00 per week, with Lombardo and M.C.A. agreeing to stand two-thirds of the cost until it paid off. It didn't take long, for by the end of the first week the place was packed and they were soon doing turn-away business. The Granada and Blackhawk were now Chicago's top entertainment spots as well as rivals for the nighttime radio audience. Lombardo became a sensation and moved on to the Hotel Roosevelt in New York in 1929, preceding the Night Hawks' eastward move by nearly two years.

Chicago had by now become identified as the hottest spot in the nation for band-building via radio. The Blackhawk continued to be one of the places where much of it happened. Hal Kemp came in soon after the Night Hawks, and he, too, became famous there. When he finally left, it was Kay Kyser who took over, eventually finding the same success as his predecessors. Both Kemp and Kyser had been around for several years enjoying only moderate success before the Blackhawk broadcasts gave them the big break they needed.

But this did not happen until the thirties were well under way, and in the meantime other Chicago spots were producing their own headliners.

The Trianon and Aragon Ballrooms, both owned by the Karzas Brothers, lost no time in putting themselves on the air. About 1927, Wayne King was heard from the Aragon, and it was these airings which made him famous as "The Waltz King." They also made the ballroom one of the best known in the nation. The Trianon kept pace with the newer Aragon, making radio names of Ted FioRito, Jan Garber, Art Kassel, and a host of others who followed later.

Although Chicago was the undisputed leader, it did not have all the action by any means. All over the country during the late twenties, hotels and ballrooms were putting in radio wires, recognizing that nothing could build a location into a top spot more quickly. It became particularly important for major hotels to be identified in this manner and perhaps prompted many of them to feature dancing if only for this purpose.

RUDY VALLEE'S first sponsored show. Sharing the mike with Rudy is famed announcer Graham Mc-Namee. — *Photo courtesy of Rudy Vallee.*

WAYNE KING'S broadcasts from Chicago's Aragon Ballroom started in 1927 and soon made him a big name and attraction. — *Photo courtesy of Coliseum Ballroom.*

TED FIORITO and his orchestra "in uniform" for a
1929 N.B.C. show sponsored by Skelly Gasoline.
— *Photo courtesy of Paul Weirick.*

WILL OSBORNE, about 1927. — *Photo courtesy of
Will Osborne.*

At the same time almost every station of any importance had its staff or studio orchestra. In many cases these groups probably performed for little or nothing in return for the use of the station as a base of operations and a means of building a following. One of these bands which broadcasted daily from a small mid-western station still stands out in my memory and there were hundreds like it. This was the orchestra of Steve Love who blanketed the Midwest with melodies from a 50,000 watt transmitter in Milford, Kansas. The owner of the station was Dr. Brinkley who did not really need the services of an orchestra to build a reputation. He became famous as the advocate of transplanted goat glands for the recovery of youthful vitality; was nearly elected governor of Kansas on a write-in ticket; and finally was driven from the state by the medical association which disagreed with his theories.

Lawrence Welk's early reputation was also built as a studio band in a small Midwestern station. Over WNAX from Yankton, South Dakota, his music was beamed out daily over the Dakotas, Iowa, and Nebraska. His first appearance before the mike was made in 1925 with a steady job at the station coming a year or so later.

Vincent Lopez became one of the early leaders to make the most of radio in the New York area, followed closely by Ben Bernie. It was his broadcasts from the Cotton Club that first brought Duke Ellington prominence in about 1927, and Will Osborne was broadcasting regularly as early as 1928.

No one was more alert to radio's potential nor more astute in making it pay off for him than Rudy Vallee. When he launched his own band in 1928, he grabbed every possible minute of air time, and through his singing and announcing of his own programs quickly made himself known. By the end of 1929, he was probably the biggest box office attraction in America, a success he attributed entirely to radio. When he lined up a commercial sponsor, he became a radio personality rather than a bandleader, even though the band continued to be featured with him. This was the beginning of a long career as one of radio's biggest names.

Not all of those in the music business shared this early enthusiasm for having their performances heard by the radio audience. Some of them felt that it did them little good, and might even reduce the public's desire to see them in person. Whether this was the reason, or simply because he was already highly successful without it, Paul

THE MILLS BROTHERS — not a band, although their vocal interpretation of musical instruments fooled many listeners into thinking they were — early 1930s. — *Photo courtesy of Bill Stafford.*

Whiteman made no early effort to broadcast. It took a sponsor with a heavy advertising budget to finally interest him, but probably this was what he had been waiting for from the beginning. About 1928, he came on for a cigarette company and for the next few years was known as "The Old Gold Orchestra".

Regular appearances on the air created the need, or at least the desirability of a trademark for identification purposes. Who was the first to use a theme song? — probably no one can really say with accuracy. Many claim it was the Kansas City Night Hawks. Others feel that Ben Bernie made the practice popular. Probably Bernie was the first to use one for opening the broadcast and another for signing off. His "Lonesome Old Town" identified his entry to the air lanes and he took leave with "Au Revoir — Pleasant Dreams". Jimmie Grier's West Coast band was not far behind

167

Bernie's in the use of dual themes, coming on with "Music in the Moonlight" and departing with "Bon Voyage-Ship of Dreams", both of these his own compositions. Needless to say, any leader who was a composer used one of his own songs for his theme.

During the years to come, radio remotes would imprint indelibly in the minds of listeners the themes of hundreds of bandleaders. Who could forget Glen Gray's "Smoke Rings", Benny Goodman's "Let's Dance", Kay Kyser's "Thinking Of You", Jimmy Dorsey's "Contrasts", his brother Tommy's "Getting Sentimental Over You", Bob Crosby's "Summertime", or Glenn Miller's "Moonlight Serenade"? Taglines would become equally familiar with few people who would not know that "The Idol of the Air Lanes" was Jan Garber, Lombardo played "The Sweetest Music This Side of Heaven", "Shuffle Rhythm" was Henry Busse, "Tic-Toc Rhythm" identified Gray Gordon or that Sammy Kaye made you "Swing and Sway".

Radio did not take long in developing from a floundering infant into a full-grown medium of communication. By the late twenties, networks had come into existence, greatly broadening the coverage. The official birth date was 1926 when the National Broadcasting Company was formed, with its officials stating their purpose was to provide coast-to-coast distribution of programs. This opened a whole new horizon for the nation's bands, multiplying many times the importance of

a remote broadcast. From the better locations, these now had a nation-wide audience, and territory bands became national attractions.

One such broadcast with an enormous audience originated from the Cocoanut Grove in Los Angeles on Sunday nights. It differed from most in that it was not a half hour program, but went on for two hours. During this time, the band took its regular intermissions while the announcer interviewed the customers when the musicians were off the stand. This feature attracted the Hollywood people anxious for the publicity involved. The band was that of Gus Arnheim, with a lot of top talent including Jimmie Grier (soon to be a leader), and the "Rhythm Boys" who had joined Arnheim after leaving Paul Whiteman.

Grier always enjoyed talking about the fun that was part of working with the "Rhythm Boys", and especially Bing Crosby. According to Grier, Bing always had a bunch of friends waiting in his dressing room for him to join them the minute he was through work. They usually had a good card game going while they waited and were equipped with a radio for catching the two hour broadcast of the Arnheim band from upstairs. On one of these nights, Bing must have been losing when he left the game for, as he finished the last chorus of his final number he delivered this message coast-to-coast:

"Deal me in, boys, I'll be right down."

RED NICHOLS doing a C.B.S. remote from Cleveland's Golden Pheasant, about 1931. — *Photo courtesy of Red Nichols.*

Limerick Gimmick May Kill Show Bernie Built

Ben Bernie, who has been blue ribbon malting for many months, and who would just about be winding up his contract but for a renewal just gone into effect, has created a brand-new reputation for himself as an outstanding radio as well as stage personality. Bernie's ready wit, the nonchalant style of emseeing his half hour, and the seeming disregard of the sponsors for the usual longwinded and serious credits attracted a great following to the period. Few who followed Bernie failed to know who sponsored the program. While Pat Kennedy's vocals and other features helped the program along, it cannot be said that the Bernie band on its own would have created undue sensations. It was primarily Bernie and his style of handling the half hour.

A change in the style of continuity now bids fair to kill off the period almost as fast as Bernie built it up. In direct contract to the carefree credits formerly given the product and its sponsors, the half hour is now loaded with a laborious limerick contest repeated more times than any intelligent person would care to hear, despite the fact that they might like Bernie.

BEN BERNIE STORY includes words of praise and a note of caution. — *Courtesy Billboard magazine.*

Network radio brought something else which was to mean a great deal to the bandleaders; a large group of advertisers willing to sponsor programs which would attract an audience to be told of the merits of the sponsor's product. Strange as it may seem, the early sponsors in most cases came seeking the music they wanted, for neither the leaders nor their agents initially recognized commercial radio's potential.

Many of the shows which soon had regular scheduling were built around bands, but whether they were or not they nearly all had to have music. As the twenties faded into the thirties, Harry Horlick and his A & P Gypsies were already a big radio attraction and who could forget the Ipana Troubadours? Rudy Vallee's popular Fleischmann Hour had been launched by the National Broadcasting Company in October, 1929. Then, in 1930, Lucky Strike Cigarettes intitiated a show featuring a different musical organization each week, picked up from some city around the nation where the band selected might be playing at the time. This program contributed greatly to making bands a major radio attraction.

Now everyone got into the act or did his best to get there. By 1932 Ben Bernie was a big radio name, both as a bandleader and a personality. His long-time sponsor became Pabst Blue Ribbon, which may sound funny to people who recall that Prohibition was still very much alive at the time he went to work for them. But the Blue Ribbon people had something more than near beer to offer — malt syrup. This was the basic ingredient for home brew and practically every home in the nation had a ten gallon jar, a tester, and a bottle capper for turning out its own version of beer.

Hollywood soon began to compete with New York as an origination point for national programs. A lot of radio's talent preferred to headquarter there so name guest stars were plentiful. Among the West Coast bandleaders to benefit from this in the early thirties, none did better than Jimmy Grier. At one period, he was doing three weekly shows, probably an all-time high. He was an important part of the Joe Penner Show, the Fibber McGee and Molly program, and was the first band used on Jack Benny's Show when it came to the Coast. In addition to all this, he was doing a nightly remote from the Biltmore Hotel where he played six nights weekly. Finally, the union eliminated some of his work when they passed a ruling limiting the number of regularly sponsored shows any leader could have at one time.

Whiteman finally came back to the air waves in 1933, having now found a sponsor willing to produce a show to his liking. The bankroller this time was the Kraft Cheese Company. Perhaps Rudy Vallee's success had some influence on Whiteman's decison to make the move. Like the Vallee Show, his was also a two hour program, and there was even a similarity in format. A trade journal story of the time gave credit to the return of legalized beer as having prompted the sponsor to spend the kind of money required since there was a direct ratio between the consumption of beer and cheese.

Fred Waring's first appearance for a sponsor was made that same year. Like Whiteman, he had not rushed into it until he got what he wanted, but once there he established himself so firmly that so long as radio remained a user of live music he was on it. His first sponsor was Old Gold Cigarettes just as it had been Whiteman's.

The cigarette people soon became one of the most active groups in buying radio time, showing a marked partiality to the dance bands. Following the Lucky Strike Show which had hopped around the country for a local pick-up, other tobacco companies began to contract important leaders. The R. J. Reynolds Company launched its Camel Caravan in 1933 with Glen Gray and the Casa Loma Orchestra featured. Three years later, Gray turned this show over to Benny Goodman whose band by that time had become the nation's most sensational.

This interest on the part of cigarette sponsors continued strong during the entire span of the thirties. It was Lucky Strike who became Kay Kyser's sponsor in 1937; Raleigh's signed Tommy Dorsey in 1938, and Artie Shaw came on for Old Gold's the same year. Chesterfield's choice about the same time was the Bob Crosby Band and it was this same company which gave Glenn Miller his first commercial program in 1939.

Kay Kyser's "College of Musical Knowledge" was probably one of radio's first audience participation and quiz shows. He had developed the idea while appearing at Chicago's Blackhawk Restaurant from where it was broadcast as a local program before attracting a national sponsor. Contestants were briefly interviewed and then asked to identify a song played by the band. The prize was a ten dollar bill which in the light of later quiz show prizes would look like nothing but tip money. Between the numbers in which the audience participated it featured the zany antics of Ish Kabibble and the capable vocal offerings of Sully Mason, Harry Babbitt and Ginny Simms. It caught on quickly and soon enjoyed high rating as a network show, making Kyser a top box office draw in theaters, ballrooms, and on one-nighters for many years to come.

By the end of the thirties the most important thing to any bandleader was identification with a sponsored radio show. Regardless of the direct

TED WEEMS was on the air for Johnson's Wax, 1932. — *Photo courtesy of Joe Rushton.*

income it was priceless in terms of boosting personal appearances. Many leaders offered fabulous bonuses to agents who could get them a sponsor. Others bought their way out of commitments to locations when these commitments interfered with a radio opportunity. In 1938 trade sources reported Jan Garber to have paid the Aragon-Trianon Ballrooms $28,000 to release him from a long term contract so that he might join the Burns and Allen Show in Hollywood.

Not all of the comedy shows gave the bandleader publicity that would warrant that kind of a price tag. In some cases his identity was kept so far in the background the listeners were hardly aware of his presence.

Outstanding exceptions to this were Bob Hope and Jack Benny, both of whom wrote the bandleader a heavy part in the script. Hope made Skinnay Ennis important in every show thereby placing

Tommy Dorsey's first show for a sponsor, 1938. Group at left of mike is Edythe Wright, Jack Leonard, and Axel Stordahl. — *Photo courtesy of Dave Jacobs.*

Kay Kyser's College of Musical Knowledge. — *Photo courtesy of Harry Thomas.*

GLENN MILLER broadcasting for Chesterfield, 1940. Vocalists Marion Hutton and Ray Eberle at mike. — *Photo courtsy of Wilbur Schwartz.*

him in heavy demand for personal appearances during the summer season. Benny did so well by Phil Harris that he was almost the co-star of the show. When he finally left after years of this kind of build-up he had no difficulty in landing a show of his own, not as a bandleader but as a comedian.

Among the radio time buyers who used dance orchestras there were a few who made an outstanding contribution to the business. Two of these built their programs completely around bands, capitalizing on the popularity which the bigger names enjoyed and giving lesser names a lift towards the top.

One of these was the F. W. Fitch Company whose "Fitch Bandwagon" was a Sunday afternoon regular during the early forties. During the winter season it was the big names who were featured. Throughout the summer season newcomers were given an opportunity to be heard, and for many this was the break they needed. The "driver" of the bandwagon was a friendly emcee by the name of Tobe Reed who handled the show most of its years on the air. Shortly after the war started they

dropped the new band summer format signing a big name for an entire 26 week season. This first occurred in 1943 with Freddy Martin contracted for the assignment.

The Coca-Cola Company with its "Spotlight Bands" was the other sponsor whose program over a period of years did a great deal to promote the music business. This show started out as a Saturday night airing which featured the band with the week's biggest record sales. But this did not work out too well since a hit record might remain at the top for several weeks, bringing the same band back repeatedly. Glenn Miller was red-hot on records at the time and an embarrassing situation developed when he appeared as the winner week after week. The embarrassment came from the fact that he had a sponsor of his own who finally requested that Miller make no more Coca-Cola broadcasts.

"Spotlight Bands" changed its format shortly after the start of the war converting to a six night weekly broadcast carried over the Mutual Network from defense plants and service camps. Fea-

172

BOB HOPE and SKINNAY ENNIS doing the weekly Hope show. — *Photo courtesy Bob Hope.*

FRED WARING (below left) did not rush into radio but finally signed to do an Old Gold show about 1933. — *Photo courtesy of N.B.C.*

PHIL HARRIS, JACK BENNY, and "ROCHESTER" (below), whose rapid exchanges of barbed humor entertained millions every Sunday night for years on the Jack Benny Show. — *Photo courtesy of Phil Harris.*

The COCA COLA SHOW had been on the air several months when World War II broke out. It quickly converted to a morale-building show originating six nights weekly from a service camp or a defense plant.

At left, FRANKIE MASTERS, one of the "Spotlight Bands" regulars. — *Photo courtesy of Freddie Large.*

Trade journal ad for the popular FITCH BANDWAGON program.

turing a different band each night, it now became not only a band building show but a morale builder as well. Between September 1942, and the war's end, the "Spotlight" personnel traveled nearly 2,000,000 miles to bring the nation's top bands to servicemen and war workers. Although everyone had his chance, it was Tommy Dorsey, Jan Garber and Frankie Masters who registered in for most repeat performances.

When the war ended the format changed once again and the show used three regulars, each doing one weekly broadcast. It was Guy Lombardo, Xavier Cugat and Harry James who carried on until the program went off the air in the Fall of 1946. From Sacramento, California, James did the final show. Thus he had launched and concluded the service show series, since it was he who had done the first camp broadcast in the Fall of 1942.

During the early forties the music business had been given, for a short time, a problem which made broadcasting extremely difficult. This was the struggle between the American Society of Composers, Authors and Publishers (better known as ASCAP) and the radio networks over performance rights, which began during the summer of 1940. The broadcasters had long been objecting to the fees which they had to pay annually to ASCAP and were threatening to refuse to sign new contracts for 1941. Unless a compromise could be reached before the deadline date the right to play ASCAP tunes on the air would cease to exist after January 1st. This would mean that a large per-

centage of each bandleader's library would be banned from broadcast after that date.

Knowledge that a showdown was brewing was common to all those in the business during late 1940. ASCAP stated its case publicly in trade journal ads. Network executives wrote bandleaders advising them to prepare libraries excluding ASCAP tunes for broadcast use after the anticipated deadline. Yet for some reason few of those to be involved took the matter seriously enough to do as suggested, with the result that they were unprepared when the ban took effect.

No agreement was reached between the two factions and the ban came off on schedule. Then there began a mad scramble to resurrect old numbers which could be put on the air. Many remote broadcasts were kept off the networks until this could be accomplished. "Jeannie With The Light Brown Hair" and other Stephen Foster numbers were played so often that Foster posthumously became a hit composer. The scope of ASCAP's coverage was such that practically every leader's theme song was included and he had to adopt a new one. Listeners who had long been accustomed to identifying their favorite orchestras by their themes were hard pressed to guess who was coming on the air when a broadcast began.

When a treaty between ASCAP and the networks was finally reached many months later there was no one who did not breathe a sigh of relief.

Remote broadcasts from ballrooms and hotels were the source of many humorous stories. One

The new band of CHUCK CABOT is introduced to the Fitch bandwagon audience by Kay Kyser, September 1, 1940. — *Photo courtesy of Chuck Cabot.*

PHIL HARRIS and ALICE FAYE get their own show on N.B.C.,
about 1946. — *Photo courtesy of Barney McDevitt.*

FREDDY MARTIN on the "Lady Esther Serenade" in early 1940s.
— *Photo courtesy of Freddy Martin.*

such tale pertained to the unusual style of introduction adopted by Joe Reichman for his broadcasts. Whether it was true or not, according to the legend it began when an announcer was seized with an irresistible urge to sneeze halfway through his introduction which came out something like this:

"Presenting the Pagliacci of the piano, Jo-o-o-oe Reichman."

Reichman liked the resulting effect so well that he insisted on it being handled by all announcers the same way from then on.

Ernie Mathias tells another story which occurred while he was working with Joe Venuti when they opened at the Venice Pier Ballroom where they would have extensive air time. Venuti had been planning to do his own announcing of all numbers and so in anticipation had been rehearsing his opening speech for a week. When it came time to do the first broadcast it developed that the station had decided to have its own announcer handle it. Venuti was considerably upset but said nothing until they got the signal they were on the air. When the red light came on the announcer pointed to Joe and said, "theme song".

To his dismay Joe stood calmly in front of the band and shouted back, "we don't have one."

Not all of the amusing incidents which occurred can be told with the use of names. Sometimes they involved serious clashes of personality and temperament between announcer and bandleader.

Tony Lafrano, who later became a vice president of KHJ in Hollywood could relate many of these from his experiences during the height of band popularity. In one such instance every announcer on the station had been sent to a popular dance spot where a well-known leader was appearing, but each declined to go back a second time. Finally the leader approached Lafrano and asked him if he would handle the remote announcements himself. Since they had practically exhausted the station's roster Lafrano honored the request, but playing a hunch he mentioned the name of the leader before every number. When the show was over he was awarded with this comment:

"Now that's the way a broadcast should be handled. Why can't those other guys learn to do it right too?"

Another of Lafrano's stories in a somewhat similar vein ended with the announcer the winner. The bandleader involved was a big name, but with a reputation for being hard to get along with. On opening night of what was to be a four week engagement he chewed the announcer out quite thoroughly at the end of the broadcast letting him know that in his opinion nothing had been done right. But if he felt he had cause for unhappiness then what happened from that point on must have made him completely furious. For the balance of the engagement the only information which went out on the air was:

"You are listening to music from the Casa Mañana."

If those who tuned in wanted to know who was playing it they could call the station and ask.

There were probably hundreds of these cold wars between bandleaders and announcers with the winning points fairly evenly divided between both sides. Shortly after he had started his own band Ronnie Kemper was booked into a St. Louis hotel from which a network broadcast was a nightly feature. Much to his dismay the announcer assigned to handle the broadcast always ate just before coming to work, soaking most of his food in garlic. Kemper could not stand the smell of garlic at all and working the same microphone with this man for a half hour show was practically unbearable. He dropped several hints hoping the situation would improve, but apparently he could not get the message through. One night on his way to work, Kemper dropped into a nearby delicatessen and picked up a piece of the strongest cheese he could find. Just before air time he rubbed it all over the microphone. That night when the band went on the air both Kemper and the announcer were having a tough time facing up to the microphone and the band vocalist refused to do her second number. Apparently Ronnie had made his point for from that point on the garlic diet was discontinued and the air was clear.

Sponsored radio continued to be a heavy user of bands throughout the war and the immediate years that followed. The big band sound still continued to be popular, and listeners could hear it played by Woody Herman on a weekly airing for Wildroot, or by Harry James and Vaughn Monroe each of whom still had cigarette sponsors. The Kyser show was still on but now for a soap company. All of these were built around the leaders plus potent name artists from other segments of show business. A lot of old perennials were still part of other shows, and even Horace Heidt came

HARRY JAMES doing the Coca Cola "Spotlight Bands" show about 1944. His foot is in a cast due to an injury while playing baseball. — *Photo courtesy of Harry James.*

out of retirement in 1947 to launch a "Talent Show" for Philip Morris Cigarettes, a program which enjoyed several years of tremendous success.

The war was not long over before the remotes from ballrooms and hotels began to lose their effectiveness. Most of them came on so late at night that they found but a limited audience. Trade journals asked if this type of air time had any importance any longer in band-building as one after another newcomer failed to make it pay off. Toward the end of the forties, the situation deteriorated rapidly when television challenged radio as a medium of communication, and began to take a big share of the nighttime audience.

Perhaps the first indication the bandleader had that something was happening came from the decline in the attention he received from song pluggers. For years the leader playing a hotel from which a nightly broadcast originated could look out into his audience and spot as many as a half dozen of them on any given night. In some spots, special tables were reserved for them. They showered the maestro with attention and favors for he had the potential to make their product a hit.

Suddenly, there were not so many of them out there and gradually they stopped coming almost entirely. The 1950s were not very far along before the new medium, television, had taken over the nighttime entertainment which came into the

179

WILL OSBORNE was bandleader on the Abbot and Costello show during the mid-1940s when the show was top-rated network attraction. Trio is shown here on personal appearance tour. — *Photo courtesy of Will Osborne.*

JERRY GRAY is the bandleader and Bob Crosby the M.C. on this "Club 15" show of the late 1940s. — *Photo courtesy of Barney McDevitt and Robert Perkins Photography.*

home. One by one the live radio programs left
the evening air waves, the locations dropped their
remote air time, and the disc jockey had a world
of his own.

Opinions on what TV would do for the dance
bands were varied. It was clear to everyone that
it could never have the flexibility of radio.

Tommy Dorsey was one of those who was pessimistic. In a 1951 interview, he blasted television
as being bad for the business and indicated he
wanted no part of it. Ray Anthony, while not quite
so emphatic, was another who publicly expressed
a complete lack of interest. Before too much time
had elapsed both were in it doing weekly sponsored shows.

These and others who were the hardy pioneers
found themselves struggling with inadequate light-
ing, poor camera work, and many other headaches.

Among the first to go all out for it was Freddy
Martin who put together a show in the Fall of
1951. His first venture was an all-band show in
which he attempted to build new musicians into
a "band of tomorrow". This was revised during
the season to a format built around his regular
band, but featuring a guest female vocalist each

week. The show received excellent reviews and
was carried nationally, but was discontinued after
its second season.

Attempts to adapt television to dance locations
in the same manner as radio were made in every
major city, particularly in New York and Hollywood. It was Hollywood which quickly took the
lead in that direction, and by the Fall of 1952 there
were seven Los Angeles area stations doing band
shows at least once a week. For a while, all of
these enjoyed moderate success. Lawrence Welk's
offering from the Aragon Ballroom was one of
these, and for a short time shows by Harry Owens'
Hawaiians and Ina Ray Hutton also were done
from the Aragon Bandstand. The latter two moved
to a studio where production was easier to handle,
and Miss Hutton with her all-girl band went on to
enjoy more television success than most of her
male contemporaries, lasting for a four year run as
a top West Coast TV show.

The Hollywood Palladium's attempt was a
one and a half hour show done on a weekly basis
which originated from their bandstand featuring
their current name band attraction. It had such
mixed reaction from the viewers, patrons, and

RAY ANTHONY at first said no TV for him but he changed his mind before the mid-1950s. — *Photo courtesy of ABC-TV.*

The bandleader playing a spot featuring plenty of airtime was "romanced" heavily by song-pluggers and composers, as proved by telegram below. — *Photo courtesy of Jan Garber.*

WESTERN UNION telegram:

WESTERN UNION 1201

CLASS OF SERVICE — This is a full-rate Telegram or Cablegram unless its deferred character is indicated by a suitable symbol above or preceding the address.

(10)

JOSEPH L. EGAN
PRESIDENT

SYMBOLS
DL = Day Letter
NL = Night Letter
LC = Deferred Cable
NLT = Cable Night Letter
Ship Radiogram

The filing time shown in the date line on telegrams and day letters is STANDARD TIME at point of origin. Time of receipt is STANDARD TIME at point of destination

IFT213 DL PD=' OSANGELES CALIF 26 343 P

1947 SEP 26 PM 5 13

JAN GARBER:

=EDGEWATER BALLROOM=

JAN "MY HOW THE TIME GOES BY" LOOKS LIKE A VERY BIG SONG FOR
ME, CHAPPELL HAS IT FOR NUMBER ONE PLUG AND BOTH JOE AND I
WOULD CERTAINLY APPRECIATE YOUR ORDERING ARANGEMENT ON IT, ITS
GOT A GOOD BOUNCE TEMPO THAT SHOULD APPEAL TO YOU VERY MUCH
THANKS JAN REGARDS:

=JIMMY MCHUGH.

THE COMPANY WILL APPRECIATE SUGGESTIONS FROM ITS PATRONS CONCERNING ITS SERVICE

ORRIN TUCKER featured in the Hollywood Palladium's second attempt to make TV pay off in 1955. — *Photo courtesy of Hollywood Palladium.*

band personnel that after two or three seasons of trying to make it pay off, it was discontinued. They discovered, as did most ballrooms, that the bulky equipment necessary for a telecast interfered with the dancers and contributed little to their interest in the spot. Bandleaders disliked it for the preparation it necessitated compared to the former ease of taking to the radio air-waves. In 1955 the Palladium tried it once again as a "Weekly Dance Party" featuring Orrin Tucker under a long-term contract, but eventually dropped it entirely.

On the East Coast, the Meadowbrook, operated by former bandleader Frank Dailey, did its best to help the bands find their place in the new medium. Early in the fifties, he had TV pickups from the spot in the same manner as the other ballrooms. In 1955, the Meadowbrook became the origination point for a full hour sponsored show called "The Cavalcade of Bands." Like many other similar attempts, it could not make the grade on a permanent basis.

Meanwhile, all the big names in the business were trying various formats in an effort to convert television into the sponsored gold mine radio had been. Sammy Kaye and his "So You Want To Lead A Band" gave it the best he had, but failed to click with the viewers. Guy Lombardo's early efforts went equally unrewarded. Vaughn Monroe was on for a while with a cigarette sponsor, and later did the first sustaining show in color called "The Voice of R.C.A." Ray Anthony finally came on for a cigarette sponsor, and the television opportunity he had said he did not want lasted a couple of seasons, which seemed to be par for most bands.

Those who had enjoyed outstanding success in commercial radio fared no better. Kay Kyser tried it with his old "College of Musical Knowledge" and then, discouraged by the ratings, retired permanently to Chapel Hill, North Carolina, to go into the drug business. Horace Heidt, whose Philip Morris "Youth Opportunity Show" had been one of radio's biggest attractions in the late forties and early fifties, tried to adapt the same format to a

INA RAY HUTTON was more successful with TV than many of her male contemporaries in the early 1950s. — *Photo courtesy of Harold Jovien.*

TV presentation. His usual "Midas Touch" failed to stand the test of the conversion, however, and after a few seasons he, too, permanently retired to look after his many other interests in California.

Jackie Gleason, one of television's biggest stars of the fifties and long a devout fan of the big bands, did his best to help them establish themselves in television. As his summer replacement in 1954, he signed the Dorsey Brothers' newly reunited band to do a production called "Stage Show" heavily featuring the band with guest stars from other segments of show business rounding out the bill. The next summer he put together as his replacement an all-band show with Paul Whiteman as master of ceremonies. This one gave four bands an opportunity to be seen on the program, each introduced by Whiteman for a fifteen minute stanza. A different group of bands was used each week offering most of the important names still in the business a chance to be exposed to the television audience under the most favorable conditions.

Response to both these shows was very good. The multiple band format was not repeated, perhaps because of the problem of lining up so many leaders. But the Dorsey Brothers won a permanent position on the winter Gleason Hour, with Gleason turning over the second half of the period to let them present their "Stage Show". They were still doing it when Tommy died suddenly in November of 1956. A week later Gleason presented a Dorsey tribute show, made up of the biggest names in the music business. Jimmy carried on with the regular show until his failing health forced him to give up shortly before his own untimely death in June of 1957.

The possibility that the Dorseys' success might indicate a breakthrough for the whole business appeared strong enough that other leaders were able to find sponsors to put them on television, some of them for the second time. In 1955 Lombardo tried again with a straight band show patterned after the old radio remotes and featuring nothing but dance music, with visiting female vocal stars. Produced by M.C.A., it received excellent reviews and was voted the best new musical television series. But before long it was gone.

In the hope that progressive jazz was what the viewers wanted Stan Kenton came on for a while in a show written by Leonard Feather entitled "Music 55". It too got good reviews but these were not enough to influence the sponsor to renew since

the ratings did not match the reviews. The same was true of a summer replacement show from New York featuring Russ Morgan in 1956. Procter & Gamble was his sponsor, and Helen O'Connell, whose voice had helped sell millions of Jimmy Dorsey records in the early forties, came out of retirement to be a regular on the show along with Morgan. For a while it seemed it would click but like most of the others, one season was the life of the program and it did not get an opportunity to repeat.

Periodic attempts were made during the balance of the fifties to find the formula for television success with a dance band. Most of these were local presentations, but a few were on a national network. None of them enjoyed any noteworthy success and were soon dropped. A limited few who landed a spot on a variety show found themselves simply playing the background music, with hardly enough recognition to let the public know they were there. Yet this appeared to be all television had for the band business.

There was one exception, however, for while the business was generally getting the cold shoulder from television, Lawrence Welk had been writing a success story into the records that far outstripped any of those which had resulted from radio.

His show which had started at Santa Monica's Aragon Ballroom in 1952 was originally a sustaining production. Before long it attracted enough attention to interest a local sponsor. The ballroom found itself doing business the likes of which it had never previously seen, and the six-week contract under which Welk had opened was renewed over and over again.

Eventually there came a slowdown and conferences were held as to the logic of dropping the weekly television pickup, or perhaps even changing bands for a while. Welk's answer was that this was no time to curtail activity, but that the real solution was to augment the band and give the public more for its money, both in the ballroom and on their television screens. Luckily for everyone concerned he won his point.

In the summer of 1955 the show went national on the ABC-TV network under the sponsorship of Dodge Motor Cars. It became a Saturday night regular, outgrowing the ballroom to move into the ABC studios for more adequate production facilities. Welk continued to play at the Aragon for nine years, with time out for occasional personal

LAWRENCE WELK's television cast in 1959. — *Photo courtesy of Lawrence Welk.*

appearance tours since the television show had made him the nation's number one box office attraction. In 1961 he deserted the Aragon for a long term contract at the Hollywood Palladium. The show itself was showing no signs of losing its momentum at the end of its ninth year as a coast-to-coast production.

Welk's TV success inspired many others to try, several of them over and over. But as the sixties were well under way most leaders looked back with fond memories to the heyday of radio. For radio had built bands and the band business, but television had never found a way to use most of them.

186

WELK pays tribute to the entire band business in a 1960 segment of his weekly show. — *Photo courtesy of Ralph Portnor.*

The KENTUCKY KARDINALS in an appearance in Atlantic City, 1928. — *Photo courtesy of Anson Weeks.*

Chicago's TRIANON BALL-ROOM, below, opened in 1922 with Paul Whiteman's orchestra playing a special charity ball. — *Photo courtesy of Andrew Karzas.*

Personal Appearances and Where They Made Them

IT WAS IN THE Fall of 1942 that a leading show business trade journal featured an editorial under the following headline, "Bands — A Billion Dollar Industry".

This was at a time when the importance of dance orchestras in the entertainment world was at its peak. That position of importance continued for a few years after the date of the editorial. During the years which made up the total span of this popularity the business could be said to consist of the following segments — records, radio, television for a limited few, and personal appearances, the most important of all.

In the beginning personal appearances made up the business in its entirety. Then came records and radio not only to provide income, but to become the potent factors in building a band to name status. Once this position had been established, however, the real payoff came from taking the product to the public. The public was as anxious as the bandleader to have this take place, for playing the record or hearing the band on radio was not enough. For the real fan it created the desire to see them in person.

To do this they flocked to the ballrooms, hotels, and nightclubs where they could dance to the music of their favorite orchestra, or to the theaters where they could listen to it playing from the stage. There were even times when they could not resist the temptation to dance to them in the theaters.

The importance of the various types of locations where bands were presented varied through the years, but each of them developed and multiplied in keeping with the growth of the band business and the popularity of dancing. Some of them stood above all the rest for the part they played in building to prominence or for their continuous use of bands as attractions.

In the years when the business was first starting to become something worthwhile, the hotels probably had an advantage over other places which offered dancing. They were already established in the business of catering to the public, and it was not too difficult to enlarge rooms to accommodate the following which a well-known band enjoyed. Many of these were already in existence having previously been supported by society's expensive private dancing parties. Perhaps because of the holdover from that era they also enjoyed a position of respect not shared by the average ballroom in operation in the early twenties and prior.

Many of the early ballrooms were "Dime a Dance" places attracting a special type of clientele. Will Osborne's description of the clubs as "The Speakeasy Circuit" can very well include a great many of the night clubs in the early twenties since a lot of them were controlled by the same people who controlled the liquor supply, a situation which continued for many years. There were, however, a great number of clubs which enjoyed favorable reputations, and where the early bands considered it an opportunity to be booked for no other reason than the fact that they were important band building spots.

Among the hotels it was those on the East Coast which dominated the scene all during the twenties, and well into the early thirties. Not only were they important to the bands which originated in New York, but they attracted those who got their start in other sections of the country, for to be booked into one of them was an indication that a band had really "arrived". Yet in some of these spots the turnover of bands was not great enough to permit outsiders to move in with any degree of regularity. Bert Lown stayed on for years at the New York Biltmore while over at the Roosevelt Ben Bernie had an equally long run. The Roosevelt was taken over in 1929 by Guy Lombardo for a stay which was to last over 30 years, interrupted only as he saw fit to go away on tour. George Hall after doing a tour for the Ambassador Hotel Chain and then a three-year stint in the Arcadia Ballroom, moved into the Taft Hotel in the late twenties and did not leave until about 1938.

To some degree the same picture existed prior to the thirties in the nation's other leading hotels, with the Chicago spots usually keeping their bands for quite extended engagements. Out on the West Coast this was even more true, for following the eastern movement of such bands as Hickman and Whiteman, those who got their starts in hotels stayed on for several years. The Ambassador's Cocoanut Grove opened in 1921 and it was Hickman who first played there. After he left the Grove would make other West Coast leaders famous, with Abe Lyman taking over and remaining there until 1926. Lyman was followed by Gus Arnheim, his former piano player, who stayed on equally as long and he, too, gained a national reputation there.

In the meantime in the Los Angeles Biltmore, Earl Burtnett had been entrenched for many years. The era of the traveling bands really got into full swing in the early thirties and when it did, most hotels across the country limited the engagements of their band attractions, but both the Biltmore and the Ambassador continued to book theirs for longer stays ranging from six months to several years.

San Francisco, the only other West Coast city with any important dance attractions featured in the hotels, also was the scene of long period bookings. During the twenties and well into the thirties it was almost entirely local bands who were featured. Anson Weeks became a big name at the Mark Hopkins where he stayed from 1927 until he went east seven years later into the St. Regis in New York. Phil Harris and Carol Lofner were at the St. Francis for several years, to be followed by Ted FioRito, the first eastern name to stay there for any length of time. FioRito was followed by Dick Jurgens, a local boy on his way up who got his first important build-up on the St. Francis bandstand.

As the popularity of the traveling bands began to increase the Mark Hopkins, St. Francis, and Palace hotels turned over their bandstands to the big names from other sections of the country for average stays of four to six weeks. In the meantime the city's own local names had become big enough to attract bookings elsewhere and became traveling bands themselves.

As shorter engagements became the accepted pattern in most of the major hotels, these hotels were no longer looked upon as the spot where the bandleader made his money, but only where he got enough build-up through radio time to cash in on one-night appearances. This was particularly true in the Midwest where the one-nighter market was big, and where by moving into a hotel in cities like Omaha, Kansas City, or Memphis, their air time over a local station would blanket the surrounding territory. Usually the leader would anticipate actually taking a loss on the hotel engagement, but the one-nighters that followed in the area which he had penetrated with his radio remotes would be most lucrative.

The big era of the ballrooms began just prior to the mid-twenties even though there had been ballrooms around the country before that time and a lot of other places which were described as dance halls. In the New York area the Roseland was well established by 1920, and there was the Glen Island Casino as early as 1918. The Arcadia started around the same time, and the Savoy also dates back into those same early years.

There was also an Arcadia Ballroom in Detroit during the early twenties, and by 1923 Jean Goldkette had taken over the Greystone in that city. In Chicago there were a number of popular ballrooms in operation, including the Dreamland and the Midway Gardens.

But the real glamour of the ballrooms, and the boom in the ballroom business, had its beginning with the opening in Chicago of the Trianon and the Aragon. The Trianon's opening night featured the largest charity ball Chicago had ever seen and Paul Whiteman and his orchestra furnished the music. Four years later the Trianon's owner, William Karzas opened the Aragon with the Ted Fio-Rito-Dan Russo orchestra given the opening assignment. By the end of the twenties they were the best known ballrooms in America, probably because they so quickly saw the importance of radio and through it made themselves famous, and at the same time established firmly in the band business those leaders who for the next several years would be among America's most successful white orchestras. From then on the building of ballrooms mushroomed rapidly across the nation.

There was a remarkable similarity of names given to some of these places during the next several years with Trianon ballrooms appearing in Cleveland, Los Angeles and Seattle, as well as in four or five other cities where they did not become quite as well known. The Aragon name was equal-

The ARAGON, Chicago, opened in 1926 by the Trianon's owner, Wm. Karzas. — *Photo courtesy of Andrew Karzas.*

Atlantic City's Million Dollar Pier, 1928. By this time Goodman and Miller had left Pollack's band, Jack Teagarden had joined. — *Photo couresty of Gil Rodin.*

TED LEWIS and his orchestra
at the Palace Theatre, 1928.
—*Photo courtesy Ted Lewis.*

ly copied, with one of the best known to become firmly established somewhat later in Santa Monica. Eventually there were a half dozen Arcadias around the country while the name Rainbow in one fashion or another was tied in with many ballrooms. There was a Rainbow Gardens in Denver, a Rainbow Rendezvous in Salt Lake City, and for several years there was a Rainbow Ballroom in Los Angeles.

During the twenties the West Coast ballroom scene included several in the Los Angeles area which were quite popular, including the Venice where Ben Pollack started his first band, and the Plantation where George Olsen was a favorite attraction. The previously mentioned Rainbow was eventually renamed the Palomar, and became for many years the West Coast's most active ballroom in the use of the big names from other sections of the country. It was here that the payoff finally came for Benny Goodman in 1934 after months of struggling to get himself established in eastern spots.

Just before the mid-thirties the Avalon Ballroom on Catalina Island added itself to the list of West Coast ballrooms using name bands. Irving Aaronson was apparently the first traveling band to play there, but for the next several years most of the nation's biggest attractions played the spot, and between the Avalon and the Palomar the West

Coast prestige as a desirable territory for names was substantially boosted.

Early in October, 1939, the Palomar burned to the ground. The fire started from a cloth left lying on the equipment of the radio engineer who had come in to do the night's broadcast. Charlie Barnet was playing there at the time, but the fire started during intermission catching the band off the stand. It spread so quickly that there was no opportunity to recover their instruments which were completely destroyed along with the band's even more priceless musical library.

The loss of the Palomar was a serious blow to the West Coast band picture for the next twelve months until the Hollywood Palladium opened in late October of 1940. Doubtless at the time the Palladium was the most glamorous ballroom in America, and was given a great deal of publicity as the first million dollar ballroom to be built. Perhaps in the 1960s that does not sound like any fabulous amount, but in 1940 a million dollars was a lot of money. Prior to its opening the Palladium management announced that its policy would be to play nothing but the best established names which created keen competition for the right to open the spot. Tommy Dorsey, having now been a big name for some three years, was given the assignment and was followed by a steady parade of the other top contenders.

THE "CALIFORNIA COLLEGIANS" AWAIT THE CUE TO BEGIN **DUNKING** FROM GEORGE MURPHY THE DANCING COMEDIAN.

BETWEEN SCENES OF THE MUSICAL HIT "ROBERTA" NOW AT THE NEW AMSTERDAM THEATRE, NEW YORK

The CALIFORNIA COLLEGIANS in "Roberta," the show which converted Fred MacMurray from saxophone to movie star. — *Photo courtesy of Lou Wood.*

At left, TED FIORITO doing a one-nighter in Bellingham, Washington, 1934. Muzzy Marcellino at mike. — *Photo courtesy of Muzzy Marcellino.*

KAY KYSER AND HIS ORCHESTRA
EL PATIO BALL ROOM
LAKESIDE PARK
DENVER, COLO. AUG. 1937.

ROCKY MT. PHOTO CO
DENVER-35838

KAY KYSER and his orchestra at the El Patio Ballroom, Lakeside Park, Denver, in August 1937. — *Photo courtesy Larry Duran.*

KAY KYSER was at the Trianon, 1937.
    — *Photo courtesy of Andrew Karzas.*

☆ ☆ ☆ ☆ ☆ ☆ ☆ ☆ ☆ ☆

SWAY WITH KAY!

KAY KYSER and his great band playing . . . . singing . . . clowning . . . acclaimed as one of the finest dance orchestras in America! . . . featuring a galaxy of stars, including Nancy Nelson, Bill Stoker, Harry Babbitt, Sully Mason, Merwyn "Ish Kabbible" Bogue, and others . . . presenting "Music As You Like It."

At The TRIANON

The Texas Centennial provided a temporary market for important names, 1936.
— *Courtesy of Anson Weeks.*

Meantime another segment of the personal appearance market had been developing which began in the twenties. Appearances in the theaters as vaudeville units had been made by a few of the bands, and by the end of the twenties some of them were making it big business. But the real boom for the name bands in the nation's theaters did not start until about 1935 or 1936. This was during the period of the strongly surging upward trend of the band business touched off by Goodman's sky-rocketing to success.

The period during which dance orchestras were a predominant part of America's entertainment reached its halfway point in 1940. Their real success began about 1920 and by 1960 little of it remained. A look at the picture at this halfway point reveals clearly that they had definitely become "big business".

One of the services of *Downbeat* magazine, which at that time covered all phases of the music business regardless of musical styles, was a band routing headed, "Where the Bands are Playing". Looking back at some old issues of 1940 this page listed approximately 800 dance bands either traveling or playing locations and enjoying local, semi-name, and name status.

The use of dance bands by the hotels had long since ceased to be something restricted to the larger cities.

Now across the nation every city of 150,000 people or more had at least one hotel where dancing was featured, and where the big names played at least intermittently. In New York City the lineup of major hotels had not changed too much in ten years, although at this point the Pennsylvania perhaps ranked the highest in terms of the number of names used in a twelve-month period. The Taft, the Roosevelt, the Waldorf-Astoria, Biltmore, and the New Yorker constantly featured names, and Maria Kramer's Edison and Lincoln hotels were in the picture although they usually attempted to book bands who were still on their way up.

Out in Chicago the Sherman Hotel had its College Inn and Panther Room, both featuring names, and there was the Palmer House, Edgewater Beach, Congress, Drake, and the Boulevard Room at the Stevens. However, if the prospective customer did not care to go to a hotel the Blackhawk Restaurant and Chez Paree offered musical attractions which competed strongly with the hotels.

In St. Louis it was the Chase and the Jefferson, and each offered the top attractions in the business. Heading into the South and Southwest the Claridge and the Peabody competed for the top names in the city of Memphis, and in Dallas it was the Baker and the Adolphus. Over in Houston there was the Rice Hotel, but perhaps the best-known spot in the South was the Blue Room of the Roosevelt in New Orleans. Here hotel owner Seymour Weiss used every well-known band in the business, and took a great deal of pride in the fact that it had been he who had given Glenn Miller his first hotel engagement.

There had been little change in the hotel picture on the West Coast, but en route there from Chicago a name band could pick up engagements at the Paxton and Fontenelle in Omaha, The

Muehlbach in Kansas City, the Cosmopolitan in Denver, and the Hotel Utah in Salt Lake City.

The Aragon and Trianon Ballrooms in Chicago were still popular places, although by the early years of the forties other spots had stolen a portion of the spotlight. The Glen Island Casino in New Rochelle, New York, had become a top band building place, and an engagement at Frank Dailey's Meadowbrook in Cedar Grove, New Jersey, put the label of success on any band which arrived there for the first time. After the opening of the Palladium in Hollywood it was accepted in the same category, and like the Meadowbrook became the target for every band in the business.

Theaters were now the best friends a name band could have and vice versa. Bands had become the top attraction in theaters and were running up fabulous grosses which became even bigger during the war years which followed. Theater owners and managers were agreed that no other form of entertainment in the nation commanded a greater audience than name bands, and from coast to coast theater marquees announced their personal appearances.

Probably the theater most universally identified with dance orchestras was the Paramount in New York. It was here that the youthful fans of Benny Goodman resisted all efforts of the ushers to control their enthusiasm, dancing in the aisles and even on the stage during one of his first appearances there about 1936. Through the years that followed, every name of importance in the music world had his opportunity at the Paramount. Several years later the Paramount management released a story to the press on the biggest business ever done for them by a name band. The readers were quite surprised to learn that it had not been one of the big names in the swing era, but dated back to the Depression Year of 1931 when the popular Buddy Rogers Orchestra did a single week's business of $98,000.00.

By 1940, college dates had become extremely important and were part of the schedule of any well-known band on tour. One of the old-time leaders recalled how in the early twenties a four or five piece band played college proms for $25.00 or $30.00. Now in the early forties, the guarantees equalled or exceeded those from independent promoters, and in most cases were quite substantially larger. Every college of every size was using several name orchestras each year and the students were periodically polled as to their likes and dislikes because their age group was considered representative of the nation's biggest dance market potential.

The wartime boom came and went although it hung on for approximately one year after the war's end. During that period, the band market continued unabated with personal appearances guarantees at an all-time high. Few of the bandleaders, unhappy with what they had been receiving from some of the ballroom operators, got into the ballroom business themselves, often to their financial sorrow. The group who became owners and operators included Shep Fields, Tommy Dorsey, and Horace Heidt. Dorsey was operating the Casino Gardens in Santa Monica, and perhaps because of his own feelings in the matter was bidding up the prices for important names who entered the Los Angeles area. The newly opened Avodon managed by Barney McDevitt bid as much as $7500.00 weekly for such names as Woody Herman and Stan Kenton, and the nearby Hollywood Palladium could do nothing but go along with them. To some degree, this affected guarantees in other sections of the country as well.

By the beginning of 1947 no one doubted that the business was heading into a decline. The theaters were the first group to drop name bands as featured attractions though a few short years before they had racked up their biggest grosses. By the end of the forties, this desertion was nearly complete. Some theater owners blamed it on the fact that television was starting to eat into their business, and that the name bands had not been able to compete with the home entertainment to the extent that they were any longer a profitable attraction. Others said, not quite so publicly, that their profit was hampered by the necessity of complying with the union's requirement of standby musicians in addition to the name attraction.

The hotels were next to move in the direction of eliminating name bands, although the trend did not have the momentum it had with the theaters. Here, too, a variety of reasons were given. One of these was that except for the wartime years, the rooms which featured dancing had not been any more profitable for the hotel operator than they had for the bandleader. Now a more realistic cost accounting was causing them to eliminate any portion of their facility which would not make money. Generally speaking, however, the decline in the use of big bands by the hotels kept pace with the

The PALOMAR, 1936. Note admission prices for a top name attraction. — *Photo courtesy of Los Angeles Herald-Examiner.*

By 1937 Catalina was a major band spot. In this Ted Weems picture, Marilyn Maxwell is seen at left while Perry Como kneels in center of front row. — *Courtesy of Ted Weems.*

197

ANNOUNCING
THE "TORRID TRUMPET" OF

CLYDE
McCOY
OF "SUGAR BLUES" FAME
AND HIS ORCHESTRA
•
OPENING OCT. 6
•
THE
PALOMAR

VERMONT AT THIRD STREET • PROGRAM WEEK OF SEPT. 26

CLYDE McCOY made his first Palomar appearance in 1936, then returned annually.

conversion of nighttime radio from band remotes to complete domination by the disc jockeys. During the days when radio from 9:00 P.M. to Midnight was a succession of remote pickups from the nation's major hotels, this had been a form of advertising which gave the hotel prestige. When the remotes disappeared from the air, one of the reasons for keeping a name band around disappeared.

The ballroom operators were in a different position. They were fighting for their lives, along with the band business, for everything they had was built around it. In 1946, the National Ballroom Operators Association of America was formed and held their first meeting in Chicago. Every major operator in the country attended this get-together which turned out to be a session in which they aired their gripes against the agencies, the leaders, and most of all the 20% cabaret tax which had included the ballrooms and which they felt did not belong there. The major complaint against the bands themselves, was that most of them insisted

on guarantees which the operators felt were too high, and that the agencies who booked the bands did not provide sufficient publicity to make the appearances successful. There was also grumbling that too few of the bands in the business at that time were playing danceable music.

This group continued to meet annually from that time on. By 1951, they won their battle to have ballrooms eliminated from the cabaret tax. In the succeeding years, their annual convention produced announcements regarding the outlook for their business which swung back and forth like a pendulum. In 1952, they were forecasting that business was once more going to be good, but they announced the next year that it was so bad ballrooms were closing right and left. One of these had been Chicago's old landmark, the Trianon, which had been placed up for auction. There was also a lot of talk that many ballroom operators would follow the example of the nightclubs and many hotels which had switched to using top-rated record names for attractions, backed by local house bands.

In the meantime, the bandleaders had formed an organization of their own called "Dance Orchestra Leaders of America", and there was talk of holding a joint convention with the ballroom operators which finally came to pass in the fall of 1955. The President of the Ballroom group at that time was Tom Archer, owner of a Midwestern chain of ballrooms which blanketed Iowa, Nebraska, and part of Missouri. Les Brown headed the bandleaders' group, and their opening session included some frank exchanges which at times were a little heated. Archer let them know that he thought many of the problems facing the business had been created by leaders who entirely ignored the taste of the dancing public. The seventy-five leaders who turned out for the convention apparently took these remarks seriously enough that their own announcements to the press inferred that jazz units which did not play dance music would be excluded from membership in their group.

That the band business was really facing a fight for its life was evident from other things happening concurrently across the nation. Early in 1952, a trade journal announced that the West Coast picture had been sagging so badly in the early fifties that opening nights were outnumbered by permanent closings. Amusement park ballrooms everywhere started to drop name band

The Palomar burns, October 2, 1939. View from rear where fire started on bandstand — *Photo courtesy Los Angeles Herald-Examiner.*

Charlie Barnet, below, was playing the Palomar when it burned. Twisted instruments and burned music were all he had left the next morning. — *Photo courtesy of Gil Harris.*

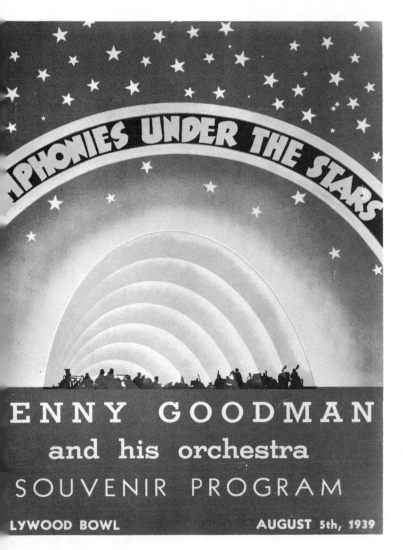

PHONIES UNDER THE STARS

ENNY GOODMAN
and his orchestra

SOUVENIR PROGRAM

LYWOOD BOWL   AUGUST 5th, 1939

Benny Goodman's was the first dance orchestra to appear in concert in the Hollywood Bowl. — *Photo courtesy of M.C.A.*

JIMMIE GRIER

JULIE GIBSON

THE
MARCH

OF
BANDS

JULIE GIBSON

LOMBARDO BROTHERS

GUY LOMBARDO

In San Francisco the St. Francis Hotel had this line-up for March
1940. — *Photo courtesy of St. Francis Hotel.*

200

bookings, claiming that they were no longer attracting crowds for them. Ten years before there had been over two hundred amusement parks who were steady band buyers. Now there was talk of shutting park ballrooms entirely. This trend even extended to the City of Denver which had been unique in that its two amusement parks, Lakeside Park and Elitch's Gardens, had been the social dancing centers of the city during the summer months. Sometime in the early fifties, the Lakeside's manager, Benjamin Krasner, decided to use his ballroom for something other than the booking of name bands, leaving the Gurtler Brothers at Elitch's Gardens without competition. They continued to bring in the nation's leading dance attractions throughout the fifties, carrying on the policy which they had started in the mid-twenties.

During the early years of the fifties, colleges began to reappraise the advantages of big bands for their important social events, versus the use of local crews which could be hired for $200 to $300. In 1951, colleges queried on this subject reported that they had paid during the previous season an average of $1400.00 per engagement for name attractions with the highest guarantee having been $4500.00 paid to Vaughn Monroe. Ralph Flanagan, Harry James, and Tommy Dorsey were next highest on the list, with some of their dates netting them as much as $3,000.00, but with most of them bringing in $2250 to $2500. The college group like most of the ballroom operators, also complained that many of the big names were not giving them danceable music, made a poor and sometimes indifferent appearance on the bandstand, and that a few of them had even considered their college prom an occasion for having a few too many drinks.

In the face of these trends, it had been necessary for bands to look around for other sources of personal appearance bookings, which they did with some degree of success. Early in the fifties, a little Frenchman from Louisiana by the name of LeBlanc parlayed a patent medicine called "Hadacol" into a business which was grossing several million dollars annually. In typical medicine show fashion, he toured the country with it, hiring name bands as part of his entourage. This one, however, lasted only a couple of years.

Canadian theaters began to use a few orchestra headliners from the States with Jimmy Dorsey and Woody Herman the first to play such engagements for substantial weekly guarantees, but with

the bandleader furnishing the other acts on the bill as well. Other foreign markets also attracted a few leaders. Tommy Dorsey made a Brazilian tour of eight weeks early in 1952 which was quite profitable, and perhaps was what prompted him to tour Europe for six to eight weeks the following year. Stan Kenton also made a South American trip, and there were rumors that some of our big names were being enticed to see what they could accomplish with bookings in Australia.

The foreign market continued to attract the better known American orchestras during the balance of the fifties. Most of their appearances were not dance dates but concerts, and their hotel accommodations ran the gamut from luxurious to unbearable. All too often travel arrangements were unreliable, and once, Harry James, on a European tour, accidentally found one of his long-standing ambitions finally being fulfilled. He had always cherished a desire to visit the picturesque city of Venice and when the tour was set up without including it on the schedule he was disappointed.

Because of the size of his group James had his own private railway car for transportation from one date to the next. Following an appearance in Milano, Italy, their car was picked up as usual and they settled back for the long trip to Linz, Austria, and a day's layoff between departure and their next showtime.

A few hours out they discovered the wrong train had taken them in tow and they would end up in Salzburg, Austria, instead of their scheduled destination. Harry and his manager, Frank Monte immediately went to work on the train personnel in an attempt to find out how they could get rerouted to their target city in time to do their concert. While they were busily engaged in this manner, the train came to a halt and they were informed a three-hour layover was to be added to their troubles. Monte, of Italian descent himself, angrily inquired as to where they were. To the surprise of both himself and James they discovered that the railroad's error had brought them to Venice, and that they would even have time for a quick tour. Finally under way again they made it to Linz with two hours to spare.

Meanwhile the concert type of appearance had developed into importance in the States. For several years such bands as Stan Kenton, Woody Herman, and Duke Ellington had been playing concert dates. Now the sweeter styled dance bands gave this one a try, with the fall of 1952 seeing

The Ballroom Operator Has His Sa

WHEN somebody is selling something with the idea of snaring a profit, and somebody else is buying same with the identical intention, and when the latter has to depend upon such intangibles and variables as public reaction, the weather and the possibly untested commercial value of the commodity, it should be obvious that life is not always a bowl of cherries for the

And Says Plenty About High Guarantees, Low Receipts, Poor Publicity and Worse Booking Office Methods—A General Unburdening of the Grievances and Pet Peeves Nursed by Dance Promoters Against the Bands They Buy and the Bookers They Buy Them From

to say, "My most common co comes from people who pay to yet feel they were fluffed off band leader.   Without those neither the band leader nor mys get along. I believe intermission be taken Glenn Miller style: Mill on the band stand, talks, visits autographs, etc., while the boy then takes his layoff for the 15 n

Listed below are the bands that drew the best business during the past season for the ballroom operators and dance promoters represented in the accompanying article. Also listed are the orchestras that went over best with the respective ballrooms' patrons, regardless of their showing at the box office. The first three are given in each instance.

It must be pointed out, of course, that there can be no basis for any comparative values or standards, inasmuch as some ballrooms play name bands only, some alternate names with territorial favorites, while still others play only territorial and local bands.

What is significant, however, is the discrepancy noted in some cases between the good business done by a band and its reception by the ballroom's clientele. The reverse may also be noted—where a band does not figure in the best gross registered at a spot, and yet may be first in the affections of the spot's patronage.

BALLROOM	BEST BUSINESS	BEST PATRONAGE REACTION
Auditorium, Knoxville, Tenn.	Cab Calloway, Count Basie, Jimmie Lunceford	Erskine Hawkins, Jimmie Lunceford, Cab Calloway
Canadarago Park, Richfield Springs, N. Y.	Guy Lombardo, Gene Krupa, Cab Calloway	Gene Krupa, Guy Lombardo, Bob Crosby
Enna Jettick Park, Auburn, N. Y.	Mike Riley, Les Brown, Rita Rio	Les Brown, Rita Rio, Mike Riley
Fairyland Park, Kansas City, Mo.	Hal Kemp, Pinky Tomlin, Cab Calloway	Jay McShann, Ben Pollack, George Hall
Fiesta Danceteria, New York City	Ben Bernie, Gene Krupa, Shorty Allen	Jack Denny, Joe Marsala, Antonio De Vera
Joyland Casino, Lexington, Ky.	Blue Barron, Ella Fitzgerald, Ted Weems	Blue Barron, Ella Fitzgerald, Ben Bernie
King's Ballroom, Lincoln, Neb.	Henry Busse, Vincent Lopez, Hal Leonard	Vincent Lopez, Hal Leonard, Nat Towles
Meadowbrook Ballroom, Bascom, O.	Carl (Deacon) Moore, Blue Barron, Emil Velazco	Carl (Deacon) Moore, Blue Barron, Tommy Carlyn
Myrtle Beach (S. C.) Pavilion	Bill Clarke, Bob Sylvester, Freddy Johnson	Bill Clarke, Freddy Johnson, Bob Sylvester
Natatorium Park, Spokane, Wash.	Phil Harris, Eddy Duchin	Muzzy Marcellino, Phil Harris
Ocean Pier, Wildwood, N. J.	Jimmy Dorsey, Larry Clinton	Lou Breese
Pier Ballroom, Buckeye Lake, O.	Ben Bernie, Jan Garber, Carl (Deacon) Moore	Jan Garber, Ace Brigode, Russ Morgan
Pla-Mor Ballroom, Lincoln, Neb.	Paul Moorehead, Jimmy Barnett, Skippy Anderson (all tied)	Paul Moorehead, Jimmy Barnett, Ralph Slade
Saltair, Salt Lake City	Jimmy Walsh, Phil Harris, Anson Weeks	Jimmy Walsh, Phil Harris, Skinnay Ennis
Sandy Beach Park, Russells Point, O.	Artie Shaw, Blue Barron, Jan Garber	Jan Garber, Blue Barron, Glen Gray
Sherman's Caroga Lake, N. Y.	Fletcher Henderson, Ray Keating, Robertshaw	Ray Keating, Robertshaw
Starlight Ballroom, Chippewa Lake, O.	Ace Brigode, Tommy Tucker, Tiny Hill	Tommy Tucker, Ace Brigode, Tiny Hill
Summit Beach, Akron, O.	Bob Chester, Clyde McCoy, Arden Wilson	Bob Chester, Will Bradley, Clyde McCoy
Turnpike Casino, Lincoln, Neb.	Glenn Miller, Ted Lewis, Paul Whiteman	Ted Lewis, Dick Jurgens, Glenn Miller
Westwood Supper Club, Richmond, Va.	Bruce Baker, Glen Garr, Barry MacKinley	Glen Garr, Bruce Baker, Barry MacKinley

The operators rate the bands, 1940 —
Photo courtesy of Billboard Magazine.

202

Art Jarrett in Chicago's Blackhawk Restaurant in the early 1940s. — *Photo courtesy Art Jarrett.*

Mitchell, South Dakota's Corn Palace was a famous Midwest spot for name band one-nighters. — *Photo courtesy of Lawrence Welk.*

The Prom Ballroom was Minnesota's Twin Cities popular name band spot. — *Photo courtesy of Prom Ballroom.*

ANSON WEEKS on the bandstand of the Sherman Hotel's College Inn, Chicago, about 1937. — *Photo courtesy of Anson Weeks.*

Philadelphia's EARLE THEATRE. — *Photo courtesy of Frankie Carle.*

Jan Garber and the Mills Brothers doing a concert tour through the Midwest as a package deal which proved quite successful. The next year Guy Lombardo followed suit playing twenty-two concert dates which grossed $175,000 for him. Two years later he tried it again with equal success, taking $270,000 from forty appearances, with the highest single take being $19,000 in Omaha, Nebraska. Release of these figures was all the Lombardo critics needed to prompt them to quickly point out that this was exactly as it should have been since Omaha was the heart of the cornbelt.

Concerts were not the only new source of income. Jan Garber discovered another in which he was to some degree a lone specialist. By this time he had moved from the West Coast to Shreveport, Louisiana, from which headquarters he concentrated on one-nighters and a few choice hotel locations to which he returned once a year. To these he added something which other bandleaders had either overlooked or had been unable to adapt their style to play properly. In Houston, Baton Rouge, Little Rock, Oklahoma City, and some three or four other Midwestern cities the annual horse shows were the big events, requiring the services of a name band. Jan found these four-day affairs to be most lucrative and soon had the entire circuit booked solidly year after year.

Garber was a person who could take a joke as well as the next one and we had a good laugh together the first time I ran into him after he began to play this type of event.

"Jan," I said, "this is just as it should be. It is about time the horses did something for you, for you have certainly done a lot for them."

Nobody loved the horses better than Garber in spite of the fact that there were many occasions when it did not appear the horses returned his love.

Las Vegas discovered the name bands for the first time in 1952. Jimmy Dorsey, Billy May, Ray Anthony, and Ina Ray Hutton were brought in for three to four week stands with their full bands. Russ Morgan made at least one appearance there at that time, and was so impressed that he considered putting together a package show tailored exclusively for that market. However, the use of big bands by Las Vegas clubs was a period of short duration this first time around, although some years later a few of them tried it again and it became a steady place of engagement for two or

Happy crowd in the Dallas Adolphus Hotel about 1940, with Red Nichols furnishing the music. — *Photo courtesy of Red Nichols.*

San Francisco's GOLDEN GATE THEATRE. — *Photo courtesy of Golden Gate Theatre.*

BUDDY ROGERS, who held the Paramount Theatre's house record for top gross by a dance orchestra. — *Photo courtesy of Paul Weirick.*

At right, VAUGHN MONROE on stage of Capitol Theatre, Washington, D. C. — *Photo courtesy of Vaughn Monroe.*

One of the rare times the "King of Swing," BENNY GOODMAN was ever photographed with Artie Shaw. Lady in center is Edison Hotel's Maria Kramer. — *Photo courtesy of Frank "Pee Wee" Monte.*

Picture at left shows CHARLIE SPIVAK's opening night at Pennsylvania Hotel, 1941. Guests include Billy Butterfield, David Rose, Stan Kenton, Jimmy Palmer, Chuck Foster, and vocalist Marion Hutton. — *Photo courtesy of Charlie Spivak.*

three big names who practically made it their base of operation.

One of these early Las Vegas bookings saw Charlie Barnet at Hotel El Rancho with a contract calling for the band to work from 11:30 at night to 5:30 in the morning. After the contract had been signed El Rancho owner, Beldon Kettleman, decided that 11:30 was too early for them to start, and asked Barnet to change his schedule to start an hour later and work until 6:30 a.m. Barnet was not one to be easily swayed, so he insisted that the original contract should hold. To carry out his end of the bargain he showed up promptly at 11:30 every evening to go to work. In order to impress Barnet that he was just as serious regarding his stand in the matter, Kettleman would turn off the public address system and lights at 11:30, then turn them on again an hour later. This might have stopped a lot of people, but not Barnet. He began playing on schedule but for the first hour his programming was limited to one number which he played without interruption. His selection of the old standard "Dancing in the Dark" was quite appropriate for the situation but if it had ever been one of Mr. Kettleman's favorite numbers, his love for it soon faded. After a week of this feuding, an agreement was finally reached whereby Barnet played the schedule originally called for in the contract.

As the 1950s drew to a close the golden era of the dance bands was fast becoming a memory for all but a very few. For those who had been successful, most of those memories were pleasant. Without exception they could recall a lot of incidents which were amusing even though some of them may not have been so at the time they happened.

One which Harry James will never forget occurred a few months after he had joined the Benny Goodman band. Goodman was riding the crest of his new-found popularity and James was particularly pleased to be part of the organization. He was additionally pleased when Goodman gave him his first raise, so he celebrated by buying himself a new trumpet. Even though he was now making good money the price of a trumpet was not an item of minor consequence, and it was with a great deal of pride that he showed it off to his fellow musicians on the job the night after the purchase.

That job happened to be a one-nighter and the place was packed. The feel of the new horn inspired him to new confidence and an evening's

List of Winners in The Billboard's Annual College Poll

Each year The Billboard conducts a poll of college editors, in reality an exhausting survey of various factors surrounding the band business. Here are the results from 1938 to 1941. List set in capitals in the vocalist section lists the five highest vocalists in male and female categories as votes were cast.

COLLEGIATE CHOICE OF ORCHESTRAS

1942	1941
1. GLENN MILLER	1. Glenn Miller
2. TOMMY DORSEY	2. Tommy Dorsey
3. HARRY JAMES	3. Kay Kyser
4. BENNY GOODMAN	4. Artie Shaw
5. JIMMY DORSEY	5. Benny Goodman
6. VAUGHN MONROE	6. Jimmy Dorsey
7. SAMMY KAYE	7. Glen Gray
8. KAY KYSER	8. Jimmie Lunceford
9. CHARLIE SPIVAK	9. Guy Lombardo
10. WOODY HERMAN	10. Will Bradley

1940	1939	1938
1. Glenn Miller	1. Artie Shaw	1. Benny Goodman
2. Kay Kyser	2. Kay Kyser	2. Tommy Dorsey
3. Tommy Dorsey	3. Tommy Dorsey	3. Hal Kemp
4. Benny Goodman	4. Benny Goodman	4. Guy Lombardo
5 Orrin Tucker	5. Larry Clinton	5. Kay Kyser
6. Jan Savitt	6. Hal Kemp	6. Glen Gray
7. Guy Lombardo	7. Guy Lombardo	7. Horace Heidt
8. Sammy Kaye	8. Horace Heidt	8. Sammy Kaye
9. Hal Kemp	9. Glen Gray	9. Jimmie Lunceford
10. Jimmy Dorsey	10. Jimmy Dorsey	10. Wayne King

COLLEGIATE CHOICE OF VOCALISTS

FEMALE VOCALISTS 1942	MALE VOCALISTS 1942
1. Helen O'Connell	1. Ray Eberle
2. Marion Hutton	2. Frank Sinatra
3. Ginny Simms	3. Bob Eberly
4. Helen Forrest	4. Harry Babbitt
5. Peggy Lee	5. Vaughn Monroe
6. Anita O'Day	6. Tommy Ryan
7. Ella Fitzgerald	7. Tex Beneke
8. Yvonne King	8. Woody Herman
9. Jo Stafford	9. Dick Haymes
10. Connie Haines	10. Art London

1941	1942	1941
1. Ginny Simms	1. HELEN O'CONNELL	1. Frank Sinatra
2. Helen O'Connell	2. RAY EBERLE	2. Ray Eberle
3. Helen Forrest	3. FRANK SINATRA	3. Bob Eberly
4. Marion Hutton	4. BOB EBERLY	4. Harry Babbitt
5. Martha Tilton	5. MARION HUTTON	5. Kenny Sargent
6. Ella Fitzgerald	6. GINNY SIMMS	6. Bon Bon
7. Bonnie Baker	7. HELEN FORREST	7. Tommy Ryan
8. Connie Haines	8. HARRY BABBITT	8. Bob Allen
9. Dorothy Claire	9. PEGGY LEE	9. Larry Cotton
10. Paula Kelly	10. VAUGHN MONROE	10. Sully Mason

BAND YEAR BOOK, September 26, 1942

College poll of popular orchestras and vocalists, 1942. — *Photo courtesy of Billboard.*

performance which won the repeated approval of the audience with each solo he took. At the end of the evening he placed the instrument carefully in its case and along with the rest of the band members assembled behind the pavilion where the bus was to pick them up for the trip to the next job. Somehow Harry's attention was diverted elsewhere while the bus was backing in to load up and when he looked around the back wheel of the bus was rolling over some of the luggage including his trumpet case. When he picked it up the instrument was mashed flatter than the top of a billiard table, and although years later he was able to enjoy a laugh over the incident he would also recall that at that particular moment the world had never seemed blacker.

Anyone who ever worked with or for Joe Venuti could probably write a book about the experiences that went along with this association. Never one to take life seriously, Joe was constantly in hot water himself and enjoyed pulling practical jokes which put other people in the same position.

Every time I go to Salt Lake City I spend an evening with Murray Williams, now a businessman in that city, who spent years playing saxophone in the bands of Woody Herman, Red Nichols, Eddy Duchin, Henry Busse and Charlie Barnet. One of his first jobs in the big time was with Joe Venuti's band and at the time he joined up he was only a kid of eighteen. Nevertheless he was an ac-

complished musician and after a few weeks Venuti promoted him to first alto. After thinking it over Williams decided that a promotion should be accompanied by an increase in compensation, so just prior to getting on the bandstand that evening he mentioned it to Joe.

At the moment he got no answer but accepted this as a probability that Venuti was thinking it over, too. Midway in the evening's program he got up to take a solo and as he played, Venuti, behind his back, signaled the other musicians to drop out one by one. Finally Williams discovered that he was the only member of the organization still playing. For one with limited experience this was a trifle upsetting so he began to falter. At this point Venuti stepped to the microphone and made this announcement:

"Listen to him folks, would you believe it, just this evening he hit me up for a raise!"

Williams told of another incident which was amusing but not necessarily Venuti's fault even though it did occur with his band. At the end of a location date at the Palomar Ballroom in Los Angeles the guitar player left the group and a new one moved in. He worked with them on the closing night following which they were to play a one-nighter in Tucson, Arizona. The next evening, when they arrived there and began setting up, there was no guitar player. The men were traveling in private automobiles and after an exchange of quer-

DEL COURTNEY's opening at the Ambassador, Los Angeles, brings out Dinah Shore and George Montgomery. — *Photo courtesy of Del Courtney.*

TEX BENEKE's first night at the Palladium below, drew 6750 dancers, 1947. — *Photo courtesy of Don Haynes.*

Dennis Day, Sammy Kaye, Skinnay Ennis and Palladium manager Sterling Way on Kaye's opening night. — *Photo courtesy of Gary Gray, Hollywood Palladium.*

ies as to who had made arrangements to transport the guitar player it was discovered that no one had. Halfway through the evening's dancing a figure appeared at the far side of the dance floor carrying two traveling bags in one hand and a guitar case in the other. He struggled across the floor through the crowd and deposited his load directly in front of the bandstand. Looking up at Venuti he put the band in stitches with the following comment, "Joe, I'm willing to play ball with you, but you're going to have to make arrangements to get me to the park."

He had hitch-hiked all the way from Los Angeles.

Put the combination of Venuti, Russ Morgan, and Wingy Manone together and anything might happen. Musicians still chuckle about a night in New York City when it did.

At the time of the incident each of them had become a bandleader in his own right and were appearing there simultaneously. Due to an acci-

dent when he was still quite young, Manone wore an artificial arm, accounting for the nickname which had been given him. After work on this particular evening the three of them got together for a tour of the late spots, finally ending up in Manone's room. Here they were having a few more nightcaps when the evening's activities got the best of Manone and he lay down on the bed and went to sleep. Whether it was Morgan or Venuti who had the inspiration neither would ever admit, but one of them called room service, and the conversation went something like this:

"Room service, this is room 598. Would you please send up a bowl of ice and a saw?"

The astonished bell captain could hardly believe what he was hearing:

"A saw? Surely you must be kidding me."

"I'm not kidding at all, I want you to find me a saw and bring it up to this room."

Finally the bell captain was convinced, so going to the hotel's maintenance shop he procured the

211

desired instrument and delivered it, probably thinking he had a couple of wacky musicians who wanted to see if they could make music on it.

Any such artistry was the farthest thing from their minds. After the bellhop had left, one of them proceeded to saw Wingy's artificial arm in two. Their job accomplished, they sat back, drinks in hand, to observe the surprised expression on Manone's face when he finally came to. The only unbelievable part of the whole story is that supposedly he thought it was even funnier than they did and broke into uncontrollable laughter.

One of Jimmy Grier's favorite stories involved a theater appearance he was making in a Midwestern city. Between shows he went back to his hotel to pick up his mail, and while there decided to take a short nap, leaving a call with the switchboard operator which should have given him plenty of time to get back to the theater for the next show. The operator gave him the call on time, and a few minutes later he was in a taxi on his way to the theater. Unfortunately the taxi took a wrong turn and got tangled up with some fire equipment. By the time they had disentangled themselves from this congestion Grier arrived at the theater with only minutes to spare before show time.

He dashed into his dressing room and made a fast change into his tuxedo, but for some reason could not find the necessary black tie. By this time he could hear the band starting to play the theme song which meant the curtain would be going up in a matter of seconds. There was no more time left for searching or delay. In his locker was a black sock which he quickly tucked under his collar, hoping that from out front the substitution would not be too noticeable.

Grier dashed onto the stage in time to make his announcement for the opening number. Unfortunately the sock which he had selected was overdue for a trip to the laundry, and this fact became increasingly apparent under the hot spotlight focused on him. As the show progressed Grier's discomfort increased, a situation which was apparently noticeable to the audience out front, and particularly to a reviewer from the local newspaper who had chosen that particular show to catch as a subject for his column. It was little wonder that he described the band as a capable musical organization, but commented that if Grier did not enjoy his work any more than he appeared to that evening, he should get into some other field.

Theater appearances produced many amusing incidents including one which happened to Tommy Tucker while he was playing the Oriental Theater in Chicago. After the curtain had raised to the sound of the band's theme, the opening number was to be a solo by the band's male vocalist. This was introduced by a drum roll and fanfare while Tucker was making the announcement. The announcement was made but there was no sign of a male vocalist coming to the microphone. Tucker motioned to his piano player to ad lib something momentarily while he composed himself and then had the band break into the old standard "Stardust". Following this the scheduled vocal number was done but by a member of the

A rare shot of the two Dorseys during the days when the feud between the two was subject to periodic flare-ups — *Photo courtesy of Hollywood Palladium.*

The Palladium marquee in the early 1950s. — *Photo courtesy of Hollywood Palladium.*

Tex Beneke and Palladium guests Peter Lawford, Lynn Bari, and Johnny Mercer. — *Courtesy of Gary Gray and Hollywood Palladium.*

RUSS MORGAN and TOMMY DORSEY, two trombone-playing leaders who both came from Pennsylvania, enjoy a few laughs about the "good old days" during one of Dorsey's early 1950 appearances at the Palladium. — *Photo courtesy of Hollywood Palladium.*

trumpet section. After the show Tucker went back stage to find the vocalist sound asleep in his dressing room.

The Glen Gray band was one of the most popular in theaters as elsewhere and made its first trip to the Paramount about 1934. The Paramount stage was one of those which rose up by hydraulic lift as the band played its theme song. In those days Pee Wee Hunt always managed to arrive late, barely having time to jump onto the rising stage before it came into view of the audience out front. One day he was later than usual and as the stage rose up he was just climbing onto it and snagged his trousers, practically tearing them apart. Since he was scheduled to come down front for a featured number something had to be done, so while the band played its first number he switched trousers in the back row with another musician much to the delight of the audience most of whom could see what was going on. They applauded wildly and after the show the rest of the band members had

their fun with Hunt over the incident telling him that anything so sensational should be kept in the act.

The opening nights in top locations would provide a lot of pleasant memories. Usually a dozen or more telegrams would be received by the incoming leader, all to wish him well and all sent for the purpose of being placed on display or read aloud over the public address system. Some of these were from fellow bandleaders, and some were the product of the agency's publicity department. Opening nights usually brought out a room full of celebrities, with every other bandleader in the area who could possibly make it dropping in for a little chat, and probably posing for a few pictures with the leader who was playing the engagement.

Often these opening nights were exciting for more reasons than one. For instance there was the night Joe Venuti, displeased with the comments of a couple of patrons, took the string bass and sailed it out over the heads of the dancers to go crashing against a wall. Some of Tommy Dorsey's openings were equally as eventful, particularly those when his brother Jimmy dropped in to pay his respects, which were sometimes misinterpreted and resulted in a renewal of the old brotherly feud.

One of these exciting evenings occurred in the early forties when Tommy opened up the summer season at the Hotel Astor roof. This was a little different from previous Dorsey openings in that he was introducing to New York for the first time his newly added string section which substantially augmented the size of his band. Every important personality in the music business from the New York area turned out, including song publishers and pluggers, disc jockeys, and other show business people.

At the time brother Jimmy was appearing at the Strand Theater which was nearby. After his last show of the evening he dropped over to join the festivities, and to get a first-hand impression of how Tommy's new band sounded. Perhaps he didn't like what he heard, but at any rate the first time Tommy came off the bandstand only a couple of words were exchanged between the two before Tommy brought a left hook up from the floor which knocked Jimmy into a corner, along with a table of four patrons who happened to be in the way. The next day good-natured Jimmy related the story to the members of his own band with tears in his eyes indicating how he really felt about the rift with his brother which dated back to

214

ENTRANCE TO THE TROCADERO AT ELITCH GARDENS

1953 band line-up for summer season of Magnolia Roof, Claridge Hotel, Memphis. The following year the hotel dropped the use of name bands entirely. — *Photo courtesy of Claridge Hotel.*

Above, one of the nation's finest amusement park ballrooms and one of the few still using name bands as this book was written. — *Photo courtesy of John Gurtler and Elitch's Gardens.*

At right, Seymour Weiss, president of New Orleans' Roosevelt Hotel, and bandleader Johnny Long in the world-famous "Blue Room," 1960. — *Photo courtesy of Seymour Weiss.*

215

ROSELAND DANCE CITY. — *Photo courtesy of Arsene Studio, N.Y.C.*

the breakup of the Dorsey Brothers band in the mid-thirties. For the next couple of days his shows at the Strand Theater were done wearing dark glasses to hide his souvenir of the encounter, a black eye.

For sheer bedlam, it is doubtful that any opening night could come close to that which accompanied the launching of Houston's Shamrock Hotel in early 1949.

The building of the Shamrock had been much publicized from the moment its foundation was laid. It was the pet project of oilman Glen McCarthy who had a reputation for making and spending money on a grand scale. The popular story when it was started was that his decision to build it came one night when the management of the Rice Hotel objected to the exuberant manner in which McCarthy and his guests were celebrating in the Empire Room.

In his determination to make it the finest hotel in Texas, no expense was spared. The swimming pool was full Olympic size and when first viewed by one columnist his comment was, "What do you plan to do, Glen, man it with lifeguards or have the Coast Guard patrol it?"

When the long awaited opening night arrived, the place was packed with Texas millionaires, Hollywood celebrities, and representatives of the nation's top newspapers and magazines, including *Life* magazine photographers.

Champagne began flowing in midafternoon in quantities indicating it must be arriving by pipeline. Russ Morgan, an old friend of McCarthy, won the coveted opening assignment and in keeping with the spirit of the occasion was throwing a cocktail party of his own in the bandleader's suite. It started out with a few invited guests but soon included everyone who walked down the hallway. Leaving the room to escape the noise while he took a long distance call, Morgan was unable to pry his way back into his own party.

Among the visiting celebrities was Dorothy Lamour who had agreed to do her network radio show from the Shamrock, an arrangement which McCarthy had apparently convinced her sponsors would be good publicity for them. It didn't work out quite that way. By the time the show went on the air the scene looked and sounded like Times Square on New Year's Eve. Miss Lamour and her cast were no match for the din, and the program was not many minutes old before the engineers decided the language their microphones were picking up should not be piped into the homes of America, and unceremoniously chopped it off the air. The gregarious Mr. McCarthy never completely forgave the press for the picturesque manner in which they described the affair to their readers.

The big event of an opening night was not restricted to the hotels. It also applied to the major ballrooms, and was particularly true of the Hollywood Palladium during the first several years of its existence. During those years, both the movie industry and the band business were riding high, with the musical personalities enjoying a status almost equal to that of the movie stars. It was not uncommon to see the great stars in Hollywood turning out for a Palladium opening, or frequenting the place with regularity. In some cases, the band appearing at the Palladium would concurrently be working in a picture, and on one occasion when Woody Herman was in Hollywood for both purposes, he brought the entire cast of the picture and half of the studio personnel in for his opening night.

Barney McDevitt was publicity director of the ballroom and he recalls how the younger starlets came to the Palladium nightly, inviting the musicians from the top bands to share their tables during each intermission. This situation progressed to the point that in some cases, getting the band back on the stand after the intermissions became a problem. During one of Tommy Dorsey's engagements it was so bad that Dorsey, standing on

the bandstand alone, shouted angrily at McDevitt, "Get those damned movie stars out of here so we can play some music," and hurled his trombone at McDevitt to emphasize his point. Apparently however, Tommy's dislike for movie stars did not include all of them for a few weeks from that evening he married one of them.

The degree to which personal appearances were the most important segment of the band business will be shown by the following figures provided by authentic sources as to the income of leaders who were big names at varying dates during "the great band era". They will, in fact, show what each segment of the business represented in terms of percentages of total income. Some allowance is necessary for the emphasis which one leader may have placed on a single phase of the business compared with another. In 1939 the Bob Crosby band moved into the big money for the first time since its beginning, and a breakdown of its gross income published in trade journals at the time indicated it added up as follows:

Locations (Hotels, Ballrooms, etc.) 16%
One-Night Engagements 29%
Theaters 31%
Radio Commercials 14%
Records and Royalties 9%

Harry James' first big year came in 1942 with total income from these sources:
Locations 10%
One-Night Engagements 30%
Records 10%
Theaters 10%
Radio 10%
Motion Pictures 30%

PAUL NEIGHBORS and orchestra, taken at Roseland Dance City, in 1961. — *Photo courtesy of Paul Neighbors.*

217

One of Freddy Martin's peak years came in 1947, and the pattern of compensation for his efforts looked like this:

Locations (all Hotels) 23%
Theaters 30%
Records 42%
Commercial Radio 5%

In addition Martin had substantial earnings from a publishing firm and a record shop.

In 1951 the band of the year was Ralph Flanagan who earned his pay in the following manner:

Locations 17%
One-Nighters 45%
Theaters 5%
Radio, Television, and Records 33%
(mostly television and records)

Flanagan's gross was topped that year by veteran Sammy Kaye who added it up from a more detailed breakdown:

Locations 15%
One-Nighters 33%
Theaters 6%
Records and Royalties 17%
Television 28%
Commercial Radio 1%

Kaye's total income from these sources added up to a most impressive figure. Not included was the revenue from another source not actually a part of the music business, but made successful through his many activities as a bandleader. Through a publishing firm of his own he was marketing a book of poems which would have supported him nicely, and probably represented separately a greater annual profit than some of his colleagues were taking from all sources at this period in the business.

By 1960 the scope of the band business had narrowed to the point that accounting for sources of income was a simple matter for the few remaining steadily active. One of these was Harry James, and the degree of changes will be well illustrated by these percentage figures given by his business manager, Frank Monte.

Clubs (all Las Vegas and Reno) 71.6%
One-Nighters (mostly private) 21.9%
Records 6.5%

And yet these statistics, or perhaps unfamiliarity with them, did not keep a few hopeful individuals from periodically predicting that "The big bands will soon be coming back."

The day he gave me the figures just quoted Monte and I had lunch with a prominent disc jockey who made a statement to that effect. Monte's reply, really a question, summed up the situation rather neatly:

"What are they coming back to? Hotels, whose entertainment rooms are long since out of operation? Night clubs now using small combos or a jukebox? Theaters featuring a double bill of B pictures? Ballrooms standing idle or converted to super markets and bowling alleys?

"How can the big bands come back when so many of the places where they made their personal appearances no longer exist?"

Wayne King's Last Waltz Closes Aragon Ballroom

2-10-64

CHICAGO (UPI) — Wayne King saved the last waltz for the faithful Sunday night when thousands of dancers drifted back to dreamland in a bittersweet farewell to the famed Aragon Ballroom.

Grandmas and grandpas who did their courting under the Aragon's make believe stars, swayed to the strains of the waltz king's theme song, "The Waltz You Saved for Me."

The sky was synthetic, as usual, but some of the tears were real.

The Aragon, a massive arabesque ballroom born in the roaring '20s, closed its doors on the big band era shortly after midnight.

Its owners plan to turn the Alhambra of the Midwest into a roller skating rink.

When Wayne King stepped to the canopied bandstand for the final set, he carried with him the same saxophone he used in his Aragon debut 35 years ago.

He was the first of a long line of band leaders to soar to fame in the shadows of the Aragon's false-front turrets and minarets. Among the others were Eddie Howard, Dick Jurgens, Art Kassell, Freddie Martin, Ben Bernie and Lawrence Welk.

"Swing" Bands

In the 1930s the "swing" bands came through — Benny Goodman, the Dorsey brothers, Harry James. The Aragon spotlight shone on the top vocalist of the day—Buddy Clark, Gloria Van, Bob Eberle and many others.

"I felt like crying," said King as his fans greeted him with hearty applause.

"There'll never be a place like the Aragon," said a gray templed dancer.

And there never will.

Wayne King returns to Chicago's Aragon Ballroom to draw capacity crowds and to play the ballroom's final dance. — *Photo courtesy of Aragon Ballroom.*

HENRY HALSTEAD, above, in an early two-reeler. Banjo player is Lew Ayres. — *Photo courtesy of Henry Jaworski.*

RUDY VALLEE and his orchestra and their first appearance in a motion picture, 1929. — *Photo courtesy of Rudy Vallee.*

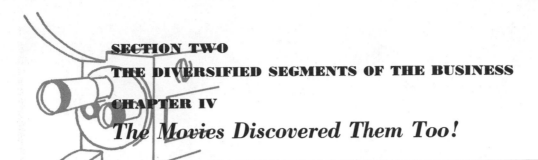

The Movies Discovered Them Too!

IT WAS ABOUT 1926 that the first "talking picture" made its appearance. Only a portion of those first attempts had recorded dialogue, with at least fifty per cent of the film still silent, and with the sound track of the recorded portion extremely noisy and often not synchronized to the lip movements of the actors. The next year the "Jazz Singer" starring Al Jolson moved a little farther towards full length sound, and was the movie industry's first important musical production.

By 1930 the "talkies" were obviously here to stay, and were starting to use dance orchestras occasionally. This was not in full length pictures, but in low budget, two reel musical shorts run in the movie houses between projections of the feature film. Production of these musical subjects dated back to about 1927 with Warner Brothers Vitaphone leading the way. Both New York and Hollywood were production scenes and many authorities credit Roger Wolfe Kahn with making the first one on the East Coast, and Henry Halstead's orchestra featured in the first one made in Hollywood. Appearing in the Halstead band at the time as a regular member was a banjo player named Lew Ayres, who would soon make a name for himself on the screen without his banjo.

Probably the first full length film to feature a bandleader was RKO's "The Vagabond Lover" starring Rudy Vallee, and made in 1929. Despite Vallee's ability as a crooner, and his effect on his vast radio public his performance in this movie was not considered particularly outstanding, nor were a couple of others which followed it. Later he was to attain picture success as a strong supporting actor in roles not related to his musical background.

In 1930 a much more ambitious production was put together, built entirely around the Paul Whiteman band, under the title of "The King of Jazz". Its producers, Universal Pictures, had negotiated with Whiteman for several months before a deal was finally worked out. At the time Whiteman was spending most of his time in the New York area where he was doing a sponsored radio show for Old Gold cigarettes. To make the most of the publicity which the picture would afford, the radio sponsor provided a special train for the entire band to make the trip to the West Coast, with a few stops on the way to make theater appearances. They arrived in Hollywood with a great deal of fanfare in the best Hollywood tradition, and in keeping with Whiteman's position in the music world at that time.

Shortly after arrival, however, they discovered that Universal's desire to make the picture had outstripped their preparation for it. No script had been prepared, so for the next several months the Whiteman band personnel relaxed in the Hollywood atmosphere and generally lived the life of Riley. Finally, they returned to the East Coast to fulfill other commitments, coming back several months later to make the picture when an acceptable script and story had been prepared.

Bing Crosby and the Rhythm Boys were still part of the Whiteman aggregation at that time. In addition to the numbers he was to do with the Rhythm Boys, Crosby had been promised an opportunity to do a solo from the picture titled "The Song of Dan". However, during the filming of the picture involvement in a traffic accident earned Bing a citation, and when he appeared in court a difference of opinion with the judge added to the seriousness of the offense and ended up with him drawing a thirty day jail sentence. Eventually Whiteman was able to work out an arrangement where Bing was released each morning in the custody of a policeman to work on the picture, and returned to confinement in the evening. In the meantime, having no assurance of Crosby's availability, Whiteman and the studio officials had assigned the solo number to John Boles, and the opportunity which could well have launched Crosby on a picture career was lost to him.

Subsequent events proved that the opportunity was not actually lost, but only delayed. Shortly

TED FIORITO's orchestra, featured in "The Sweetheart of Sigma Chi," 1933. Betty Grable had just joined the band as vocalist. Muzzy Marcellino is the guitarist and at the end of FioRito's piano stands Leif Erickson. — *Photo courtesy of Muzzy Marcellino.*

BING CROSBY and the BOSWELL SISTERS worked together in some of Crosby's early movies.
—*Photo courtesy of Anson Weeks.*

222

after this the Rhythm Boys left Whiteman and joined up with Gus Arnheim at the Cocoanut Grove. Here his talents were exposed almost nightly to Hollywood personalities and executives and it was not long before they recognized his potential drawing power as a picture personality. Since no picture in which Crosby was featured at that time could be made without a format built around the music business, those pictures provided work for a number of bands. Among these was Jimmy Grier who was a well-known leader, and had already been quite active in pictures through the making of a number of musical short subjects and in arranging scores for pictures which did not involve his own band.

One of the early pictures which starred Crosby was "The Big Broadcast of 1932". Actually, this picture had many stars who were big attractions on radio at that time. The list included the Mills Brothers, the Boswell Sisters, and the band of Cab Calloway who Hi-De-Ho'd his way through scenes in costumes which were the predecessors of the "Zoot Suit".

In the meantime, in addition to the West Coast bandleaders, pictures were bringing other important names out from the East to appear in movies. One of the first of these was Ted FioRito, and among his early pictures was "The Sweetheart of Sigma Chi" made in 1933. This picture gave Fio-Rito and his entire band coverage which was a strong factor in making him a top national attraction. Appearing in the picture as a band vocalist was Betty Grable, who soon after gave this up for a movie career, and quickly became one of Hollywood's biggest stars.

After the strong upsurge in the band business, touched off by Benny Goodman, each of the new bands who rose to the top were picked up by Hollywood for one or more pictures. In some they played important roles and in others they simply provided background music. One of Goodman's first pictures was "Hollywood Hotel" made about 1936, and he was followed by Tommy Dorsey, Artie Shaw, Duke Ellington, and all of the other big names of the thirties. Even though the picture producers were indicating a reluctance to let most of them play roles which were more than incidental to the story, they were admitting that the bandleader's name on the theater marquee added substantially to the box office appeal and total gross.

By the early forties the big business status of the dance bands was so impressive that Holly-wood had to go along with it whether it wanted to or not. Each year saw an increasing number of pictures produced using the current big names. As a result of his "Pot of Gold" radio show Horace Heidt and his band were featured in a movie built around the show's idea and using the same title. After Jimmy Dorsey's big year on records in 1941, he and his entire band were featured in two pictures made in 1942. One of these was "The Fleet's In" made on the Paramount lot, and the other "I Dood It" at MGM.

Glenn Miller appeared in an interesting production titled "Sun Valley Serenade", along with Sonja Henie, in which the band was afforded several opportunities to display its musical talents with some of the tunes which had made them famous. In 1942 his band was featured in a story written about the music business and titled "Orchestra Wives", depicting an acceptably realistic version of the life of a dance orchestra on the road. The Miller band appeared in the picture fairly intact, but with the piano player giving up his place for Cesar Romero, the bass player moving out for Jackie Gleason, and the trumpet section augmented by George Montgomery. Romero and Gleason gave convincing performances as sidemen, but Montgomery's attempts to finger the trumpet valves convinced no one that he was playing the solos heard on the sound track, and provided a lot of laughs to musicians who dropped into the nation's theaters to catch the picture. However, with allowances made for these shortcomings music people generally rated it one of the best pictures made to date about their business.

Whether or not the roles given them in most productions were particularly strong the motion picture industry was now using a lot of dance orchestras. In June of 1943 Downbeat magazine, in an article devoted to the subject, listed nearly thirty pictures which were under production at the time in which one or more name bands were featured. One of these, "Jam Session", made by Columbia had a very impressive total of seven bands around which the picture was written. The line-up included Louis Armstrong, Glen Gray and the Casa Loma Orchestra, Teddy Powell, Alvino Rey, Jan Savitt, Charlie Barnet, and Jan Garber who at that stage of his career was fronting a big swing band in keeping with the trend of the times.

There was some argument about the manner in which Hollywood was using these dance bands, and whether or not they were doing as good a job with them as they might. The music people complained that most of the stories were weak and unrealistic, either over-glamourizing the music business or in some cases making the musicians appear ridiculous. The movie people countered with the complaint that all too few of the bandleaders were actually capable of acting well enough to deserve a major role, and that those who had been given such an opportunity had often appeared so ill at ease that they generally weakened the picture. Regardless of these differences of opinion the arrangement was mutually advantageous to both the bandleader and the picture producer from a profit standpoint, and fans across the nation flocked to the theaters to see the finished product. Music lovers in the Los Angeles area benefited in another way since the appearances in pictures brought every major name in the orchestra world to Hollywood. While they were making the picture they appeared nightly to play for dancing at the Hollywood Palladium, or some other of the eight or ten location spots using name bands during that boom period.

Although the use of name bands in pictures continued after the war, it was during the wartime years that it had reached its peak. It began to decline quite rapidly within a year or so after the war's end, and the type of picture in which bands were used also changed considerably.

The production of musical shorts continued, but in late 1946 the movie companies indicated that they were attempting to upgrade the caliber of this type of production and would use only the top names available. They also indicated that the number produced would be reduced in the face of rising costs. Before the war it had been possible to make a two-reel band short subject for a cost ranging from six thousand to seventy-five hundred dollars. It had now risen to a minimum of thirty-five thousand, with most of them going beyond that. Two major studios were producing a series of this type of picture, with RKO doing a "Popular Bandleader Series" and Columbia calling their series "Film Vodvil".

About this same time Hollywood started to produce the first of its series of supposedly authentic stories of America's musical history. One of these came out in 1947 titled "New Orleans", and was billed as the frank and actual lowdown on sinful old Basin Street. It was authentic at least to the extent that it featured Louis Armstrong and a few other musicians who were a part of the early New Orleans scene. There was also a substantial part for Woody Herman written into it.

That same year United Artists produced "The Fabulous Dorseys" in which the story of Tommy and Jimmy and their careers was apparently related exactly the way they wanted it told. It had quite a line-up of names, including Paul Whiteman, Woody Herman, Charlie Barnet, Henry Busse, and Jimmy's two vocalists who helped him rise to fame, Bob Eberly and Helen O'Connell. The reaction to it at the box office was not outstanding, but a few years later when television introduced

The GOODMAN band was intact for "Hollywood Hotel" with only Johnny "Scat" Davis added to trumpet section — 1936. — *Photo courtesy of Don Haynes.*

RUSS MORGAN's new band, right, in a Paramount picture, 1937. Linda Lee is doing the vocal —*Photo courtesy of Russ Morgan.*

In this publicity shot for Harry James' first movie, 20th Century-Fox overlooked a credit for one of show business' biggest stars of a few years later — Jackie Gleason. L. to R. — Cesar Romero, Carmen Miranda, John Payne, Betty Grable, Edward Everett Horton, Charlotte Greenwood, Gleason, Helen Forrest and James. —*Photo courtesy of Harry James office.*

The MITCHELL AYRES orchestra appears in a Universal Production with the Andrews Sisters, 1943. — *Photo courtesy of Universal Pictures, Inc.*

Nautical is the word for the Dorseys. With Tommy it was *Ship Ahoy*, while Jimmy's last was *The Fleet's In*, with Dorothy Lamour

Kay Kyser? Shucks, he's a Hollywood veteran now! Here he is night-spotting it with Paul Whiteman and Ginny Simms

Harry James also was in *Syncopation*, but his newest release is *Private Buckaroo*, with our Dick Foran

THE MOVIES

It's the dawn of a new era, dance band fans! Your favorites are now being tapped for the movies, and you'll soon be seeing a whole raft of your musical heroes turning into Gables and Boyers. One after another, the big studios are rushing plans for elaborate musicals, and what was formerly an isolated trip by a Lombardo or a Vallee to Hollywood will soon become a mass invasion of the flicker colony by the leading hepcats of the airlanes and the ballrooms. So get set to choose the great lovers of Swingdom!

With a profile like that, Sweetheart of the Campus was a cinch for the handsome Ozzie Nelson

Orchestra Wives will find Glenn Miller with two new musicians—Cesar Romero and George Montgomery!

Glen Gray (not bad, eh?) went histrionic in a thing called *Time Out for Rhythm*, with Joan Merrill and that old actor, Rudy Vallee

45

This 1942 page from popular fan magazine *Dance Band* shows Hollywood's interest in the orchestras. — *Photo courtesy of Fawcett Publications.*

its "late late show" it was exposed to a lot of people through this medium.

The potency of the disc jockey and his influence on the music world was recognized in 1951 in a movie production titled "Make Believe Ballroom" starring the West Coast's original disc jockey, Mr. Al Jarvis. To support him in this rather weak but interesting full length picture, substantial footage was given to the bands of Jimmy Dorsey, Ray McKinley, Charlie Barnet, Jan Garber, Gene Krupa, and Pee Wee Hunt.

The production of "Young Man With a Horn" in 1951 was both reputed and denied to be an attempt to record the life story of Bix Beiderbecke. The author of the story which was the basis for the movie was Mrs. Dorothy Baker, who stated that while it was the life of Beiderbecke which had inspired her to write the story its hero, Mr. Rick Martin, and all of the events related were fiction. Acting the part of the trumpet playing Martin was Kirk Douglas, with the sound track of all the trumpet choruses played by Harry James. Hoagy Carmichael played the part of the pianist in the band which was prominent throughout the picture, and another strong part was given to Doris Day. The public reaction was not overwhelming and most of the critics insisting that it had been intended to portray Beiderbecke's life, pretty well tore it to pieces.

By the early 1950s the use of the bandleaders in motion pictures bore little resemblance to the situation which had existed ten years earlier. As a matter of fact, the motion picture industry itself was rumored to be in trouble, with theaters all over the country closing their doors. A story in a national magazine devoted to this subject concluded that it had now become the popcorn concession in the lobby which was the theater owner's major source of profit rather than the pictures on the screen inside.

However, Hollywood was now beginning to take a serious look at the lives of some of the big musical names as worthwhile material for feature pictures in themselves. There were rumors that the life of Ted Lewis might be produced under the title "When My Baby Smiles At Me", and two or three possible approaches to making a movie about Ben Pollack were written up in trade journals. 20th Century-Fox was indicated as about to produce something covering the early years of Harry James' experiences while traveling with his father's circus band, and bringing it on up to his

status as one of the nation's top orchestra leaders. A lot of other big names were being mentioned in the same capacity, but most of these rumors did not materialize. However, some of them did.

One of the best of these was the "Glenn Miller Story" produced in technicolor by Universal International in 1954. Mrs. Miller had delayed for several years giving her consent to the making of such a picture, and would only agree when she finally got complete assurance that the story would be done factually. To further insure this, Don Haynes, who had been Miller's manager for many years, served as technical adviser on the picture. Miller's part was very well played by Jimmy Stewart, who spent countless hours learning the positions on the slide trombone to make sure that his use of the instrument in the picture would look authentic. Mrs. Miller's part was played by June Allyson. Many of the original sidemen portrayed themselves, as did Ben Pollack, one of Miller's earliest bandleading employers. Elitch's Gardens in Denver, Colorado, was chosen for the site of some of the sequences, but identified in the picture as the Glen Island Casino where the Miller band first clicked. In view of Miller's terrific popularity the picture could not have failed to be a financial success, but it received excellent reviews as well.

The life stories of other important leaders followed the "Glenn Miller Story" in rapid succession. "The Eddy Duchin Story" was produced with Carmen Cavallero playing the sound track, but with the role of the former great piano leading maestro who had passed away in the prime of his life going to Tyrone Power. Benny Goodman's life story was done with Steve Allen in the starring role, and was full of the good music which it would have been expected to include. "The Gene Krupa Story" with Sal Mineo playing the part of the drummer did not come off so well as the others, and was considered weak by all of the reviewers who took the time to write about it.

Production of many of these biographies involved countless delays and revisions before they finally reached the screen, or even got into production. Contracts for the life story of Red Nichols were signed in 1954 at which time the title was supposed to be "Intermission", and Nichols' part to be played by Van Johnson. Sometime later the title was changed to "The Red Nichols Story", and the part to be played by Johnson was temporarily vacant when that arrangement did not work out. Finally Danny Kaye was chosen for the part, and

CHARLIE SPIVAK and his orchestra, right, followed the parade to Hollywood in 1943. Here they appear in a scene from "Pin-up Girl". — *Courtesy Charlie Spivak.*

PEE WEE HUNT, JIMMY DORSEY, CHARLIE BARNET, and JAN GARBER swap stories on the set of "Make Believe Ballroom." — *Photo courtesy of Capitol Records.*

RAY ANTHONY works with his orchestra in a Fred Astaire picture
with Leslie Caron in the early 50s. — *Courtesy of Capitol Records.*

Louis Armstrong blows it sweet while Danny Kaye, playing the part of Red Nichols, looks on in a poignant scene from the movie of Nichols' life, "The Five Pennies," released in 1959. — *Photo courtesy of Red Nichols.*

some footage was shot which was later junked when additional changes were made. Part of the delay was because Mrs. Nichols objected to the original script and the manner in which Red and the other musicians were to be portrayed.

Eventually production got under way at Paramount early in 1959. Nichols himself acted in the capacity of technical adviser and assisted Danny Kaye in mastering the apparent playing of the cornet. A touch of humor was added when Nichols played a minor part in the picture himself, portraying the role of an Eskimo. There was a lot of good music in the picture, including some excellent contributions by Louis Armstrong, and the story turned out to be about a seventy-five per cent factual coverage of Nichols' long career, though

some liberties were taken with the truth to permit Danny Kaye's own personality to be used to greatest advantage. During the course of production the title was changed once again, with the picture finally released under the title of "The Five Pennies".

At the time this chapter is brought to a close the movie industry has portrayed the life stories of a mere handful of the important names who made the big band era what it was, and that period appears to be permanently dead. However, like other phases of America's history there are millions of people who would like to see it temporarily brought back to life on the screen, and it is hoped that in years to come the motion picture producers will offer that opportunity.

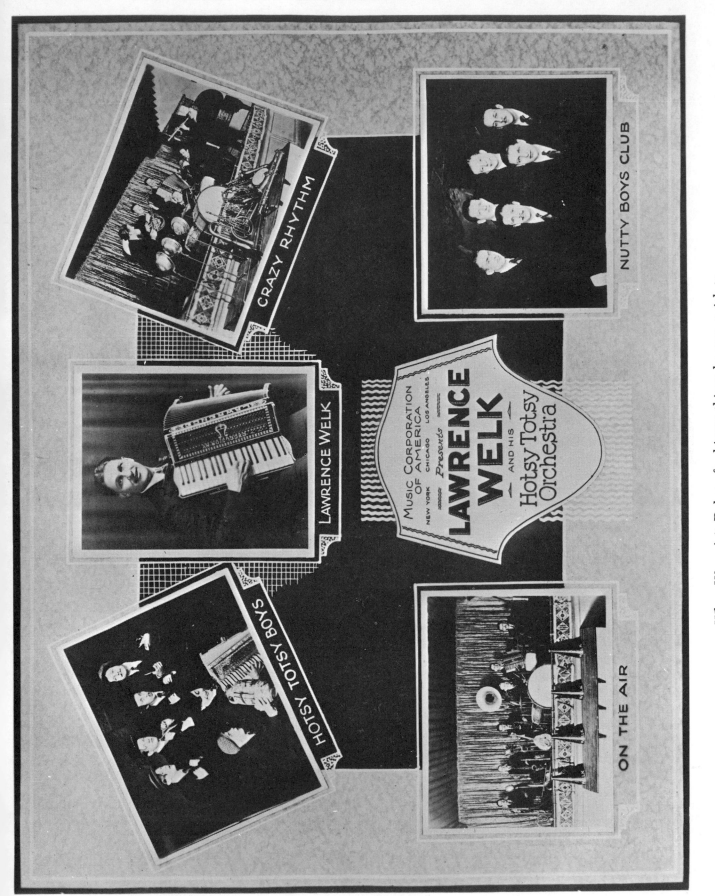

CRAZY RHYTHM

NUTTY BOYS CLUB

LAWRENCE WELK

Music Corporation
of America
NEW YORK   CHICAGO   LOS ANGELES
Presents
LAWRENCE
WELK
— AND HIS —
Hotsy Totsy Orchestra

HOTSY TOTSY BOYS

ON THE AIR

When WELK left Dakota for bigger things he was quick to sign with M.C.A. — *Photo courtesy of Lawrence Welk.*

Agencies Built Bands and Then Forgot Them

WHEN THE BIG band era was at its peak a leader, struggling to make ends meet until his big break came was asked what kind of arrangement he had with his agent. He answered:

"I guess it's the usual ten per cent arrangement. He gets ninety per cent of all I make and I get ten."

Agents and agencies have probably been the butt of more bad jokes than any other segment of the music business. They have been damned by bandleaders, nightclub and ballroom operators, theater managers, and one-night promoters, and, in fact, occasionally blamed for all of the ills of the industry. Yet the truth remains that had it not been for the agencies the band business would never have been built to the pinnacles it attained.

In the early stages of the business those bands which did any traveling at all were poorly organized to arrange their engagements. Some of them worked through an advance man while others attempted to book engagements through direct correspondence between the bandleader and the promoter. Both of these methods left a great deal to be desired for everyone concerned.

In many cases it was not uncommon for the advance agent to arrange more than one engagement for the same date. Usually this was not because of any misunderstanding on his part, but simply because after having made the first booking he found another more lucrative job for the same time. Far too often they proceeded to take the second date without the formality of notifying the first promoter that the band would not appear for his engagement. Consequently, any money which the owner spent for advertising went down the drain and he ended up on the night of the dance with a red face when customers showed up but not the band which had been advertised. When this happened he had very little recourse since the band in question was probably not intending to route itself into his area again anyway.

As some of the leaders became established names they began operating small agencies themselves with several groups working under the leader's name and booked by him. Probably the pioneer in this was Meyer Davis who was already well organized by 1920. Certainly it was he who was to enjoy the longest success in this manner although in those early years Harry Yerkes, another New York leader, may temporarily have had more units than Davis. Probably because of the example set by these two the other names of the New York, Chicago, Detroit and Boston areas followed suit.

This system of booking also left something to be desired. Too many times the patrons came expecting to see the "big name" himself on the stand and were disappointed if it turned out that he was not there. Initially, at least, the leader with multiple units actually made an attempt to appear with each of them and a lot of the advertising used permitted the impression that this would be the case. As his booking activities grew it became impossible to make all the dates involved, although some of them continued to attempt it by spending a small portion of the evening with each of several groups if the area in which they were appearing was compact enough to permit it.

The advent of organized agencies whose sole purpose was the handling of bands did much to change all of this. They lent dependability to bookings and assured the operators that appearances would be made by the band booked. They also gave respectability to the business to a degree which had not previously existed. Through their organized sales efforts the market for personal appearances was greatly expanded, and it was only through the building of agencies to national status that nationwide tours could become a reality for any but a very few.

In the beginning these people, just as the bandleaders, were local operations. Some of them remained in that category, finding all the prosperity they sought on that basis or as a territorial supplier of the lesser known attractions.

Out of this group there emerged a number who handled dance orchestras on a national and even international scale. Among the better known of these was the Rockwell-O'Keefe Agency which later became General Artists Corporation. Such big names as Glen Gray and Jimmy Dorsey were handled by this agency during most of their careers. The William Morris office, originating in 1898 for other show business fields, added a successful band department for many years. Consolidated Radio Artists came into the field a little later, as did Joe Glaser who built his Associated Booking Corporation into a strong contender. From out in Kansas City, Fredericks Brothers, Inc., eventually gained strong national stature, and on a somewhat lesser scale so did another agency from the same city, McConkey Music Corporation. Omaha, Nebraska, had its National Orchestra Service run by Serl Hutton which supplied territory bands to the Midwest, and at one time also indicated it might go nationwide.

In addition to these, there were a number of successful independents, most of them specialists in particular fields. Moe Gale was well known in this category, and Harold Oxley's expert handling of such names as Jimmie Lunceford put him in touch with every dance promoter in America. A little more diversified was the activity of the Stanford Zucker Agency.

Yet it was another agency which came to mean "dance orchestras" to America's band buyers and dancers as well. Organized in Chicago, Music Corporation of America, usually referred to by its shortened trademark M.C.A., eventually came to be the leader in all forms of show business and entertainment. Still it was for the purpose of booking dance bands that it was first organized and in this field they became outstanding specialists. Their activity became the driving force which made the business big and set the pattern for others to follow. There are many who believe the story of M.C.A.s growth and the history of the expansion of the band business are synonymous.

The start of M.C.A. dates back to 1924. Its beginning was not particularly auspicious and gave little indication of the big things to come. Dr. Jules Stein, a graduate of the University of West Virginia and Rush Medical College, returned from World War I to serve an internship at the Cook County Hospital. He was a musician, and to help finance himself during this internship he augmented his income by playing in a dance orchestra. Soon he also took to booking engagements for other bands in the Chicago area.

About this time he met W. E. Goodheart who was a graduate of the University of Chicago Medical School. Goodheart was interested in the booking of dance bands and worked together with Stein, and the two of them gradually enlarged the scope of their operations. By 1925 it became apparent they might have something big developing, so they both gave up their medical careers to establish the agency under its soon to be famous name of Music Corporation of America. In 1928 the business they were doing warranted opening a branch office in New York, soon to be followed by many others.

Countless contradictory stories have been told as to which were their first bands. Many of the old-time leaders claim that they accounted for the early success of the agency. According to vice president Karl Kramer, M.C.A.s own files indicate the first band they ever sent on the road was King Oliver, and this for a short tour of Pennsylvania and Ohio at nightly guarantees of $125. The first to be signed to an exclusive booking contract was the Coon-Sanders orchestra enticed by Stein to leave Kansas City and move into Chicago where he signed them for a long stay at the Blackhawk Restaurant.

What may have been M.C.A.s first trade journal ad was a full page which appeared in *Billboard* magazine on May 15, 1926, proclaiming the agency to be the originator of "The Circuit of Orchestras", and listing twelve of the Midwest's top bands as available for engagements. The prices quoted were somewhat fantastic in relation to those name bands were able to ask and receive not too long after that date.

There are also many stories about what encouraged Mr. Stein to broaden his scope of operations to what finally became the biggest nationwide agency in existence. One of these stories, which appears to have some authenticity, comes from Elitch's Gardens in Denver. This very popular amusement spot was owned then, as it is now, by the Gurtler Family. Mr. Gurtler had known Jules Stein personally, and contacted him one summer to line up a band for him to open the summer season. Since the band procured for him was satisfactory, Mr. Gurtler continued to have Stein function in this capacity and this led to other

This was probably the first trade journal ad placed by Music Corporation of America, 1926. — *Photo courtesy of Billboard magazine.*

Among the big names handled by ROCKWELL-O'KEEFE was the Casa Loma band, below. This agency, formed by Tom Rockwell and Cork O'Keefe, later became General Artists Corporation. This picture was taken in the late 1930s. — *Photo courtesy of Tony Briglia.*

"RED" PERKINS
and His
ORIGINAL DIXIE RAMBLERS

Exclusive Management
NATIONAL ORCHESTRA SERVICE
OMAHA   MINNEAPOLIS

National Orchestra Service in Omaha was a very successful territorial operation with a branch in Minneapolis. Red Perkins was one of their hottest names for several years.—*Photo courtesy of Eddie Sheffort.*

engagements for the orchestras involved. At the outset these consisted of several one-nighters between Chicago and Denver on both the outbound and return trips.

The fame of the M.C.A. trademark grew rapidly. Bandleaders strove to get into the fold for it was considered a mark of "having arrived" when they made it. Part of the attraction to the leaders was that M.C.A. gave them a build-up under their own name instead of simply identifying them with the spot where they played as had been common practice before. To ballroom operators and dancers alike the three magic letters on a dance poster soon became a guarantee of quality comparable to the Good Housekeeping Seal of Approval on a product for the home.

This is making it sound as though success came easily, which was not the case. In spite of all the outward appearances of prosperity they did not show a profit until 1931. As the Depression gained momentum in 1929 and 1930 the fortunes of M.C.A. had declined with it. One story has it that Dr. Stein was at the point of being ready to dispose of the agency, and that an agreement had practically been reached for Ralph Wonders and some of his associates to purchase. For one reason or another, however, this deal did not go through and sometime during 1930 "Billy" Goodheart came up with his idea for a weekly radio program featuring the pickup of a well-known dance band with a different major city used as an origination point for each broadcast. He took the idea to the American Tobacco Company who liked it so well they bought it for Lucky Strike Cigarettes. The program became a hit and not only launched something new in radio, but did much to build the bands to greater prominence, firmly establishing M.C.A. in the agency business at the same time.

The repeal of Prohibition made hard liquor legal at the beginning of 1934. It did not, however, assure an unlimited source of supply as of that date. Through a very astute move on the part of an M.C.A. official, they gained possession of approximately one million dollars worth of high-grade liquor and were able to set up their own distribution facilities. This put them in a position to offer many hotels who featured dancing a package deal consisting of talent and the basic ingredient which made the operation profitable. Needless to say, this was an arrangement which made it

236

JIMMY LUNCEFORD was Harold Oxley's hottest property, although Oxley had other strong Negro attractions.

During WALLER's all-too-short bandleading career he was handled by Ed Kirkeby. — *Photo courtesy of Barney McDevitt.*

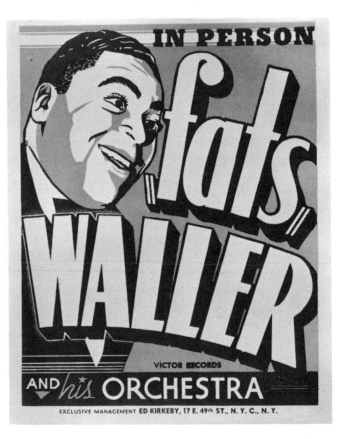

This unidentified cartoonist at left, hints that band buyers may be smarter than some agents credit them with being — (from the mid-40s).

237

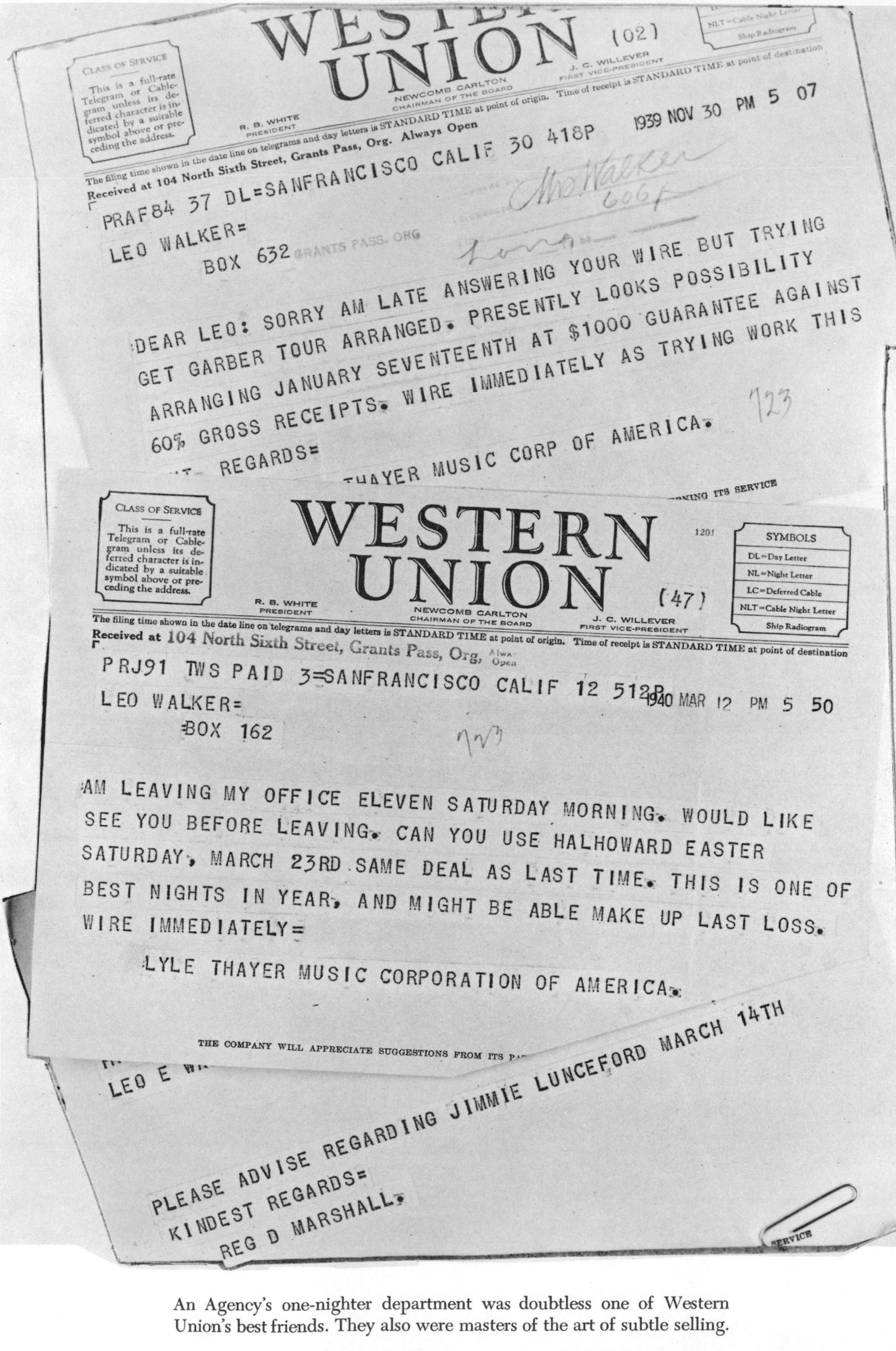

PRAF84 37 DL=SANFRANCISCO CALIF 30 418P   1939 NOV 30 PM 5 07

LEO WALKER=

BOX 632 GRANTS PASS. ORG

DEAR LEO: SORRY AM LATE ANSWERING YOUR WIRE BUT TRYING GET GARBER TOUR ARRANGED. PRESENTLY LOOKS POSSIBILITY ARRANGING JANUARY SEVENTEENTH AT $1000 GUARANTEE AGAINST 60% GROSS RECEIPTS. WIRE IMMEDIATELY AS TRYING WORK THIS

REGARDS=

THAYER MUSIC CORP OF AMERICA.

PRJ91 TWS PAID 3=SANFRANCISCO CALIF 12 512P   1940 MAR 12 PM 5 50

LEO WALKER=

BOX 162

AM LEAVING MY OFFICE ELEVEN SATURDAY MORNING. WOULD LIKE SEE YOU BEFORE LEAVING. CAN YOU USE HALHOWARD EASTER SATURDAY, MARCH 23RD. SAME DEAL AS LAST TIME. THIS IS ONE OF BEST NIGHTS IN YEAR, AND MIGHT BE ABLE MAKE UP LAST LOSS. WIRE IMMEDIATELY=

LYLE THAYER MUSIC CORPORATION OF AMERICA.

LEO E W

PLEASE ADVISE REGARDING JIMMIE LUNCEFORD MARCH 14TH

KINDEST REGARDS=

REG D MARSHALL.

An Agency's one-nighter department was doubtless one of Western Union's best friends. They also were masters of the art of subtle selling.

extremely difficult for any other agency to comete with them.

By this time, M.C.A. was a very well organized operation with strategically placed offices throughout the nation and in London. The personnel in each of these branches consisted of highly trained and skilled sales people. Their roster of attractions was fast beginning to include the majority of the big names in the orchestra field.

If you have never been sold by an agency, then you just haven't been sold at all. Most of their business is done by long distance telephone or telegram, and it is beneath their dignity for any letter to be sent in any fashion other than air mail, with many of them going special delivery. Phone conversations and correspondence are usually on a very personal first name basis, regardless of whether the recipient of the communication is personally known or has ever been met face to face.

On various occasions bandleaders and promoters have been heard to make the statement that all agents are habitual liars. In each instance this was probably traceable to the heat of the moment and was not a true expression of their opinion. However, a somewhat more generous appraisal would still have to include recognition of the fact that many of them displayed a fair amount of talent and dexterity in arranging the facts to fit the situation.

The arrangement between bandleader and the agency which represented him had some variation, depending on how big he was at the time he was signed and the contract which he was able to negotiate. Basically, however, they were the same, calling for a percentage of all he earned from personal appearances. From one-night engagements it ran as high as 20%. So-called location jobs of a week's duration or longer paid the agency 10%. All of this came off the top before any expenses were deducted and was payable even when the leader closed the deal himself.

Like any other sales organization the agencies had field men to handle the band-buying accounts. A good many of these were former bandleaders who had decided there was more money in handling musicians than in being one. Their efforts were almost entirely concentrated on the locations or long term buyers who used music regularly. They can hardly be criticized for this since it was from here their largest revenue came. Seldom did the promoter of one-nighters ever find himself on their personal contact list, unless he was located on the natural route to what they considered major accounts.

One-nighters were booked through other, and what would appear on the surface, less expensive methods. The band's availability was made known in some cases by letter but usually by telegram giving possible open dates and the asking price. If the promoter was interested in the band submitted and on the date indicated an agreement was arrived at by the simple exchange of telegrams.

To assist him in advertising the coming attraction he was then mailed a minimum number of window cards, a press manual of frequently unusable publicity material, and a few photos of the leader and featured members of the orchestra. Much of this material was usually charged against the leader's account.

During the late thirties and early forties I spent some time promoting name bands for one-night stands in the Pacific Northwest. To the degree possible I used all the major musical organizations who passed through en route to Portland's Jantzen Beach, and other amusement spots in that area. There was really no room for complaint in the treatment given me by the agencies involved, for since I was located in a spot where a break in a trip was desirable I got some price concessions. But it is amusing to look back at some of the communications regarding bookings. Being by nature a string saver I still have most of them in my files, and some of them are reproduced here. For the most part they were masterpieces of subtle high-pressure selling.

In each instance, the potential engagement was described glowingly as the year's greatest opportunity. The most amusing of these was one offering me a band for the Saturday night preceding Easter Sunday, and describing it as one of the best dance nights of the year. It's possible the sender of that wire had not heard the old joke that the year's absolute low in show business was always Holy Week in its entirety, and any week in Boston. However, I doubt this. It's much more likely that he thought I hadn't heard it.

Almost without exception any band submitted to an operator was offered at a price with enough cushion in it to permit the operator the luxury of beating it down. No such courtesy, however, was usually shown to colleges who booked names for proms and other affairs. Not only would these bookings be taken at full price, but at a price usually higher than normal guarantees. Many times the college date would be booked first and then a tour of other one-nighters booked around it with the independent promoter buying the band at prices as much as fifty per cent below what the school paid. Some of this differential, it should be pointed out, was justified by the fact that all contracts with independent promoters included a percentage clause beyond the actual guarantee. For the most part, however, it was made possible by the fact that the school affair was the big event of the year for which all of the students were willing to go overboard, and because the people who bought the band for the school were probably not inclined to bargain and may have been slightly dazzled by the prospect of negotiating for the services of the top name bandleader.

If the foregoing comments make it seem that all of the problems of the business were on the side of the promoters and bandleaders, such was far from the case. The agencies, too, had many headaches in spite of the prosperity which they appeared to enjoy. Any reader who by chance is a salesman will know the problems which go along with selling any type of commodity. Just imagine how much these would be multiplied if you had to sell a product which could talk back to you!

It is probably human nature for a bandleader, or any other artist, to feel that the engagements lined up for him by his agent are not as well chosen or as well negotiated as they might be. In some cases this feeling resulted in constant hassling which could easily have left the agency wondering if any amount of money could make it worthwhile. Many one-night promoters seemed to have the opinion that all they had to do was sign a contract for the band's appearance, and with little or no advertising of the event, still get a crowd to turn out. When this did not occur they blamed the agency and if the attendance was so bad that a band could not be paid off it was the agency's responsibility to somehow recover for the bandleader, a feat which in many cases was impossible. The agency also received complaints for any on-the-stand misconduct of the leader, or for any less than first-class appearance of the musical organization.

In addition, many of the agencies actually financed some of the bands through that painful period when they were getting started. In some cases they were left holding the bag when a leader became so discouraged that he simply threw in the towel and decided not to continue.

Witnessing a feud between a bandleader and his agency is an interesting experience. I sat in on one of these myself and received a liberal education in the art of diplomatic cold war. The leader involved was Jan Garber and the year was 1940. The agency which was the target of his displeasure was M.C.A.

Garber was on a tour of the West Coast, with heavy publicity built around the fact that this was his twentieth anniversary as a leader. Actually the anniversary had occurred two years earlier, but this was of minor consequence. Somehow everything on the trip went wrong, and as they moved northward each date seemed more jinxed than the last. Periodically the bus would be halted while Jan placed a collect call to the agency's office to complain about the bookings. Almost without exception these collect calls were refused. They were replaced by a steady exchange of collect wires, with both the office and Jan refusing to accept charges, but only after somehow managing to read the messages.

At Medford, Oregon, the worst blow of the trip was delivered. During a mediocre Monday night "one-nighter" he was called off the bandstand by a long distance operator. I stood beside him as he was given the news that fire was at that moment destroying the ballroom in Astoria where he was scheduled to play a lucrative three-day celebration. He immediately got the M.C.A. agent, who had booked the tour, out of his Beverly Hills bed, and for the next half hour of telephone conversation you'd have thought the agent had personally supervised the starting of the fire.

The financial soundness of the leader was a matter which directly concerned his agency for unless he was solvent he could not take a band on the road and keep them going. Al King related a story of an agency's attempts to keep a well-known leader afloat by handling his money for him.

King's own part in the band business dates back to the mid-twenties and includes time spent running his own outfit for a while followed by years of acting as a playing manager for several important names. He eventually wound up in the agency business himself in San Mateo, California.

In 1929 Mr. Goodheart of M.C.A. called King to go on the road with one of Chicago's better known leaders. In addition to being well known as a musician, this leader had developed a reputation for a love of all types of games of chance far greater than his ability to master them. King's job was to collect all the money earned on the tour

Two of General Amusement's strongest contenders,
1940. — *Photo courtesy of General Amusement Corp.*

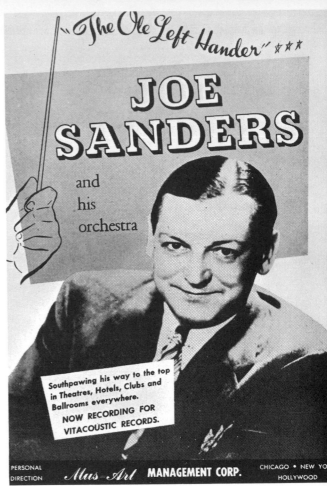

Mus-Art, a new entry to the agency field in the late 1940s, lined up a few names along with their newcomers. Success was not to be for them however and they abandoned the venture after a few short years. — *Photo courtesy of Billboard.*

This 1951 McConkey ad indicates they were successfully invading former sacred M.C.A. territory. — *Photo courtesy of McConkey Artists Corp.*

since the agency was already holding tabs for sizeable advances. Nothing was to be given to the bandleader in cash, but King was to pay all of his hotel bills and personal expenses and collect for each job they played.

This proved to be no handicap to the leader, however, for he quickly figured out there was something he could do about it. No sooner would they be checked into a new hotel than he would arrange for a cash advance of a hundred dollars or more which would be posted on his room account and King could do nothing but pay off to the hotel

when it came time to check out. There are many stories which would parallel this one with every major office being faced with the difficulty of working apparently successful orchestra men out of financial problems created for themselves.

Equally numerous were the stories of incidents involved in collecting from under-financed promoters the money due both the attraction and the agency. Usually a deposit was collected in advance against the guarantee called for by the contract, and getting the balance was chiefly the responsibility of the band's road manager. Sometimes he worked directly for the band but often he was sent out with them by the agency.

Probably few in the business can tell more of these stories than Eddy MacHarg who had years of experience on the road with bands and other musical attractions, handling the financial end of their business. In the early thirties he gave up a successful career as a ballroom operator himself to enter the personal management field handling various attractions booked exclusively by Rockwell-O'Keefe.

MacHarg had his own definition for "operators" and "promoters" the first of which he identified as someone who was in business from year to year, while a promoter was often in business for one day or sometimes for only one event. My own experience as a promoter would cause me to agree basically with MacHarg's appraisal although I would have to elaborate slightly. For the most part "promoters" were also suckers, who seldom made any worthwhile money for their efforts, except during the boom of World War II, or who made it on one attraction and lost it on the next. Often they were practically "conned" into the business by agencies anxiously trying to keep attractions working. The "operator" probably could not have made it either without many things besides dance admissions going for them including bar, food, and other concessions.

In the early thirties the Mills Brothers were just hitting the big name category and Rockwell-O'Keefe sent them on tour, booked as a package deal with the band of Tiny Bradshaw. MacHarg was sent along and found himself in Norfolk, Virginia, on a rainy night with a contract calling for a one thousand dollar guarantee, plus a percentage privilege clause, and with fifty per cent of the guarantee having been deposited in advance. The way the rain was pouring down it was apparent there would be no percentage and MacHarg decided he'd better get his other five hundred dollars before the Mills Brothers did the first of their two shows or he probably wouldn't get that either. He began to pressure the promoter for the money, but without success. Finally after delaying the Mills Brothers appearance a half hour he threatened to stop the dance also unless he got paid. At this point the promoter stated flatly that he could not pay off in money but finally offered to sign over a deed to two lots, and went to the office safe to produce the deeds. The documents looked impressively legitimate so in desperation MacHarg agreed,

feeling this would at least give him something to show for the evening. Next morning he mailed them to Warren Pearl, the treasurer of Rockwell-O'Keefe. Back in New York a few weeks later he entered the office to be greeted by Pearl:

"Say Eddy, I see you're putting us in the real estate business."

"I guess you mean those lots in Norfolk," Eddy replied. "The papers looked in order to me and I thought you'd rather have them than nothing at all."

"Congratulations, Eddy, it was quite a deal," said Pearl, but before MacHarg could break into a smile of relief he went on, "we had the deeds checked out and guess what? You just made us the proud owners of two cemetery lots."

Competition between agencies to put their attractions in the nation's top spots was very keen. This certainly included the hotels, for in spite of the fact that most of the leaders complained they could not make any money in the hotel jobs there was a certain amount of prestige involved in playing them, and particularly in opening a new hotel room. An example of the sharpness of this competition was told me by a representative of one of the major agencies, involving an incident which occurred about 1940 when the Kenmore Hotel in Albany, New York, was new and preparing to open an elaborate room for dining and dancing.

A few weeks before they opened one of the representatives of this agency decided he would make a trip from New York to Albany to sell the place a band. When he got on the train he was surprised to find a salesman for another major agency, so both of them suspecting the reason for the other's trip they visited all the way, discussing baseball, boxing, and everything except the band business. In Albany they took a cab to the hotel, where another surprise awaited them. Signing the register as they walked in was still another agent representing a third major office and of course he was there for the same purpose.

What happened from that point on could best be likened to a pickpocket's convention where everyone kept his hands in his pockets to be sure someone else's were not there. Each of the three decided the only way to protect his own interests was to keep the other two in sight so they went out on the town making all of the better night spots, ending up back at the hotel after everything in

243

Tommy Dorsey's M.C.A. contract expires and he tells the world in a full-page ad. — *Photo courtesy of Billboard.*

town was closed. The next morning around 10:30 they met in the coffee shop for breakfast, each feeling much the worse for wear. While they were having breakfast the manager of the hotel entered the room, and spying them came over to their table. He bowled them over with this remark:

"What brings all of you fellows here, a bookers convention? You could have saved me some money if you had let me know you were coming. Just ten minutes ago I completed a call to M.C.A. in New York and booked Ben Bernie to open our new room."

By the time the 1940s rolled around, M.C.A. had diversified in many directions beyond the band business which had been their initial venture. In the next few years they were to discover, like many another successful corporation, the price of diversified leadership is diversified trouble. Radio had given them an opportunity to manage many of the big names who were in it, and the same had now become true of the movie industry. These branches of show business were so important and lucrative that the band business started to assume a minor role in their over-all picture. Considering that, by this time, they had under contract a large percentage of all the biggest names in the business, this apparent lack of interest on M.C.A.s part could do nothing but create unrest on the part of the leaders.

Before the forties were very far along, this unrest started to make itself evident. Some of their top names made an effort to break M.C.A. contracts or get out from under them peacefully. Part of this stemmed from their contention that M.C.A. was no longer properly representing them, and part of it from the feeling that they were important enough to handle their own bookings through a personal manager. The booming business which existed during the war years doubtless contributed to this trend of thought.

Among the first to put real pressure on the agency were Benny Goodman and Horace Heidt. Neither were successful in getting relief from their contracts, and towards the end of the war Goodman disbanded. He was followed very soon by Heidt, who elected to be inactive during the remaining period of his contract which was to expire in February of 1947.

The common complaint was that M.C.A. would neither aggressively represent them nor release them. However, many of those who did switch agencies discovered that M.C.A. was still a very potent factor in the band booking picture to whom the best location spots in the nation still looked for top dance attractions. Breaking into many of these accounts through another agency was not as easy as they assumed it would be.

Nevertheless, the trend continued on the part of their important names to go elsewhere as contracts expired. Vaughn Monroe and Sammy Kaye pulled out in 1947. Russ Morgan made the switch in 1948. Early in 1949, Jan Garber switched to William Morris after having been handled by M.C.A. since the mid-twenties. An M.C.A. official

This was a promotional piece mailed to band buyers in early 1943 and gives an idea of Glaser's talent lineup. Later, Glaser's agency became the Associated Booking Corporation. — *Photo courtesy of Associated Booking Corp.*

once told me that because of his love for "one-nighters" on which they collected their highest commission rate, Garber had been one of their most consistent money-makers. Others of major and minor importance took leave, though many of them returned to the fold later as other connections proved even less productive.

Most of these leaders who left did so quietly and signed with other offices. This was not true, however, of Tommy Dorsey when his contract expired, an event which occurred in late 1950. He immediately purchased a full-page ad in *Billboard* magazine proclaiming to the world that he was now on his own and had, as a matter of fact, formed his own agency known as "Tom Dor Enterprises, Inc.". He continued to handle his own bookings through this agency until his death a few years later.

Unhappiness with M.C.A. was not restricted to the bandleaders. A number of ballroom operators and promoters were also beginning to be displeased, and at least one of them decided he should do something about it. In 1945, Larry Finley filed a damage suit against them in the amount of $3,000,000 charging them with conspiracy to restrain trade, and with operating a dance band monopoly. Earlier that year he had taken over the Mission Beach Ballroom in San Diego. His complaint was based upon his inability to buy important names from M.C.A., alleging they had an agreement with another San Diego Ballroom to give it first opportunity to book all their attractions of importance. He further claimed that M.C.A. had such a large percentage of the biggest names under contract that the number available through other agencies would not permit him to operate on a competitive basis and that because of this he had suffered heavy financial losses.

The case was argued at some length in the courts, with most of M.C.A.s top agents of the Los Angeles area called as witnesses. Finley was awarded a judgment in the amount of $65,000, but the case continued to be drawn out in the courts with appeals, reversals, etc., and with the final disposition rather hazy.

While all this had been going on the other major offices had been having their problems, too, although they were not given the publicity which M.C.A.s received. The lush days of the business were coming to an end, and in an attempt to improve their individual positions many leaders decided a change of agents might be the answer. Refusals to renew contracts was general, and many big names made switches or tried handling their own bookings. Finding this not too satisfactory they next experimented with short term contracts, some for a single season, or in some cases for a single tour.

In the immediate postwar period a few new agencies appeared in the field, and one which showed bright promise was the Mus'Art Management Corporation with offices in Hollywood and Chicago. It was made up of several of M.C.A.s former top agents, assisted by recruits from some of the other offices. The M.C.A. people who formed the agency were Jack Whittemore, Russell Facchine, Lyle Thayer, and Eames Bishop. Together they were a combination of sales talent who knew all the artists in the business and all the operators of locations. Their enthusiasm influenced some of the newer leaders, and even a few old-timers to sign with them.

Unfortunately, their timing was very bad. They entered the field when the business was starting its lengthy decline, making competition for that which already existed keener than ever. In addition they soon learned that selling bands for an agency with a big roster of talent such as that of M.C.A. was different from trying to compete with them with a handful of names or semi-names. After a couple of years of mediocre but declining success, the agency dissolved and each of its principals went his separate way.

Other changes continued to occur in the over-all agency picture. Some dropped their band departments or sold them to other people. William Morris was one of those who made such a move, disposing of their band interests to the General Artists Corporation late in 1949. Soon after this, Fredericks Brothers liquidated entirely, releasing the artists under contract to negotiate with other agencies. Bill Fredericks became a very successful insurance man in Atlanta, Georgia, and when I saw him there in the spring of 1957 he did a lot of reminiscing about his years in the agency business, but indicated he had no regrets that it was all behind him.

Meanwhile with the growth of television, M.C.A.s interest continued to get farther and farther away from the dance bands. Television not only offered them additional opportunities to sell talent, but they soon began to be complete producers of many of the top shows.

Their band department was still in operation at the end of the fifties, and it would appear at that

G.A.C., with a strong lineup including many former Music Corporation of America stars, tries to bolster the sagging dance business with this 1951 ad. — *Photo courtesy of G.A.C.*

time they were continuing to do the biggest share of the business which still existed. Perhaps what that business needed then to give it a revival was for a new Music Corporation of America to inject into it the vigorous sales effort with which they had approached it in the early years. No one who was part of the music industry could deny that the agencies had played a major role in building the band business to the peak it once enjoyed. Many agencies participated in this building, but M.C.A. had led the way and others followed. They managed a lot of people into great success, and the

success they enjoyed for themselves in the process was well-deserved. But eventually they had to give it up or relinquish some other interests.

In July, 1962, under heavy pressure from a Justice Department anti-trust suit, they voluntarily disbanded their talent agency, retaining their television production interests. This move released simultaneously a fair share of the biggest names in all categories of show business touching off a mad scramble on the part of all other agencies to sign them to contracts.

A picture on a copy of sheet music was one of the
most valuable forms of publicity in the early 1920s.

Publicity Was Where You Found It

TOWARD THE END of 1945 a well-known bandleader was quoted in a music magazine article as having offered five hundred dollars to anyone who could get his name in Walter Winchell's column.

At the time it supposedly happened this leader was far from unknown and seeing his name in print would have been no new experience. He was, however, acutely aware of the value of the right kind of publicity and his offer, if it were really made, was an acknowledgment of the potency of a Winchell plug.

Several years later his name was mentioned by Winchell with some regularity. Enough time had gone by to dispel any idea that there existed any connection between the supposed offer and the plugs he received and he had become famous not only as a leader but as a composer of a dozen or so top song hits.

No business ever prospered without some form of publicity, but in no field is it so important as in show business; for here life depends on it. The dance band field was no exception. The success of its people individually was in direct proportion to their ability to get their names before the public, and keep them there.

Those who might be described as pioneers faced some difficulty in accomplishing this. Communications in general were quite limited prior to radio, and it was a real problem for them to make themselves known beyond the area which was their base of operations. Newspaper coverage was effective only in its own local area; there were very few magazines with national circulation. Building a coast-to-coast reputation was no easy task under these conditions which did not improve much until radio became well established and records became geared to national distribution in quantity.

The absence of these things gave something else an importance which would diminish later. Home entertainment was built around the piano, making the sale of sheet music a big business. Music stores of any size employed a full time pianist to play the numbers displayed on the rack for the prospective customer. Some of the bigger ones even had a vocalist to sing the lyrics, and the influence on sales was much the same as the effect of the demonstration booth in the record shop a few years later.

The covers of this music were quickly developed into a publicity medium for the dance orchestras and other artists as well. But the bandleaders particularly made capital of it, assuming an implied sponsorship of the number with the indication that it was "First Introduced By" or "Featured By" Monty Metronome and his orchestra. As the number of Monty Metronomes in the business increased so did the competition for the space on the cover. Photographs of the leaders were used, and as often as possible the whole orchestra was pictured.

In some cases, the publisher handled the competitive situation by special releases, each featuring sectional favorites, thus permitting as many as a half dozen bands to be tied in with the same song.

That which resulted was instrumental in promoting the interests of everyone concerned. The publishers helped make the leaders become better known — the leaders helped sell sheet music. The bigger they became the more their name on the cover meant. The practice of using bandleader photos in this manner never completely disappeared, but the use of full group photos diminished rapidly after the end of the twenties.

One of the oldest jokes among show business people is that there is no such thing as adverse publicity so long as the performer's name is not misspelled. Exaggerated though this may seem there is some evidence to support it. Particularly in the movie industry has this appeared to be true, with Fatty Arbuckle having been practically the only one forced into oblivion because of involve-

Identification card for members of Coon-Sanders fan club, in the early 1930s. — *Photo courtesy of Edna Mae Nesbitt.*

ment in a scandal. Others who came after him seemed to become even more popular after making headlines not generally considered conducive to building public acclaim.

The music people also had their examples, too, even though not so many in number. Tommy Dorsey's short temper continually had him in the headlines for clobbering someone. At a Hollywood party he nearly removed the nose of a prominent male movie star, but it left no visible damage to his own prestige. Neither was there any apparent decline in the box office appeal of one of the most successful leaders of the early fifties when he went for a daytime stroll along an East Coast beach in the nude. However, it's probably the only known instance of a bandleader getting that amount of publicity without a press agent taking credit for the idea.

Actually, however, examples of disregard for public opinion were few. The maintenance of favorable press relations was of such importance that no one intentionally neglected it. The band business was not very old before every artist who was established followed the example of other show business stars and employed someone to make sure he and the fourth estate were on good terms.

Such a job required imagination, as well as the ability to get along with people in order to make sure the leader's name made the news with regularity. Any press agent worth his salt could always put together a little news item for publicity purposes when none developed through the natural course of events. In the fall of 1926 the Detroit papers carried a story of Jean Goldkette's an-

nounced intention to organize a jazz band among the wild animals at the New York Zoo. He explored the subject at some length, maintaining that all animals had an ear for music, and that properly handled these could be developed to the point where they might play instruments quite proficiently.

There is no evidence that the organization of such a band ever got as far as the rehearsal stage. Perhaps it was not as farfetched as it sounded in the light of what the music business was to produce in later years. Mr. Goldkette is well recognized as a pioneer, and with this idea he may simply have been thirty years ahead of his time. During the mid-fifties the sounds which were reproduced on top selling records would have permitted a band such as this to become a strong competitor for a high rating on the popularity charts.

Bandleaders were quick to discover one always available source of publicity. Politicians, either in office or trying to get there, needed publicity as badly as the music people and could always be depended on to cooperate for pictures with any important personality who was newsworthy. This took whatever form fit the occasion at the time. A favorite picture story involved having the name leader made honorary "Mayor For a Day" in the city where he was currently appearing. This type of promotion was encouraged by the agency handling the band, and was usually arranged through the promoter of the local appearance.

Ted FioRito was one who consistently tied in with the local atmosphere in this fashion. Few leaders had a greater sense of publicity value than he, or the ability to get it. As one of the earliest to appear regularly in movies featuring his entire orchestra, he had many friends among the picture stars. These always could be counted on to cooperate, and during the early thirties he was constantly pictured in poses with celebrities of the Hollywood scene.

By this time radio was a major business, and a versatile medium for publicity in many forms. For the most part everything which came about through the airwaves was well planned, but occasionally it just developed.

The famous Winchell-Bernie feud of the early thirties falls in the latter category. Whether or not either of them needed the publicity which resulted is questionable for both were well-known at the time. Of the two, Winchell would have needed it

The RAY MILLER band on the White House lawn during the Coolidge re-election campaign, 1924. Facing Miller is famed entertainer Al Jolson. — *Photo courtesy of Ward Archer.*

JIMMIE GRIER vs. ABE LYMAN in a bicycle race — a publicity stunt staged in 1933. Starter is movie star Alice White. — *Photo courtesy Margie Grier.*

Three bandleaders, VIC MEYER, also Lt. Gov. of Washington, TED FIORITO, "acting Mayor of Seattle" and HAL GRAYSON, in the mid-1930s. — *Photo courtesy of Muzzy Marcellino.*

Judging a beauty contest was sure-fire publicity, and interesting work too, if the look on FREDDY MARTIN's face is any indication. — *Courtesy Barney McDevitt.*

FIORITO also had the cooperation of Hollywood talent for publicity releases. Here he meets Buster Keaton and Jimmy Durante. — *Courtesy of Muzzy Marcellino.*

At left, a RED NICHOLS publicity shot when he was on radio for Kellogg's. Apparently he believed that if you work for them you should eat their product. — *Photo courtesy of Red Nichols.*

In the late 1950s this might have been the cover shot for a record album titled "Music To Drown By." But in 1939 it was just a run-of-the-mill picture made by VINCENT LOPEZ and his orchestra at Atlantic City. — *Photo courtesy of Arsene Studio, New York City.*

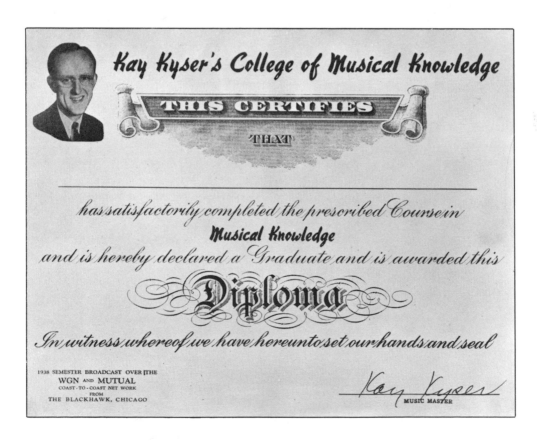

Kay Kyser's College of Musical Knowledge

THIS CERTIFIES

THAT

has satisfactorily completed the prescribed Course in

Musical Knowledge

and is hereby declared a Graduate and is awarded this

Diploma

In witness whereof we have hereunto set our hands and seal

1938 SEMESTER BROADCAST OVER [THE
WGN AND **MUTUAL**
COAST-TO-COAST NET WORK
FROM
THE BLACKHAWK, CHICAGO

Kay Kyser
MUSIC MASTER

In 1938 fans of KAY KYSER were awarded this diploma in appreciation of their devotion to his top-rated radio show. — *Photo courtesy of Harry Thomas.*

Champagne Music
WELK-O-GRAM

WELK TO N.Y. CAPITOL IN FALL

Photo Glimpses . . .

Crowds throng the Trianon, Chicago's wonder ballroom, to greet Welk on his 11th repeat engagement in less than four years. Band has nine air shots a week over WGN-Mutual from the Trianon.

Lieutenant Commander Eddie Peabody welcomes Welk on his fourth trip to entertain the boys at Great Lakes Naval Training Station.

Welk interrupts his show for Camp Grant soldiers to introduce two of his former bandsmen to their fellow messmates. L. to R.: Jayne Walton, "Little Champagne Lady of Song"; Pvt. Dave Kavitch, former Welk trumpeter; Welk, and Pvt. Jay Jackoskie, former Welk sax man.

$17,000 in bond sales during the noon hour at Chicago's Treasury Center!— That was the record Lawrence Welk hung up recently. War Savings officials congratulate Welk at the conclusion of the program, which was also aired over WGN. L. to R.: Milt Wolf, Special Events Div.; John C. Gallaher, Regional Manager; Lee Bennett, WGN Announcer; Lawrence Welk; Kenneth Carpenter, Mgr. Information Division; Don McKiernan, Mgr. Special Events Division.

Eastern Theater Tour Follows Current Chicago Trianon Stand

> **NEW DECCA RELEASE**
>
> New recording of Lawrence Welk released by Decca Records during July is an all-instrumental tune entitled:
>
> **SOUTH**
> Decca No. 4420

Band Busy Playing Servicemen Dates

Like all of the nation's leading maestros, Lawrence Welk is "all out" for playing as many servicemen dates as his busy schedule permits.

Ever since Pearl Harbor the band has adopted the policy of devoting every free day to an engagement at some Army or Navy post, a bond rally, a veterans' hospital, USO's, Service Men's Centers, etc.

More than 100,000 servicemen have enjoyed the "Champagne Music" since the first of the year. Band is a favorite with the boys at the Great Lakes Training Center, where it has appeared four times. Three times it has packed them in at Camp Grant in Rockford, Ill. Among other camps visited have been Fort Snelling, Minneapolis; Jefferson Barracks, St. Louis; Fort Benjamin Harrison, Indianapolis; Bomber Base, Sioux City, Iowa, and Fort Crook, Omaha. Band has also made frequent appearances at Chicago's Treasury Center, Service Men's Centers and USO's.

Maestro is also planning to include as many camps as possible on his Eastern tour.

Champagne Music Zesty as Ever

More fortunate than some maestros, the war has not affected the long-established style of Welk's Champagne Music.

No key member of the band has been eligible for selective service as yet, as all are heads of families. Since Pearl Harbor only five men have had to be replaced.

Welk himself is the proud father of three budding accordionists.

Skedded to start November 1 after wind-up of band's 11th repeat in less than four years at Chi's Wonder Ballroom

Lawrence Welk and his Champagne Music will invade the East this fall for his first swing thru the Eastern Seaboard's leading theaters. Outstanding date in the tour will be skedded stand at New York City's Capitol Theater. Engagements are also being lined up by Frederick Bros.' Music Corp. for leading theaters in Philadelphia, Washington, Baltimore and other seaboard cities.

Tour will begin as soon as Welk winds up Oct. 31 his current four-month stand at William Karzas' Trianon Ballroom in Chicago. Current Trianon date is the eleventh in less than four years for the Champagne Music Makers.

Consistent Top Grosser

Welk has long been in the forefront of Midwestern maestros— consistently hanging up greater grosses in ballrooms, theaters and one-nighters in the land west of the Alleghenies than some of the nation's top-moneyed bands.

Welk's following on the nation's juke boxes, plus his frequent airings over WGN-MUTUAL, have expanded his popularity to both coasts so that his "fans" no longer can be classified as dwelling only in the Midwestern area.

Top men in the music business already are predicting that Welk is a dead cinch to follow in the footsteps of many other maestros who came out of the West to become the "rage" of the East.

LAWRENCE WELK's publicity releases during the early 1940s took this form. — *Photo courtesy of Ralph Portnor and Lawrence Welk.*

the least since he was firmly established in radio. Perhaps for Bernie it supplied the final touch to make him a radio personality as well as a bandleader.

Just who fired the first microphone salvo is now forgotten. Winchell had his regularly scheduled show at the time, and Bernie had a nightly bandstand remote. One or the other made an uncomplimentary remark on the air which brought forth an immediate rebuttal from the one who was the target. Total verbal warfare was soon under way and continued to get hotter by the week, with the listening audience increasing as it went along.

Eventually the two "buried the hatchet" and appeared together in a motion picture which incorporated their feud into its theme, but the duration of their much publicized disagreement had embraced several years. While it was still in progress other people decided it was proof that if you had the right kind of enemies you didn't need any friends. Seeing the value of the Bernie-Winchell feud in terms of the publicity it received, Ian Garber and Jimmy Grier collaborated to stage one of their own on the West Coast. This, too, was in the mid-thirties. At that time Grier was one of the West Coast's biggest leaders, headquartering in the Biltmore Bowl and featured on at least two network shows. Garber came to the Coast for an extended engagement at what was then California's glamour spot, Catalina Island. The fact that they were actually close personal friends was known only to those who helped put the "argument" together.

Nightly broadcasts were featured from both the Biltmore Bowl and Catalina's Avalon Ballroom. Grier was scheduled to go on first each evening, and during the course of the broadcast he would always make some cutting remark about the quality of the music Garber was dispensing at Catalina. Garber would naturally retaliate when his turn on the air came a little later the same night.

This went on for a matter of weeks with the comments becoming increasingly caustic. Finally, on one of his Saturday night broadcasts Grier announced that since the next day was his day off, he intended to sail to Catalina and have it out with Garber. Next day, having borrowed Biltmore owner Baron Long's yacht for transportation, he sailed into Avalon Bay accompanied by another bandleader friend, piano player Eddy Duchin. The usual number of newspaper reporters and newsreel photographers were on hand to record a pre-

tended argument between Garber and Grier on the deck of the yacht followed by the signing of a peace treaty.

Red Nichols was another leader whose sense of the value of publicity was extremely sharp. In his case, his name lent itself readily to special promotions for his billing as "Red Nichols and His Five Pennies" which was a natural. For many years the public in those cities where he was scheduled to appear began to get the message that he was coming several days prior to his appearance and in a very subtle manner. From some mysterious source a supply of five cent pieces dipped in red paint would flood the area and it became almost impossible to receive your change for a purchase without receiving at the same time a silent reminder of Mr. Nichols.

One of Red's publicity stories received widespread news coverage in 1941. The cities of Oakland and Alameda, California, were plagued with a population of rats which efforts of the city governments had been unable to control. Red was appearing in the area at the time, and in a public interview suggested that perhaps a re-enactment of the Pied Piper of Hamelin bit would get rid of the rodents. He made it known that he was available to play the part of the Piper, and was pictured signing with the city fathers to do the job. The coming event was given advance coverage in the papers coast-to-coast for several days. At the appointed time, Nichols and his band marched through the streets playing their music to the accompaniment of flashlight bulbs and newsreel coverage. There is no record of just how many rats Nichols was able to sell on the idea of marching off the pier into San Francisco Bay, but there's no doubt the performance of the original Pied Piper was not nearly as well publicized as was this modern version.

By the mid 1930s dance orchestras and their various activities had developed into one of the entertainment industry's most important segments. As their status in this regard increased, so did the coverage allotted them in such show business trade journals as *Variety* and *Billboard*. Others such as *Metronome* and *Downbeat* were devoted entirely to the music makers, as were a few lesser known publications which came and went for want of adequate circulation.

Favorable coverage in these was sought by all and made the most of when it occurred. Each weekly issue of *Billboard* reviewed from one to a half dozen bands observed in action by a magazine representative. This department titled "On the Stand" was widely read by the trade. The leader who received there treatment to his liking usually was quick to reproduce it in a brochure for mailing to prospective band buyers. Similar coverage from *Variety* was made use of in the same manner.

Special service departments were also available to the musical organizations who wanted to provide information as to where they were appearing. *Billboard's* complete coverage was headed "Orchestra Routes" and for many years took up a page or more in order to accommodate the great number of bands in operation. Another section published complete advance itineraries under the heading "Bands on Tour". *Downbeat's* "Where The Bands Are Playing" similarly required at least a page to give the same type of information.

But the really coveted spot was on the cover of those magazines which used pictorial material. Both *Billboard* and *Metronome* reserved this place for photographs of the important ones, and it became a status symbol of the highest order to appear there. No less desirable was *Downbeat's* cover. This magazine, with much of its space devoted to pictorial news stories, permitted a little more latitude with its cover subjects. An imaginative publicity man who could come up with an unusual shot of his bandleader client found them co-operative in making their most desirable space available.

Band publicity had now become big business for the people who handled it. In the fall of 1940 a widely circulated syndicated news story announced and simultaneously deplored the overnight building of a new band to "Name" status. The band referred to was that of Will Bradley. Nonexistent a year before, it had at the time of the article, bookings scheduled in all of the top hotels, theaters, and ballrooms in the country, and a phonograph record which was a smash hit. All of this the news writer credited to, or blamed on, high pressure publicity arranged by the band's handlers at heavy financial cost. Just why this was considered objectionable was not quite clear since it was acknowledged that the musicianship within the band was of high caliber and assured the patron his money's worth.

The Bradley band building actually made news only because it was the first to occur in that manner. Before too many more years had gone by it would be accepted as standard procedure, and the band which could not project itself rapidly into the big time would probably never make it at all.

The part the agencies took in using all forms of publicity and promotion to sell the services of the orchestras represented by them was substantial. It divided itself into two phases, the first of which was aimed at the band buyers of hotels, ballrooms, etc., who were the potential users of somebody's orchestra if only for one night.

In this regard most agencies were experts as might be expected. Through well-written trade paper ads they broadcast the accomplishments of their bands in personal appearances, on records, and most of all their position on radio, either sponsored or remote pickup. Reproductions of these ads were converted into direct mail pieces, elaborate brochures, some of which covered the activities of a single band and others perhaps picturing the agency's entire roster. These became part of the mail which went regularly to their list of clients.

TOMMY TUCKER makes the coveted *Billboard* cover. — *Photo courtesy of Billboard.*

The Billboard
The World's Foremost Amusement Weekly

NOVEMBER 23, 1940   15 Cents   Vol. 52. No. 47

"It's Tommy Tucker Time"
TOMMY TUCKER
and His Orchestra
Personal Representative For Calkin

While all of the agencies gave their artists this kind of publicity, there were some who stood out for the consistency and quality of their efforts. Music Corporation of America, having the largest talent roster, was bound to be one of these. But few could do a better job than one of the smaller independents with only a few leaders under contract.

Harold Oxley was the agent who enjoyed this reputation, with his own office in New York, and represented on the West Coast by Reg Marshall. Oxley specialized in the handling of top Negro talent although his stable included a few others as well. His gold mine, and perhaps vice versa, was the Jimmie Lunceford orchestra and his efforts in Lunceford's behalf left little to be desired. His mailing list was probably the most complete in the business, and where those of bigger agencies were largely made up of prior purchasers of their talent his included even the smallest one-night promoters. Each of Lunceford's openings in a major hotel was made known to these people through some form of direct mail, and holidays were the signal for a special brochure. From some uncanny source of information he even learned the date of the promoter's birthday, favoring him with a card signed jointly by himself and Lunceford. He kept the band booked solidly, and it was a real tragedy that Lunceford's untimely death in 1947 put an end to what may have been the greatest team of leader and agent the business ever saw.

Although not so consistent as Oxley, other agencies with one or more outstanding artists did good jobs on somewhat similar build-ups. Commendable performances were turned in by William Morris for Count Basie, General Artists for Jimmy Dorsey, and the job Joe Glaser did for such leaders as Les Brown and Louis Armstrong left little to be desired.

For some reason never quite clear, the second phase of publicity in which they should have excelled was generally poorly handled by all the agencies. This involved providing the band buyer with material intended to help insure public support of the band's appearance. Since this was the publicity which had the greatest effect on the box office, it's surprising that it was not given greater importance.

Each location or promoter who contracted for the band received a standard promotional package. It consisted of window cards, photographs, newspaper mats, and a press manual. The window

THE ORCHESTRA · WORLD

"Mirroring Modern Music For 20 Years"

May, 1945

15¢
Foreign Canada 25¢

TONY PASTOR
And His Orchestra
Currently:
HOLLYWOOD PALLADIUM
Direct from:
HOTEL SHERMAN, CHICAGO
VICTOR RECORDS
Personal Management
CY SHRIBMAN
Direction
GENERAL AMUSEMENT CORP.

Another popular music business publication. — *Photo courtesy of Orchestra World.*

cards and mats were adequate for advertising purposes, but the real publicity was intended to be found in the press manual.

With this manual the promoter was supposed to encourage the local press and disc jockeys to write and say those things about the band which would create a desirable image of musical ability worth spending money to hear in person. Most of them were so poorly done that they could not be used at all as written. Some of them rambled so far afield that no newspaper entertainment editor would be party to using them. Often they were devoted only to proving that the leader had a pleasing personality, got good marks in grade school, and turned down an opportunity to take over a rich father's successful business because of

CAB CALLOWAY'S
"Hepster's Dictionary"

A

AIN'T COMING ON THAT TAB (V)—won't accept the proposition. Usually abbr. to "I ain't coming."
APPLE (N)—the big town, the main stem, Harlem.
ARMSTRONGS (N)—musical notes in the upper register, high trumpet notes.

B

BARBECUE (N)—the girl friend, a beauty.
BARRELHOUSE (A)—free and easy.
BATTLE (N)—a very homely girl, a crone.
BEATUP (N)—small change. Ex.—"Can you lend me a little beatup?"
BEAT UP THE CHOPS (or the gums) (V)—to talk, converse, be loquacious.
BLACK (N)—night.
BLUES AND GRAYS (N)—colored and white folks.
BLIP (N)—something very good. Ex.—"That's a blip."
BREE (N)—girl.
BRIGHT (N)—day.

C

CAT (N)—musician in swing band.
CLAMBAKE (N)—ad lib session, every man for himself, a jam session not in the groove.
COMES ON LIKE GANG BUSTERS (or like test pilot) (V)—playing, singing or dancing in a terrific manner, par-excellence in any department. Sometimes abbr. to "That singer really comes on!"
COOLING (V)—laying off between engagements, not working.
CREPT OUT LIKE THE SHADOW (V)—"comes on," but in smooth, suave, sophisticated manner.
CUT RATE (N)—a low, cheap person. Ex.—"Don't play me cut rate, Jack!"

D

DIG (V)—(1) meet. Ex.—"I'll plant you now and dig you later." (2) look, see. Ex.—"Dig the chick on your left duke." (3) comprehend, understand. Ex.—"Do you dig this jive?"
DILLINGER (N)—a killer-diller, too hot to handle.
DIME NOTE (N)—ten dollar bill.
DOGHOUSE (N)—bass fiddle.
DOSS (N)—sleep. Ex.—"I'm a little beat for my doss."
DRAPE (N)—suit of clothes, dress, costume.
DRY GOODS (N)—same as drape.

E

EARLY BLACK (N)—evening.
EARLY BRIGHT (N)—morning.
EVIL (A)—in ill humor, in nasty temper.

F

FALL OUT (V)—to be overcome with emotion. Ex.—"The cats fell out when he took that solo."
FAUST (N)—an ugly girl, a hag (see battle).
FEWS AND TWO (N)—money or cash in small quantity.
FINAL (V)—to leave, to go home. Ex.—"I finaled to my pad" (went to bed), "We copped a final" (went home).
FRAUGHTY ISSUE (N)—a very sad message, a deplorable state of affairs.
FREEBY (N)—no charge, gratis. Ex.—"The meal was a freeby."
FRISKING THE WHISKERS (V)—what the cats do when they are warming up for a swing session.

G

GATE (N)—a male person (a salutation), abbr. for "gate-mouth."
GOT YOUR BOOTS ON—you know what it is all about.

LEARN YOUR JIVE TALK FROM AN OLD MASTER—THE HI-DE-HO MAN!

GOT YOUR GLASSES ON—you are ritzy or snooty, you fail to recognize your friends, you are up-stage.
GROWL (N)—vibrant notes from a trumpet.

H

HARD (A)—fine, good. Ex.—"That's a hard tie you're wearing."
HAVE A BALL (V)—to enjoy yourself, stage a celebration. Ex.—"I had myself a ball last night."
HIDE-BEATER (N)—a drummer.
HIP (A)—wise, sophisticated, anyone with boots on. Ex.—"She is a hip chick."
HOME-COOKING (N)—something very nice.

I

ICKY (N)—one who is not hip, a stupid person, can't collar the jive.
IGG (V)—to ignore someone. Ex.—"Don't igg me!"
IN THE GROOVE (A)—perfect, no deviation, down the alley.

J

JEFF (N)—a pest, a bore, an icky.
JELLY (N)—anything free, on the house.
JIVE—(1) (N)—Harlemese speech or lingo; also stuff and things. Ex.—"Did you bring the jive (liquor)? (V)—to kid along, to blarney, to give a girl a line. Ex.—"He can jive his way into any chick's heart."
JOINT IS JUMPING—the place is lively.

K

KILL ME (V)—show me a good time, send me.
KNOCK (V)—to obtain. Ex.—"I'm gonna knock me some food."
KOPASETIC (A)—absolutely okay, the tops.

L

LAY SOME IRON (V)—to tap dance. Ex.—"Jack, you really laid some iron that last show!"
LEAD SHEET (N)—a top coat.
LEFT RAISE (N)—left side. Ex.—"Dig the chick on your left raise."
LILY WHITES (N)—bed sheets.
LINE (N)—cost, price, money. Ex.—"What is the line on this drape?" (how much does this suit cost)? (Also, in replying, all figures are doubled. Ex.—"This drape is line forty" (this suit costs twenty dollars.)
LOCKED UP—to acquire something exclusively. Ex.—"He's got that chick locked up." "I'm gonna lock that deal."

M

MAIN KICK (N)—the stage.
MAIN QUEEN (N)—favorite girl friend.

(Continued on page 73)

an uncontrollable urge to be a musician. Usually they had not been rewritten in years, and any musical accomplishments listed were ancient history even though there may have been recent newsworthy ones.

No bandleader who could afford to do something about it left the matter of his publicity to chance. Instead he hired his own publicity and promotion expert who either worked full time, or whose activities on a free lance basis insured proper coverage. It was the job of this expert to originate ideas to build up interest in advance of and during an appearance, or to provide audience tie-ins which endeared the leader to his public. Most of these would be something usable as a stock part of the band's publicity, but some were local through co-operation with the management for whom they were playing. Actually, the man was a combination publicity and public relations expert.

Over the years a lot of interesting things developed, most of which reflected much ingenuity, were reasonably successful, sometimes had humorous sidelights, but generally contributed to the welfare of the business.

Some of Ted FioRito's approaches to publicity have already been related. During the late thirties he had another going which was a natural tie-in with his reputation as a song writer. He was well known, and the possibility of anything he wrote becoming a hit could not be overlooked. For one entire season he conducted a "Name the New Song" contest, with the winner promised a share of any royalties the song might earn. This type of promotion had a way of backfiring and eventually this one had to be discontinued.

In the early forties another FioRito promotion became so successful he regretted ever becoming involved in it. One of the major airlines was sold the idea of a tie-in streamer for advance announcement that the band was coming to town. At that time he was billing himself as "Ted FioRito and his Musical Pilots" and it was this which gave the airline its interest in participating. In addition to the advance streamers, a card made as an airline cutout was placed on each table where the band appeared, with the suggestion the fans get them autographed by "Captain FioRito". The reception to the idea was so great that FioRito often had to beg off on the autographing because of writer's cramp, and some of his featured artists had similar trouble.

About the same time a Dick Jurgen's promotion was, strangely enough, pointed in the other direction. While appearing at Catalina Island his nightly broadcasts asked for the autographs of his fans, along with a letter "I like Dick Jurgens because—". The response to this new approach was terrific and gave Jurgens the biggest load of fan mail the island had ever seen.

Probably the best known audience participation gimmick ever used was Sammy Kaye's "So you want to lead a band", in which three or four guests from the audience competed for the title of "best bandleader" awarded from the volume of applause their friends gave them while they waved a baton at the Kaye sidemen. Gray Gordon encouraged camera fans to stand in front of his band while a friend photographed them posing with baton in hand. Lawrence Welk's fans of the forties were invited to request a birthday dedication followed by a presentation of a Welk autographed birthday card.

JIMMY JOY invades California and informs promoters coast-to-coast with a broadside mailing, 1940. — *Photo courtesy of M.C.A.*

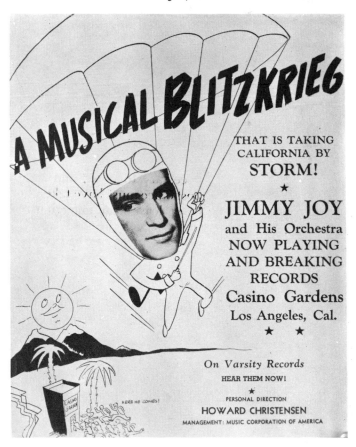

A MUSICAL BLITZKRIEG

THAT IS TAKING
CALIFORNIA BY
STORM!

★

JIMMY JOY
and His Orchestra
NOW PLAYING
AND BREAKING
RECORDS
Casino Gardens
Los Angeles, Cal.

★   ★

On Varsity Records
HEAR THEM NOW!

★

PERSONAL DIRECTION
HOWARD CHRISTENSEN
MANAGEMENT: MUSIC CORPORATION OF AMERICA

259

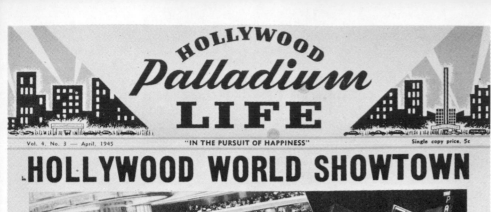

HOLLYWOOD *Palladium* LIFE

Vol. 4, No. 3 — April, 1945   "IN THE PURSUIT OF HAPPINESS"   Single copy price, 5c

HOLLYWOOD WORLD SHOWTOWN

the bandstand

By BUD MAJOR

It was just little over a year ago when your columnist sat with Frankie Carle and his charming wife on the famed Palladium Terrace and listened
(Continued on Page 8)

This picture montage provides a quick tour of Hollywood. Above left is a crowd shot at the Palladium, with Maestro Frankie Carle seated at the piano below. Lower left show a premier night at Grauman's Chinese. In the center is an exterior view of the Florentine Gardens, while alongside is the "Wall of Fame" at Earl Carroll's, with the Palladium neon sign above. Below is the NBC studio and a panoramic view of the famous Hollywood Bowl.

Film City Now Famed Hub of Entertainment

Not so many years ago, Hollywood was a land of orange groves, bean and barley fields and wide open spaces. Scarcely 30 years have elapsed since the first motion picture studio was built here. Today, it is the film capital of the world.

More than that, Hollywood is the greatest showtown on the face of the earth. Endless opportunities for en-
(Continued on Page 6)

Opening—May 1
TONY PASTOR

Now—FRANKIE CARLE

COMING
TOMMY TUCKER

Hollywood's Palladium had a newsy fan magazine which it released monthly. — *Photo courtesy Palladium.*

Below, BARNEY McDEVITT and client RONNIE KEMPER make the "Dixie Dugan" comic strip. — *Photo courtesy of Ronnie Kemper.*

Trianon Ballroom DANCE TOPICS

COTTAGE GROVE — SIXTY SECOND

Published at Chicago, Ill.   Issue of March 27, 1937

On The Avenue!

Trianon's bandmaster, Kay Kyser (right); his charming songstress, Nancy Nelson; and Aragon maestro Freddy Martin, pictured in front of the magnificent new Michigan avenue display on the night they formally set it in motion.

The whole town's talking about the newest creation in advertising—the mammoth, breathtaking animated display of Trianon and Aragon, located on fashionable Michigan Avenue, at Pearson Street—just south of the Palmolive Building!

In a setting that is a faithful reproduction of the magnificent Aragon, the display features couples actually gliding about the floor in an amazingly lifelike manner. Through ingenious scaling and decorating the illusion of a spacious ballroom is created, a ballroom filled with happy dancing couples, moving rhythmically about to the music of the orchestra that can be seen in the background.

At nightime is the display especially attractive, with its many-colored lights blending perfectly with the multi-hued interior and the costumes of the dancers.

The display was conceived by Mr. Andrew Karzas, managing director of Trianon and Aragon, and was designed and executed by the skillful artists on the staff of the General Outdoor Advertising Company.

By all means, see this magnificent creation. You'll find it well worth even a special trip downtown!

The TRIANON had its own publication. — *Photo courtesy of Andrew Karzas.*

Below at left, WOODY HERMAN and RED NORVO, 1946. All leaders cooperated for product endorsement publicity. — *Courtesy of Minnesota Mining & Mfg. Co.*

Below is a sample of what a press manual often included.

A sample of HAROLD OXLEY's excellent handling of Jimmie Lunceford's publicity.

Tommy Dorsey's appearances were announced in advance via paper napkins imprinted with his name and displayed in any restaurants which would use them. During one of Cab Calloway's New York appearances he managed to cover all the taxicab bumpers with a placard requesting, "Take a cab to see Cab Calloway". In Des Moines, Iowa, a publicity man working for a local promoter nearly died in an attempt to adequately publicize an appearance of Ben Pollack and his "double-barreled rhythm". He dressed himself in a fur coat and a coon skin cap and walked up and down the streets carrying a double barreled shotgun. It might have worked at a different time of year, but he was trying it in August when the temperature was one hundred degrees in the shade.

A tribute to the genius of some publicity man hit the wire service some years back, indicating that Russ Morgan was not only a prolific song writer, but an inventor as well. The story related that for some time Morgan had been on the verge of perfecting a new trombone, his favorite instrument. The new horn differed from the conventional model in that it would be built to move side-ways instead of forward. One of its advantages would be to make playing easier for short armed trombonists, but its real purpose was for use in marching bands where it would eliminate bruises on the posteriors of those musicians marching directly in front of the trombone section. Instrument dealers have not yet started displaying Morgan's version of what a trombone should be, and when last observed he was playing the standard model.

Another Morgan promotion in a more realistic vein, was very successfully used for years and consisted of making available to all promoters who had a mailing list, playable miniature records of one chorus of the Morgan theme song.

There were always product manufacturers anxious to co-operate with a name bandleader in arranging publicity to their mutual advantage. These usually involved an endorsement, stated or implied, but sometimes were in the form of news stories when the type of product and the circumstances could be tied together in a logical manner. The public relations department of the company involved could be depended on to get the neces-

262

sary coverage with the story, and special advertising to tie in was normal procedure.

In some cases the leader was financially compensated for these endorsements, but in most cases he went along for the publicity alone. Rudy Vallee was one of the first to make real capital of this form of publicity, but practically every name of importance had offers at one time or another. Almost without exception they tried to identify themselves with a product which was well thought of.

Endorsements were not limited to products alone. Large chain stores made a practice of promotions of this type and transportation companies too, particularly those which hauled the orchestras on cross-country tours.

One season during the early forties, Ben Bernie agreed to the endorsement of a product which was distributed through a major mail order house. This resulted in his picture appearing in the company's catalogue which had a circulation blanketing the entire Midwest. Since this was the prime source of merchandise to the Midwestern farm trade, Bernie felt that a tour of personal appearances through the farm belt should benefit from this exposure and pay off handsomely.

Because of other commitments it was early fall before he booked the tour, but somehow things didn't work out as he had hoped. Heading west from Chicago on one-nighters the turnouts through Iowa, Nebraska, and South Dakota were quite disappointing. By the time they had doubled back into St. Joseph, Missouri, Bernie was taking quite a ribbing from the band. He must be slipping, they told him, if he couldn't get the rural people to turn out by advertising in their favorite publication.

Bernie was never known to be without a comeback and this time was no exception:

BASIE makes the most of his "One O'Clock Jump." This was only one page of an elaborate brochure. — *Photo courtesy of William Morris Agency.*

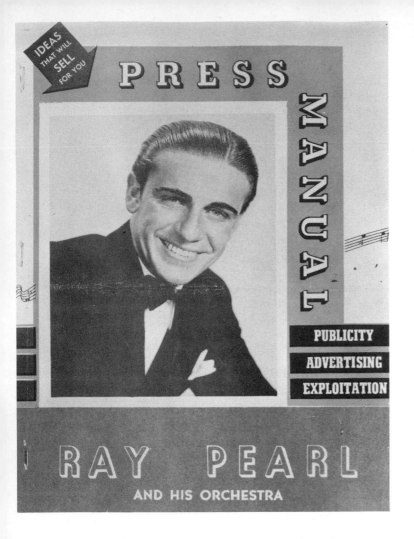

Press Relations Department
Music Corporation of America
9370 Burton Way
Beverly Hills, California

"THIS AND THAT" ABOUT
HAL HOWARD

Hal Howard is 6'0" tall - weighs one hundred and sixty five pounds - has blue eyes - and brown hair.

Some of the featured entertainers Hal Howard will present will be SAMMY CONOVER, "THE TRIO", AND TWO PIANOS.

Most people call Hal Howard, "The Eddy Duchin of the Piano." Not only does Hal play a sweet tune but sings a good song too. The Rhumbas and Tangoes that he plays would make any dance- lovers feet tingle.

Anybody couldn't help but like to have Hal's presence around. His jolly attitude and pleasing personality makes you feel very welcome in his presence. All and all, Hal is "just one swell fellow!"

MCA

The agency's press manual was supposed to provide the band buyer with material to entice the dancers out.

Another sample of an agency's "makes you wanta dance" press releases.

SPIKE JONES' record of "Chloe" resulted in this publicity stunt dreamed up by Jimmie Grier and Leo Walker at California's State Fair, 1948. The picture made national coverage in a trade publication.—*Photo courtesy of Pope Studios, Sacramento, California.*

"This simply proves that we waited too late in the season to make this swing. Now we know it's really true that by this time of the year the farmers have gotten way past the slick pages and are over into the harness section."

The foregoing story was told to me by veteran publicity man Barney McDevitt, who, like Jimmy Durante, probably "has a million of them". He should have. During a career which dates back to his association with the early Fred Waring band, he has handled publicity for practically every big name in the business, either full time or on a free-lance basis.

When a substantial portion of the band business moved headquarters to the West Coast during the 1930s McDevitt came West with it. Here he continued to handle big names, eventually taking over the publicity for the Hollywood Palladium when it opened in the fall of 1940.

In later years the use of bands by the Palladium dropped off to week ends only, and his time became divided between the ballroom and one of the country's largest music publishers. This would have been enough to keep most people busy, but somehow he still found time to handle an average of a half dozen musical names who would trust no one else with their publicity.

His desk was usually a pile of correspondence and handwritten notes in such disarray that you would have sworn he could find none of them, although somehow he knew where everything was. Probably he didn't need most of them anyway for his memory was fantastic. Out of his head he could quote the telephone numbers of anyone associated with the music business, and most of the movie big names as well. Most of these were unlisted numbers, but he had access to the information when few others did.

For several years he maintained space in two offices, one with the music publishing firm in the Capitol Records Tower, and the other at the Palladium Ballroom. His day usually started at 9:00 a.m. when he arrived at the publishing company's office where the morning was spent with the mail and on the phone. Around lunch time he usually departed for the Palladium on foot since it was only four blocks away. The trip would be subject to pauses at every unoccupied phone booth en route where he would dart in and place a call to one of his clients, a newspaper, or disc jockey, about an idea which had just occurred to him.

What better way to get publicity than to be photographed with Hollywood's best-known columnist and a movie star? Louella Parsons, bandleader Jack Fina, and Mona Freeman. — *Photo courtesy of Barney Mc-Devitt and Irving L. Antler.*

A 1946 recap of Ted Lewis' career. — *Photo courtesy of Billboard.*

CLAUDE GORDON, winner of the 1959 National Band Contest, poses with the kind of glamor which should lure vacationers to Catalina Island.
— *Photo courtesy of Claude Gordon.*

BARNEY McDEVITT, a veteran of many years spent in band publicity. What would a publicity man do without the telephone? — *Photo courtesy Barney McDevitt.*

McDEVITT enters the gate at N.B.C. Studio with one of his most cooperative clients, Phil Harris. — *Photo courtesy of Barney McDevitt.*

Chuck Cabot and full band pose on the Palladium's marquee. — *Courtesy of Chuck Cabot.*

APPEARED WITH
Dinah Shore · Bob Hope · Eddie Fisher
Elvis Presley · Jack Carson · Gordon MacRae
George Gobel · Ann Jeffreys and Bob Sterling
Marge and Gower Champion · Gale Storm
Guy Cherney · Lucille Ball and Desi Arnaz

At left is an excerpt from a brochure proving that band publicity was not dead yet in 1961. — *Courtesy Benny Strong.*

Even the seals got into the
act as BOB CROSBY makes a
bandstand visit to see his
friend Jimmy Dorsey. —
Courtesy Barney McDevitt

LES BROWN's agents were quick to tell the trade
the results of the 1958 band poll. — *Photo courtesy of Don Kramer.*

Saturday was his day to catch up on correspondence which he tried to accomplish while the
publisher's office was officially closed. Many times
I would join him there at noontime for a Saturday
luncheon, getting the building security officer to
let me in the back door. Usually I'd find him with
at least two telephone conversations in progress,
and one of these might be with composer Dimitri
Tiomkin while Harry James was competing for his
attention on the other phone. Sometimes when
things became too complicated for him he would
hand me one of the phones with a simple introduction to the other party like, "I'd like to have
you meet a good friend of mine who has something he would like to ask you." When this happened there was nothing to do but ad-lib it, and on
one occasion I found myself trying to carry on a
ten minute impromptu conversation with one of
Hollywood's most important gossip columnists
who didn't know me from a load of hay, and probably thought I belonged on top of one.

Whether McDevitt could be called a typical
publicity man is debatable, but he was typical of
what most of them would like to be. His contacts
were unlimited, and he had more friends than the
man who hands out checks at the unemployment
office. The gathering of material for this book in-

volved contacting a lot of important people in the music world. Some of them I knew quite well myself, some only slightly, and some not at all. McDevitt was the entree to all of them. Mentioning his name was like flashing a pocketful of credit cards on a restaurant headwaiter. From that point on anything you wanted you could have.

In a business which required many personal contacts, he carried on without ever driving a car himself. No one else could ever have done it, but he did. Somehow when he needed to make the rounds of the radio stations to romance the disc jockeys there was always a friend to drive him. If he asked for the lift he had a way of making it seem as though you were making the trip for yourself rather than for him, and since you were going in that direction he would just ride along. Even though you knew you were being conned somehow you didn't mind it for in most cases before you had completed the round trip he would have done something for you which made the trip worthwhile.

One night we were driving across town to take some publicity material to Freddy Martin. The car radio was on and tuned to one of Hollywood's most popular disc jockeys. Without planning it that way, we were driving a route that took us right past the station from which he was broadcasting. As we approached the area, McDevitt suddenly grabbed my arm and said:

"I've got a record in my briefcase which would fit in with the stuff he's playing tonight. I'll bet you $5.00 I can get it on the air in five minutes."

Knowing I was probably a sucker I agreed to the bet anyway, and we pulled to a fast stop at the curb in front of the station. McDevitt hit the sidewalk running while I stayed in the car listening to the radio and watching the second hand reel off the minutes on my watch. McDevitt lost but it wasn't really his fault. He had forgotten to check the time and when he burst into the studio they were playing the last record before the hourly news break. Still before the news went on it was preceded by this announcement:

"Barney McDevitt just came into the studio with a new Harry James record which you'll hear immediately following the news."

The time since McDevitt had left the car was just two minutes and thirty-five seconds.

One of McDevitt's favorite stories was about one of the many personal radio interviews arranged by him for bandleader clients during the heyday of the big bands. This one actually involved two leaders who were to appear, one after the other, on the program of one of the better known disc jockeys of that period.

It was in the early 1940s and the Southern California music scene was booming. Among those in town were Joe Reichman, playing at the Cocoanut Grove, and Count Basie who was appearing at the Casa Mañana in Culver City. McDevitt was handling publicity for both of them.

The radio appearance called for them to be on for consecutive fifteen minute sessions, with Reichman being up first. The Reichman interview went off as scheduled. However, while the disc jockey was interviewing Joe, a telephone call was received from Basie saying he was not going to be able to put in an appearance. This news was not passed along to the disc jockey until Reichman was through being interviewed. Needless to say such a short notice cancellation made it impossible to arrange for another name guest to fill the spot.

When the news that Basie would not appear was received, Reichman, an accomplished mimic, started clowning and imitating Basie complete with voice inflections. During the ensuing commercial a hasty decision was made. Instead of announcing that the Count would not be able to be on the show, he was introduced at the time indicated. Reichman went back on the air, this time in Basie's place and answered all the questions which had been prepared in advance for the Basie interview. Having spent a lot of time around Basie's former home town of Kansas City, he knew him very well and was able to carry it off. His imitation of Basie's voice and expression was so nearly perfect that the listeners were never aware that the Count himself was not in the studio.

To the surprise of the station personnel, and the amusement of Reichman and McDevitt, most of the fan mail received as a result of the two interviews was addressed to Basie.

During the lush days of the band business there were many Barney McDevitts who contributed a great deal to making it what it was. His story and theirs are deserving of much greater coverage than has been given here and someday perhaps it can be written into the big story which actually it is.

Jean Goldkette's orchestra on tour in the mid-1920s. — *Photo courtesy of Jean Goldkette.*

Lawrence Welk's band of the 1920s toured the Midwest in this big Graham-Paige sedan.
    — *Photo courtesy of Lawrence Welk.*

The Road Trips Were Rugged!

To THE FANS who crowded ten to twelve deep around the bandstand to get a close view of their favorite band in action, the life of the bandleader, his musicians and entertainers, probably appeared glamorous. A lot of the members of the band were probably there because it had looked the same way to them. To some of them it may never have lost that appeal. But for most it took only a couple of road trips to dull the glamour and convert it into a job; a job which only their love for music or a burning ambition could make worthwhile.

Perhaps to the crowd out front it looked like an easy life. But they could not know what hardships might have been involved in getting the band on the stand at the appointed hour ready to deliver a top performance, and give the impression they enjoyed doing it. Maybe they had just gotten off a train and scrambled madly to change clothes and set up the instruments before the patrons arrived. More likely they had bounced around in a bus for ten or twelve hours, or fought the highway in a private automobile.

It was in the early twenties that the dance bands began to go on the road to any extent. In those days several factors combined to place limitations on the distances between engagements. Public transportation left much to be desired, and the automobiles were not capable of long distance travel. The superhighway was not yet even in the dream stage; instead there were only poorly marked and even more poorly maintained dirt roads. Perhaps the concept of the range of the automobile was best emphasized by the tire manufacturers. In the early twenties two or three of the more daring ones began to guarantee their tires to have a life of 5,000 miles, publicizing the fact widely as a sales advantage.

Early pioneers in the one-nighter field included Joe Kayser's band, although most sources indicate that it was the Jan Garber-Milton Davis orchestra which was first to do one-nighter tours with regularity.

Kayser hit the road about 1921. He had led one of Meyer Davis' units for several years, and prior to that had worked his way through school with a five piece band. The first group he organized for himself was also five men, and included saxophonist Frankie Trumbauer. A little later he increased the band to eight men, eventually giving up the drumming chores done by himself to let a newcomer by the name of Gene Krupa handle them.

He first operated along the East Coast, but moved into St. Louis sometime in 1921 where he headquartered for a while and then established Rockford, Illinois, as a base. From these points he ranged out into the hinterlands on swings which kept him on the road most of the time. The average jump was less than one hundred miles, but even then they encountered road conditions which made it difficult to arrive on time. When winter weather piled the roads with snow they sometimes could not make the date at all.

The promoters who hired them usually could not be prevailed upon to give them a guarantee, possibly because they too wondered if the band could be depended on to get there. When they did get guarantees they ran from $75. to $150., with the last figure being the rare exception. Usually they took the date on the basis of 75% of the admissions, but often it was on a 50-50 arrangement.

Kayser's experiences were typical of most of the leaders who depended on travel to keep their group working steadily. The trail blazing done by the Kaysers and Garbers soon made one-night stands a standard operation, and made it possible for hundreds of "territory bands" to come into existence. Many of these outgrew this status to become names on a national scale. Some became very prosperous with the following they built up in their own locale.

Transportation for most of these orchestras was the passenger car. Henry Ford, who had openly expressed a strong dislike for popular dance music, was very much part of the business and probably didn't really object to the part he played. A lot of Model T Fords transported musicians on these junkets, but as soon as they could afford it, they usually grabbed off a big secondhand sedan of some type. The two "jump seats" which were standard equipment in the high priced limousines made it possible for an eight or nine piece band to ride in one vehicle, with the instruments on top in a luggage rack. The bandleader on his way up could usually find one of these on a good used car lot so there were a lot of them carrying musicians on the dance circuit. Among these was a big Graham-Paige which became a familiar sight on Midwestern highways in the mid-twenties, with the instrument rack painted to tell the world it was carrying "Lawrence Welk's Novelty Orchestra" to its next dance date.

As some of the bands grew to a dozen or more members, it took a couple of these limousines to transport them. In almost every instance these would be owned by the leader for he assumed full responsibility for getting the band to the job. Eventually, they began to charter buses and a few even bought them outright. Jean Goldkette was one of the first to send his units on the road in buses.

The bigger names like Fred Waring and Paul Whiteman usually went by train. For the most part, both of them played only the larger cities, leaving the one-nighters in the hinterlands pretty much alone. By the end of the twenties, Whiteman's band totalled 34 performers and would have found it extremely difficult to travel by any other means.

But even when they went by rail, things could go wrong. About 1930 the Waring band was scheduled into Buffalo, New York, for a theater date. They were making the trip from Philadelphia which was an overnight sleeper trip, and they arrived in Buffalo in mid-forenoon. Their opening show was scheduled for 12:45 that afternoon, which meant they would really have to get organized in a hurry to make it.

Barney McDevitt was the publicity man for the band, usually traveling ahead by four or five days. But that time he had doubled back and made the trip with the rest of the group. The minute the train stopped, he took over to see that the

instruments, uniforms, etc., were rushed to the theater.

Approaching one of the porters, he asked the location of the baggage car. The porter gave him a funny look and said: "Baggage car? Man, there ain't no baggage car on this train. We took it off last night in Harrisburg."

A quick check made it clear that he spoke the truth and there was no possibility of recovering the delayed baggage by showtime. Waring looked at McDevitt and said:

"Barney, with that Irish luck of yours there must be something you can do. It's up to you to have us on that stage when the curtain goes up."

Rudy Vallee and his orchestra had just closed an engagement in the same theater the night before. McDevitt dashed over to the hotel where the Vallee band was still sleeping in and roused Vallee from a sound sleep. Telling him of their predicament, he prevailed upon Rudy to loan him all the instruments from his band, and enough uniforms to dress up the front row members so that they, at least, would appear to belong to one group with common interests.

The first show went off right on time and the story should end there — but it doesn't.

The tuba player in the Waring band had purchased a new instrument during a New York engagement about six months before the Buffalo date. Since that time he had been on the road quite steadily, and for one reason or another had not mailed any payments on the account. The music store from which he had made the purchase also had a branch in Buffalo. Learning of the band's scheduled appearance there, they had notified their Buffalo store manager to repossess the instrument. And so the opening show crowd included two men from the music store, firmly determined to have either the money or the tuba by the time they left the theater.

As they sat in the audience watching the performance, they probably congratulated themselves on one fact which appeared obvious. Even if the guy hadn't made any payments on the horn his personal pride had still apparently prompted him to keep it in first class condition, for it still shone like a new instrument. What they couldn't know was that coincidentally, Vallee's tuba man had also purchased a new one, and it was this they were admiring.

TED FIORITO goes Greyhound, 1933 —
Photo courtesy of Muzzy Marcellino.

When the show ended, they dashed backstage and accosted the musician as he came into the wings. He readily admitted his identity and the fact that he owed the money, but was not in a position to pay off. Unable to collect, they got hold of the tuba and let him know they were going to take it with them. His protests that it was a borrowed instrument and not the one in question only made them more determined. However, they did congratulate him on what they considered quite an imaginative cover-up story.

For a while it looked as if both the Waring and Vallee bands would be without tubas. The situation was finally saved by McDevitt who got Waring to advance the necessary bail money.

There were many other stories of mix-ups in destination, often involving band members. During 1930 the Ted FioRito band, playing one-nighters, had their last date of the tour scheduled in Marion, Virginia. Somehow when they checked

out from their previous night's engagement, half the band, apparently confused as to the itinerary, drove instead to Marion, North Carolina. When they discovered their mistake, it was too late to do anything but call FioRito in Marion, Virginia, and let him know they would be unable to make it in time to play the job. There was nothing he could do but find enough local musicians to fill in and play the job without them.

The Irving Aaronson Band had an even more frustrating experience primarily because the distances involved were greater. They had been playing on the West Coast and when they left to return to the East, their first engagement was in Mound City, Illinois, a distance of 2400 miles. There they played a one-nighter and continued on to Parkersburg, West Virginia. Immediately after that job they got into their cars and drove all night and all the next day to arrive in Erie, Pennsylvania, at 8:00 p.m. for another one-nighter. When they

273

Denver, 1934. The truck hauled the instruments, the band members rode in passenger cars. — *Photo courtesy of Ernie Mathias.*

June Christy prepares to board the bus during a Stan Kenton tour. — *Photo courtesy of Capitol Records.*

walked into the Pavilion, they found another band already playing. Apparently, the agency had made a mix-up in the bookings.

One of the worst features of being on the road was the layover on open dates for which no engagement had been booked. A territory band attempting to broaden its scope of operation was probably most vulnerable in this situation for subsistance of its members was often a day to day affair, dependent on a nightly payoff. During the depression years of the early thirties, this was particularly true.

Among the memories I'll never forget was a week in the early part of 1931 when we pulled into Grand Island, Nebraska, on a Sunday night with no job booked until Thursday. After a little searching, we found a small upstairs hotel a couple of blocks from the Hotel Yancey, which was then the leading hotel in that city of 25,000 people. There were nine of us in the band and not very much money. Five of us registered into the hotel—the rest of us simply moved in.

At that time I was a kid not too long away from a much smaller town than Grand Island, and there were a lot of the facts of life no one had told me. That the occupants of the other rooms in the place were predominantly girls between the ages of 20 and 35 did not impress me as being anything other than an unusual coincidence. Neither did their extreme friendliness disturb the illusion that they probably worked at a nearby Woolworth's store or neighborhood cafe. It was not until we had pulled out of town on our way to North Platte that the conversation of some of the older boys woke me up to the fact that the possibility of their having been sales girls or waitresses was extremely limited.

But the problem of being "on panic" with no immediate jobs lined up was not restricted to the territory bands. Few were the big names who, on their way up, did not find themselves temporarily stranded in a tank town or sometimes even the largest cities with no work in sight and nothing coming in.

The Hal Kemp Band was no exception when it first left its North Carolina base to move into New York. Kemp's start had been made at the University of North Carolina, and a good many members of his orchestra had been with him there. Fred Waring became interested in them and it was under Waring's sponsorship that they made the New York move.

They came into the big city under what looked like ideal circumstances with an extended booking lined up at one of the major ballrooms, but something went wrong on opening night. The band got into a hassle with the ballroom manager and the next morning they were out of a job, a status which continued for several weeks. Old-timers with the band in later years could recall with amusement those weeks which were not at all funny while they lasted. Waring looked out for them until something else could be lined up, but there had to be some limitation to his support. He guaranteed their hotel bills, and every morning his manager met the Kemp sidemen in the hotel lobby, giving each of them $1.00 as his subsistence for that day. They didn't live very high on the hog, but they managed to survive until something else could be lined up.

Similar experiences could probably be recalled by most of the other leaders and their sidemen. The Negro bands, in particular, found the going rough on road trips. Unfortunately, with the possible exception of the bigger names, their problems did not disappear completely even in the heyday of the band boom. Some of the best bookings were not open to them, and even after they had made money they often could not spend it where they chose.

Anyone who has ever been associated with the music business in even a minor way will know what I mean when I say it's impossible to get it out of your blood. Consequently, during the late thirties and early forties, I found myself taking a fling at being a dance promoter and bringing name bands into Southern Oregon where at Grants Pass and Medford we caught the bands en route to or from the Pacific Northwest. Almost without exception, these bands were booked through one or another of the major agencies. But in the summer of 1940 we brought in a San Francisco Negro band billed as "Gene Coy and his Harlem Swing", booked through an advance agent on a straight percentage deal. It turned out to be a terrific dance band, but unfortunately no one knew this beforehand. Had we not had a date which was the night before a middle of the week holiday, we would doubtless have laid a big fat egg.

When the band hit town, the first problem we faced was getting them a place to sleep. The hotels where we normally routed our bands turned us down. Finally we got them into a rooming house

GENE COY was finding the one-nighter trail no bed of roses in the early 1940s.

near the railroad yards, and on to the bandstand on schedule.

From the first number, the response from the dance crowd indicated they liked what they heard, with their approval increasing as the evening wore on. Around midnight, I decided their music deserved an expression of appreciation in more usable form than applause and whistles, and sneaked a couple of fifths of gin onto the bandstand along with a few bottles of Seven-Up. Between midnight and the 2:00 a.m. quitting time, the momentum of the band built up to a point where neither they nor the dancers wanted to call it a night.

In the meantime, I was trying to figure out how fourteen musicians could possibly get that much mileage out of two fifths of gin. When I paid off Mr. Coy after the dance, I got my answer. They had ridden all day in their battered old bus without eating, having no money for food until they collected for playing the night's job.

As the number of bands enjoying "name" status increased during the mid and late thirties, the necessity of making road trips and playing one-nighters increased at the same time. The increase in the number of places able to support a big band for a one-nighter unfortunately did not keep pace. Consequently, the distance between one night's engagement and the next often involved as much as a five hundred mile jump with little time out for sleeping.

Whether or not distance was the direct cause accidents on the highways began to involve one band after another. In a great many of these, Lady Luck seemed to be looking out for her musical friends, for most got off with minor injuries. Not all of them were quite so fortunate.

The death of Hal Kemp in a head-on crash near Madera, California, shocked the music world and its followers in December of 1940. Kemp's friends had done their best to talk him out of making an overnight drive from Los Angeles to San Francisco. But he wanted to make sure everything was in order for his Mark Hopkins opening the next evening. Leaving immediately following his closing at the Cocoanut Grove seemed the only way to accomplish this. There was nothing unusual about what he was doing, since overnight trips were common travel practice in the band business at that time.

What Kemp perhaps may not have known was the treacherous nature of the road he was taking. During the winter months it is not uncommon for the San Joaquin Valley to be blanketed for days with what natives of the area describe as a "tule" fog. This was the condition encountered by Kemp during the early morning hours, and when the headlights of an oncoming car suddenly appeared coming towards him on his side of the road, there was no avoiding the crash which followed. Kenneth LaBahn, only member of the band traveling with him got off with minor injuries, but Kemp died in the Madera Hospital on December 21st in spite of all efforts to save him.

Two months later the crash of a bus on a Midwestern highway involved another well-known band and its popular leader in a near-fatal accident. This time it was Anson Weeks, who while appearing regularly at Chicago's College Inn, had been induced to accept an Iowa one-nighter on a Monday night, the only night of the week they were not busy on their regular job.

It was several years and a lot of operations later that Weeks told me about the tragic incident as he recalled it:

"For some reason that I could not put my finger on, something kept shouting at me not to play that date. Hal Kemp had been a good friend of mine, and the memory of what had happened to him was still fresh in my mind. I knew how treacherous those Midwest roads can get in February, and this was a longer round trip than I cared to make on them.

"So when the agency first came to me about the job, I quoted them a figure which I was sure no one in his right mind would pay me. Much to my surprise, it was accepted by the Iowa promoter.

Hal Kemp Dies Of Injuries In Madera Hospital

Noted Dance Band Leader Is Pneumonia Victim; Fresnan Faces Arrest

(McClatchy Newspapers Service)
MADERA (Madera Co.), Dec. 21.—James Harold Kemp, 36, better known as Hal Kemp, internationally famed dance band leader who was injured in a headon automobile crash Wednesday on the Golden State Highway near here, died at 6:30 o'clock this morning in the Dearborn Hospital from pneumonia caused by a punctured lung. Drs. Ray R. Dearborn and Coe Swift, the hospital physicians, said the lung was pierced by a broken rib.

Immediately following Kemp's death a warrant was issued for the arrest of Casimiro Azbarren, Fresno restaurant operator, who, according to the California Highway Patrol investigators, was attempting to pass Kemp's automobile without ~~~~~~nt clearance when the head-
~~~~~~~~~d. It was in-
~~~~~~nt~

An all-night drive ends tragically, 1940. — *Photo courtesy of McClatchey Newspapers.*

"Then I tried to get out of it by demanding the agency guarantee the chartered bus would be one of the latest models, of which there were only a few then on the road. When they assured me this would be provided, I had nothing to do but accept. It was too late to back out when the time came for the trip and they wheeled up with a beaten-up old model instead.

"When the crash came, I was dozing in one of the front seats. I was thrown out of the bus and somehow under it; then dragged until it came to a stop. My arm was badly mangled, and to a bandleader who also played piano, this looked like the end of a career."

It came near to being just that. During the next several years, Weeks was forced to disband for long periods while he underwent treatment and surgery. Unfortunately, some of these years were the most lucrative the business saw, and while his fellow bandleaders reaped the harvest, Weeks was forced to be almost a sideline observer.

During the next few months, other well-known leaders made headlines with transportation accidents. The Jimmy Lunceford Band was involved in a crack-up with several of its members injured. The Red Nichols band, making a one-night jump from Akron, Ohio, to Perth Amboy, New Jersey via bus was involved in a head-on crash with a passenger car. The same week, members of the Isham Jones' Orchestra (he had come out of retirement to try his hand once more) miraculously escaped injury when the station wagon in which they were cruising along a Georgia Highway left the road, totally demolishing it and destroying the band's instruments.

In the face of the rising casualty list, the Musicians Union finally took action to remove some of the apparent causes. It established maximum mileage permitted for one-day travel between jobs, and indicated it would approve no contracts which involved travel in excess of those limitations.

In the meantime, the nation had been precipitated into World War II. Before many wartime months had passed, the band business found its road trips involving headaches never previously dreamed of. The travel restrictions established by the War Department caught the dance orchestras squarely in the middle and it was a long while before any relief was granted them.

First of these to take effect was the 35 m.p.h. maximum speed limit intended to conserve gasoline and tires. This came in the summer of 1942 and made previously spaced one-nighters impossible. One trade journal story illustrated its effect on bookings already scheduled when the ruling took effect. The story concerned Blue Barron with a dance date in Washington, D. C. which would be concluded at 2:00 a.m. The next afternoon at 2:00 p.m. he was scheduled to open at a theater in New Haven, a date which also involved a network radio show broadcast coast to coast. The distance between the two jobs was in excess of 300 miles, meaning the band would have to sleep and dress on the bus in order to be on the theater's stage at show time.

Following the reduced speed limit came gasoline and tire rationing, with entertainment people in all categories well down the list of those whose travel was considered essential. For a while it appeared this would take out of circulation all those units whose practice had been to travel by private automobile.

The railroads were quickly swamped with business. Every train was overcrowded by transferring military personnel, families trying to keep up with military personnel, and civilians unable to get gasoline. Schedules became meaningless and bands who attempted to make their jumps by train found themselves arriving late for a lot of their dates. In many cases, the railroad was unable to get their instruments on the same train with the orchestra, or they could not get them transported to the ballroom after they had arrived in their destination city. In the Fall of 1942, the Jimmy Lunceford Band made a 500 mile trip by train, with only two of its twenty members able to find seats in the chaircar. The rest of them stood up for the entire trip.

Buses for charter were equally at a premium although eventually some relief was provided. Towards the end of 1942, the Office of Defense Transportation recognized the part played by the dance orchestras in morale building. Buses were made available as long as the band's schedule included not less than two U.S.O. shows weekly. Most of the leaders had volunteered their services for entertaining military personnel at the beginning of the war and were already exceeding these requirements.

Some of the buses provided were often virtually fugitives from the many scrap metal drives. Many bandleaders considered "prima donnas" before the war now had to adjust their travel standards or stay off the road. Actually, the majority of them took it in stride and considered it a minor inconvenience during a period when others were making greater sacrifices. Although the situation remained virtually the same for the duration of the war, somehow everyone managed to maintain a schedule, and when it was all over get a lot of laughs out of some of their experiences.

Legally or not, a lot of the fans cooperated to help keep their favorite bands on the road. Ration stamps were required for the purchase of gasoline, but during the course of an evening, enough of these usually could be promoted from the crowd to insure the next day's driving.

Joe Venuti could always be counted on to get a laugh out of any situation, and gas rationing did not dim his sense of humor. While checking out of an Omaha hotel at the end of an engagement there he ran into Russ Morgan in the lobby coming in to replace him. After the usual greetings, Morgan asked:

"Where are you headed from here, Joe?"

"We're going into the Baker Hotel in Dallas," Joe replied.

"Dallas," said Morgan, "that's quite a jump. How are you fixed for gasoline stamps?"

"Who needs gas stamps," was Venuti's retort, "Take a look at the map, it's all downhill, isn't it?"

Crowded hotel conditions created another serious problem all during the war years and I particularly remember chatting with Stan Kenton on this subject during a one-night stand in Sacramento on a Friday night in early 1944. At that time, Kenton was the regular band on the Bob Hope Show which was aired every Tuesday night, usually from some service camp. The broadcast for the next week was to originate from an Army base in Tennessee, with two one-nighters booked for the band en route.

Kenton and his orchestra were traveling in automobiles, and in order to make the schedule would have to start driving immediately following the Sacramento job. They had not been able to secure hotel reservations for any of the nights to be spent on the trip, and were anticipating the necessity of sleeping in their cars.

When the Hope show came on the air the next Tuesday night, I fully expected to hear some other band furnishing the music, but they had made it, as the distinctive Kenton style in the opening

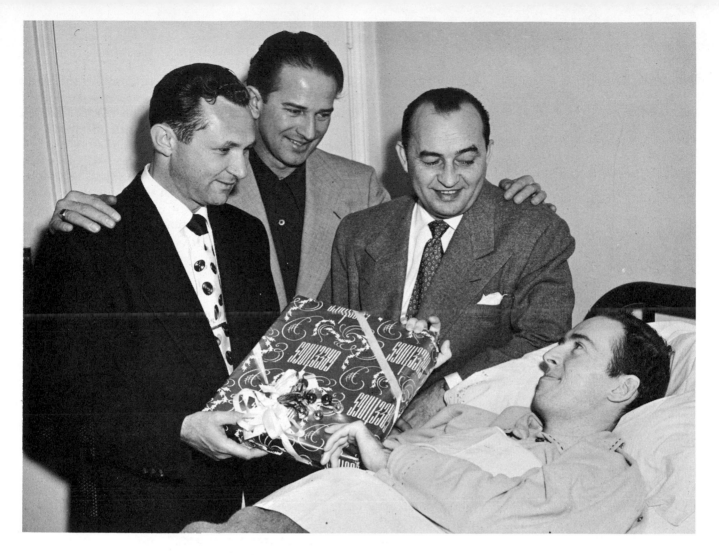

FREDDY MARTIN visits BARCLAY ALLEN in his hospital bed after he had been paralyzed in a 1949 accident while driving all night to his next engagement. — *Photo courtesy of Freddy Martin.*

number clearly indicated. Halfway through the show, however, Hope announced that Stan himself was not on the stand. He was in a local hospital suffering from an acute attack of appendicitis with which he had been stricken during the hard drive.

The hazards of a long road trip took many other forms, too, as one well-known Chicago leader discovered in the mid-forties. This particular leader had strong feelings regarding the comparative virtues of a bank account versus cash in a safety deposit box. He favored the latter arrangement and, consequently, most of his savings were put away in that manner. As is the case with most married men, the box was taken in his name and that of his wife.

Things were going quite well for the maestro and the nest egg in the neighborhood bank con-

tinued to pile up. Those who told the story later maintained that it had grown to approximately $150,000. when the band was booked on a swing to the West Coast, including one-nighters, a location job, and participation in a movie. It was to be nearly four months before they would return to their Midwestern base of operations.

Bouncing along in the bus with the rest of the group was the band vocalist, a very cute and shapely brunette. Perhaps all was not serene with the leader's home life, or perhaps the trip was just too long. At any rate, the farther they travelled, the cuter the brunette seemed to be, and eventually he could not resist letting her know that he would like to consider her more than just an employee.

Somewhere on a lonely one-nighter in the Pacific Northwest, they decided they were meant for

When success came to RALPH FLANAGAN he bought his own plane, flying it from one engagement to the next while the band travelled by bus. — *Photo courtesy of Barney McDevitt.*

one another, and that he should get a divorce to permit them to marry. Being an honest and forthright individual, he felt it unfair to wait until the end of the trip to break the news to his wife in Chicago. Consequently, he dashed off a letter telling her how he felt, suggesting that mature adults such as they should be able to work out a solution quietly and quickly.

The little woman at home was quite capable of making decisions and taking action as she now demonstrated. She saw no reason to force him to continue a marriage he wanted to terminate, so by return mail gave her consent to the divorce necessary to make him happy. The route to the post office must have taken her right past the bank, or at least near enough to remind her of something which he had apparently forgotten. The safety deposit box had two keys, and with the use of the one in her possession she picked up the accumulated cash to compensate her for the loss of his companionship. When he returned from the trip and discovered what had happened, he was fit to be tied, but there was nothing he could do about it.

When the war ended, the world looked rosy for everyone in the business, particularly the leaders.

Travel restrictions were lifted, gasoline rationing was terminated, and buses for charter were readily available. Returning service men made sidemen plentiful, eliminating the necessity of constantly outbidding someone else to get qualified musicians. The demand for name bands was never greater for one-nighters, theaters, and hotels. New ballrooms were built as restrictions on materials were made easier.

But this happy condition lasted less than a year.

During the war all commodities and services had been subject to price ceilings regulated by O.P.A. Now these also underwent adjustments and were soon removed entirely. Gone were the $2.50 hotel rooms and the ability to eat three meals in a restaurant for $3.00. The cost of chartering a bus went upward from its prewar level of $.40 per mile to an eventual $.75.

The upward spiral of prices was equally hard on the cash customers who had been lining up at the box office to hear and see their favorite orchestras. With their cost of living up, they simply had less to spend for entertainment. When the attendance began to drop, band buyers found it more and more difficult to show a profit on a name band appearance involving a heavy guarantee.

Hampton's Bus Driver Remains On Critical List

George Alliston, 45, Newark, N. J., driver of the chartered bus which blew a tire and plunged into an arroyo near Socorro Saturday, injuring 21, remained in critical condition in Presbyterian Hospital Tuesday.

Meanwhile, band leader Lionel Hampton, whose troupe was aboard the chartered bus, was transferred Tuesday from the Truth and Consequences Hospital to St. Joseph's Hospital. He suffered a broken ankle in the accident. Also transferred to St. Joseph's Hospital from the T-C Hospital was Ed Preston, 25, Cleveland, who was still suffering shock.

Three other members of the Hampton organization were reported in good condition at St. Joseph's Hospital. Others were hospitalized at Belen, T-C and Socorro.

The accident factor was not eliminated by modern equipment, as indicated by this crash on a New Mexico highway involving the Lionel Hampton band in the mid-1950s.

Once on the road the KENTON OR-CHESTRA reads, plays cards and enjoys a snack while Maestro Kenton kibitzes.

— *Courtesy of Capitol Records.*

BUTCH STONE, Les Brown's comedy vocalist and sax man, demonstrates his dislike for flying by kissing the ground when the plane lands after a flight which was somewhat less than smooth.

— *Courtesy of Barney McDevitt.*

One-nighter promoters had made a lot of money during the 1941 through 1946 period, and most of them could see little reason to lose it back in the same manner. After a few promotions on which they took a loss, a great many of them decided to get out of the business. So, too, did theater operators, thus eliminating a very lucrative part of any extended road tour.

Now the bandleader was caught in the middle of a situation about which he could do little. His own cost of traveling made it imperative that he receive high guarantees. The decline in the public's ability to pay increased admission prices which those guarantees made necessary reduced day by day the number of band buyers willing to pay his price. It became increasingly difficult to get top musicians to go on the road except at the high salaries they needed to survive the expense of living away from home and still support their families while they were away.

The situation grew steadily worse with some semblance of previous prosperity existing through the late forties. But as the early fifties moved along, the rate of decline became more rapid. One-nighters became fewer and fewer, automatically stepping up the travel distance between them. By the mid-fifties, they had practically become a Thursday through Sunday operation, with bookers reluctant to try to entice a crowd out on the other nights of the week. This meant that the traveling band was faced with costly lay-overs, with no work available on an average of three nights out of the seven.

Only the biggest and best established bands could do better than that, and only the most hardy could survive. During the late fifties, the number of dance bands hitting the road with any regularity was decimated. Without private dates on their schedules they too would have had time on their hands. In some cases, distances between dates made travel by plane both necessary and economically feasible.

And so it would seem for those who were seeking an answer to the question, "What happened to the big dance bands" the part played by basic economics should be given the credit it deserves.

For even though the road trips involved many inconveniences and even hazards, it was here that the bandleader made his big money from personal appearances. Location jobs in hotels and ballrooms were taken for prestige, air time build-up, or to give a travel-weary group of musicians a rest. When he wanted to pick up some real money in minimum time he went on tour. When the market which he found for his product on those tours died, that which we all called the "big band business" died with it.

It came a long way from the $150.00 one-nighters played by Joe Kayser and his fellow pioneers of the early 1920s. Guarantees moved steadily upward during the twenties, and then suffered a serious setback during the depression years of the early thirties. A strong upsurge of the business sparked by Goodman's success in 1934 touched off a spiral which had much longer life. The leader's asking price and his ability to get it came to be in direct proportion to his position on radio and records.

In terms of averages, prices reached an all-time high during the boom years of World War II and immediately after. There was no one who could not command a guarantee of $1,000. for a one-nighter, with the privilege of taking 60% of the gate if that figure were greater. Benny Goodman, Harry James, Tommy Dorsey, Artie Shaw, and a few other top names were signing contracts at $4,000.00 nightly by the time the war ended. The first time I caught the James Band on a one-nighter, the box office receipts were in excess of $11,000. of which he took 60% after amusement tax was taken off the top.

These figures are impressive, and additionally so because of the number of bands simultaneously in that bracket. However, the business had seen a few leaders in previous years able to command guarantees even higher and more out of proportion to the rest of the field. During the peak of Rudy Vallee's popularity he received as much as $6500 nightly, and Paul Whiteman at about the same time was getting in excess of $5,000. A little later, many of Lombardo's dates were taken at around that same figure.

But all this occurred during the years when the business was building towards its peak or had reached it. The "Era of the Big Bands" is generally meant by most who speak of it to be that period starting its build-up in the early thirties and its tobogganing decline just after the mid-forties. The biggest success story of the band business actually occurred after the business had been quite officially pronounced dead and the post-mortems were being held to see what killed it.

This story was not written by a new discovery, for the music business had practically quit dis-

The band business, or what remained of it, goes modern as Les Brown
and his orchestra are the first to fly by jet from coast to coast in 1959.
— *Photo courtesy of Don Kramer.*

covering newcomers. Instead, it was Lawrence
Welk, who had been around as long as Lombardo
and not too many years less than Whiteman. Since
his start in 1925, he had seen many musical trends
come and go, a lot of leaders rise to prominence
with these trends, and fade away with them. During the years his original format changed little except that he added to the size of his band. He
continued to maintain that a danceable tempo was
necessary, and with it went steadily along enjoying success so moderate it created no great impression on anyone. He was often ridiculed by his
contemporaries as a "Mickey Mouse" bandleader.

The tide turned in the early fifties after an extended engagement on the West Coast. He followed this with an Eastern tour resulting in heavy
grosses everywhere he appeared. Trade journal

coverage of that tour made interesting reading
later on, for unable to believe what was happening, the heavy turnouts were credited to lucky
timing with other events, etc.

But Welk returned to the Coast and a television show which by the mid-fifties made him
America's biggest musical attraction. He became
so in demand for personal appearances that he
was able to ask and get minimum guarantees of
$10,000 nightly, with an almost unheard of per-
centage privilege of 70 per cent. Usually his guarantees ran well above that figure, and for concert
appearances, he sometimes walked off with as
much as $50,000 for a single date.

The long years of many rugged road trips were
paying off handsomely for Welk, but for most of
his fellow bandleaders, they had ceased to exist.

Best wishes — Bing

THE RHYTHM BOYS — Al Rinker, Bing Crosby and Harry Barris. — *Photo courtesy of Gus Angelo.*

* * *

Study in Sinatra:—Frank Sinatra is doing a pretty quick job of winning over Tommy Dorsey's fans and making new ones for himself. Like his novel idea of asking all those who request his picture to send theirs in return. (Must have an interesting collection!) Poised and friendly in appearance, which links strongly with a very capable voice. Gets the biggest thrills from ex-boss Harry James' trumpeting, Dorsey's trombone solos and Bob Eberle's tone, quality and perfect pitch. Thinks Bobby Byrne has the coming band (yippee!) and's been trying to meet Byrne's vocalist, Jimmy Palmer, for ages, and vice versa. Proudly displays a wedding band and boasts of the Mrs. and an expected addition to the family in June. Lad's full of pipe dreams with a collection of over 30—not dreams, pipes! Nice guy, Sinatra!

* * *

Johnny Drake is doing local club dates until his union card comes through and he can rejoin Dick Stabile as featured singer. . . . Connie Haines joined that newsy man (careful of misprints), T. Dorsey, directly following his appearance at the Paramount Theatre. That makes two James' ex's singing in the band. (Harry's a good judge in the other man's opinion). . . . On Kay Kyser's recent tour Ish Kabibble stole the show—when nobody was looking! . . . Bobby Byrne's band, youngest and newest to play at Glen Island Casino, opened there on May 14.

News of the vocalists was read by an avid public in 1940. This clipping from June issue of Swing magazine.

At left is the great MILDRED BAILEY who sang with Whiteman, later with Red Norvo.

284

The Vocalists Made Their Contribution

IN THE EARLY 50s Frank Sinatra was reported to have stated in an interview that over-emphasis on singers contributed to killing the band business. Coming from one who got his start as a band vocalist and who did much to pave the way for others to find success as a single attraction, this was a rather surprising comment.

Perhaps, however, Sinatra was right, for there are others who shared that opinion. But neither can it be denied that vocalists and vocal groups did much to assist many of the biggest name bandleaders to attract the attention which brought about their initial success and helped them to maintain it.

Sinatra may in fact be one of the best examples of this contribution. Tommy Dorsey was already a big name when Frank joined the band but during the three years he stayed there the Dorsey band was a richer musical organization because of his presence. Remember some of those great Sinatra vocals on such records as "This Love of Mine", "Neani", "I'll Never Smile Again"?

Like Jack Teagarden's entry into the musical big leagues, the Sinatra story is full of people who claim to have discovered him, or were there when his big break came. If they were all true, he would have been "discovered" a hundred times. Actually he "discovered" himself and sold his way into the newly-formed Harry James orchestra. There he shared the bandstand microphone with Connie Haines, who would also later become a member of the Dorsey band. Frank's leave-taking from Harry James was on a friendly basis — a situation which apparently did not exist when he left Dorsey in early 1943. James waived the contract between the two of them. Dorsey was not so inclined and continued to take a healthy cut of Sinatra's earnings as a single attraction until Frank could buy his way out of the pact.

Sinatra may have become the best known of all Dorsey vocalists but he was not the first. From the time he left brother Jimmy, Tommy had featured top caliber singers, including such greats as Jack Leonard and Edythe Wright. Leonard's departure for military service created the opportunity for Sinatra to move in.

Who was the first band vocalist? You can get a thousand answers to that question. During the early years of the band era little emphasis was placed on singing. When it was felt a vocal chorus might contribute something to the cause, one of the instrumentalists simply moved up front and handled it. Even Paul Whiteman's "Rhythm Boys" were required to hold violins equipped with rubber strings and go through the motions of playing them. In his book "Call Me Lucky" Bing Crosby emphasizes his opinion that the chance to join the Whiteman orchestra was the luckiest break he ever got, thereby pointing up the fact that the contribution to success was a two-way street — good vocalists helped the bandleader and band singing experience launched the career of many a big show business star.

Crosby also recalls in his book that during the early twenties male singers with dance groups were often subjected to much ridicule by fellow members of their own sex, probably largely jealousy stemming from an indication that their dates were impressed by the singer's personality. When Rudy Vallee became the nation's singing sensation in the late twenties he too encountered a great deal of the same reaction and, like Bing, was often hard-pressed to hold his temper when the needling became too personal. But eventually this attitude disappeared and Crosby and Vallee were not only accepted as great talents but were widely imitated by other singers.

Of these two Crosby was the first to begin his singing career but Vallee was the first to enjoy big success. By the early thirties they were both identified as crooners and in one of his early movies Crosby did a song entitled "Learn To Croon" which became a national hit and was one of the finest tunes of that period.

285

DALE EVANS when she was the vocalist with Anson Weeks' orchestra.
— *Photo courtesy of Anson Weeks.*

PERRY COMO who gave up barbering to sing with Ted Weems. — *Photo courtesy of Freddie Large.*

RUSS COLUMBO, below, whose singing style closely resembled Crosby's. — *Courtesy of Gus Angelo.*

Crosby and "The Rhythm Boys" had come to a parting of the ways with Whiteman in 1930 and joined Gus Arnheim at the Cocoanut Grove. Arnheim had a star-studded organization including, in addition to the "Rhythm Boys", Donald Novis and a beautiful girl singer named Loyce Whiteman, who later married Harry Barris. In the violin section was Russ Columbo who also sang and who eventually developed a style so closely resembling Crosby's that listeners could hardly tell which one was on the air. His unfortunate death in 1934 put an end to Columbo's career at a time when his future appeared very bright. Before this occurred both he and Crosby had left Arnheim and set out on individual roads in search of bigger things.

By this time vocalists of both sexes were an accepted part of any band enjoying a degree of prominence and success. The bigger ones also featured girl trios, a practice which expanded as the business grew. Fred Waring had the Lane Sisters, (Lola, Priscilla, and Rosemary), Gus Arnheim used the "Three Cheers", Ted FioRito called his "The Debutantes". FioRito also featured for a few years a beautiful blonde whose presence did much to enhance the band's reception — Miss Betty Grable.

Miss Grable soon went on to greater success in motion pictures. So too did many other band vocalists. Dorothy Lamour was spotted by Hollywood scouts while singing with her husband Herbie Kay's orchestra. Marilyn Maxwell had been Marvel Maxwell with Ted Weems. Frances Langford, Alice Faye, Kay St. Germaine, Georgia Gibbs, Connie Haines, Janet Blair, Jo Stafford, Anita O'Day, Helen O'Connell, Dale Evans, Ginny Simms, Peggy Lee, Doris Day, Harriet Hilliard, Kay Starr, Jane Russell, Betty Hutton, Rosemary Clooney, Dorothy Collins, Gale Robbins, Eydie Gormé and dozens of others got the experience and attention necessary for success in the rarefied stratosphere of movies, radio, records, and television by first singing with a dance orchestra.

The number of male stars who came up along the same route is doubtless just as large. It would include Tony Martin, Dick Powell, Nick Lucas, Johnny Desmond, Andy Russell, Perry Como, Dick Haymes, Art Lund, Mel Torme, Merve Griffin, Buddy Clarke, Tony Bennett, Art Carney, and even Gene Barry, better known as "Bat Masterson", who got his start singing with the Teddy Powell orchestra.

287

TED FIORITO with his most famous vocalist, Betty Grable.

THE DEBUTANTES and MUZZY MARCELLINO below, were featured by Ted FioRito for several years. (This picture 1934). — *Both photos courtesy of Muzzy Marcellino.*

EDYTHE WRIGHT was the featured vocalist with Tommy Dorsey's first great band. — *Photo courtesy of Barney McDevitt.*

FRANK SINATRA and CONNIE HAINES, Harry James' vocalists when this 1939 photo was made, stroll the Atlantic City Boardwalk with fellow band member JACK PALMER.
> — *Photo courtesy of Fred Monte.*

TED WEEMS and MARVEL MAXWELL who later became Marilyn Maxwell.
> — *Photo courtesy of Coliseum Ballroom.*

BETTY HUTTON—CASA MANANA, 1938

Lopez Vocalist Looks Like Real "Personality"

Beatty Hutton, a young and pretty blond doing a jitterbug trick singing act at the Casa Manana, New York, in addition to vocalizing with the Vincent Lopez Band is a cinch show stopper. She uncorks terrific vitality (reminiscent of Martha Raye), sing-shouting rhythm numbers of the *Old Man Mose* type. Looks like a real personality discovery. With proper build-up she'd be sensational on the screen.

DICK HAYMES followed Sinatra into both the Harry James and Tommy Dorsey orchestras. — *Photo courtesy of Fred Monte.*

"WEE BONNIE BAKER" the "Oh Johnny" girl vocalist with Orrin Tucker. — *Photo courtesy of the Hollywood Palladium.*

At right, GINNY SIMMS and HARRY BABBITT, stars of the Kay Kyser band, 1937. — *Courtesy of Larry Duran.*

HELEN FORREST sang with both Goodman and Harry James, then went into radio as a single. — *Photo courtesy of Fred Monte.*

Jo STAFFORD sang with Tommy Dorsey in the early 1940s, left in 1943 to become a single. — *Photo courtesy of Hollywood Palladium.*

The famous PIED PIPERS when they were star attractions with Tommy Dorsey.
— *Photo courtesy of Hollywood Palladium.*

RAY EBERLE, Glenn Miller's featured male singer. — *Photo courtesy of Don Haynes.*

MARION HUTTON, vocal star of the Glenn Miller band.
— *Photo courtesy of Don Haynes.*

PAULA KELLY AND THE MODERNAIRES, Glenn Miller's
great vocal quintet. — *Photo courtesy of Don Haynes.*

ANITA BOYER, left, worked for Tommy Dorsey, Leo
Reisman, Artie Shaw, Jimmy Dorsey and Harry James.
— *Photo courtesy of Hollywood Palladium.*

Usually the pay scale for a featured vocalist was slightly less than that earned by a featured instrumentalist. Crosby, Barris, and Rinker were each drawing $150 weekly from Whiteman in 1928 while the pay for sidemen ranged from $175 to $350. In the case of either it was no doubt the highest in the business at the time, for Whiteman believed in paying well. Sinatra worked for Dorsey in the early forties for $75 weekly and this was probably as good or better than most of his contemporaries, for Tommy was one of the top names at the time.

Jimmy Dorsey, like his younger brother, gave his vocalists a chance to share in the spotlight. Bob Eberly joined the band shortly after the brothers formed separate organizations, with Helen O'Connell coming in later. These two made a combination which was hard to beat and it was their performances on records which contributed greatly to Jimmy's moving up into the top brackets in 1941. When Helen retired in 1942 she was replaced by Kitty Kallen. Miss Kallen joined Harry James when Eberly went into the service and somehow Jimmy's band was never quite the same from that point on.

Many of Glenn Miller's best records featured Ray Eberle (Bob's brother) and the Modernaires. Benny Goodman did not put the same emphasis on singers but did cut a substantial amount of wax on which the work of Helen Ward, Louise Tobin, Helen Forrest, and, later, Peggy Lee was an asset of no small dimension. Goodman seldom used a male vocalist — among those who did appear with him the best known was Art Lund.

On the other side of the coin there were several leaders who did not support the popular theory that having an attractive female on the stand was a necessity. Throughout his entire career Freddy Martin resisted the trend with the exception of his television appearances. The Casa Loma Band had no female vocalists until the early forties, at which time a trio was added for a short time. They were followed by Eugenie Baird who went on to become a regular on Bing Crosby's radio show.

Sammy Kaye was slow in adding girl singers to his group and supposedly fired his first one a few days after hiring her for the reason that she was taller than he. Guy Lombardo, had only one in nearly forty years as a maestro and in that instance kept the money in the family by using his sister Rose Marie. Jan Garber had dozens of them over

KAY WEBER did vocal chores for the Dorsey Brothers' orchestra and then spent several years with Bob Crosby's band. — *Photo courtesy Barney McDevitt.*

BOB EBERLY, below, was featured with the Jimmy Dorsey band. — *Courtesy of Hollywood Palladium.*

LEE BENNETT sang for twelve years with the Jan Garber orchestra. — *Photo courtesy of Jan Garber.*

KITTY KALLEN sang first with Jack Teagarden, then Jimmy Dorsey and Harry James. — *Photo courtesy of Harry James.*

Below, veteran vocalist ANITA O'DAY is pictured with Stan Kenton and Capitol Records prexy, Glenn Wallichs. — *Courtesy of Gary Gray, Hollywood Palladium.*

HELEN O'CONNELL below, whose singing contributed greatly to Jimmy Dorsey's record success in the early 40s. — *Photo courtesy Barney McDevitt.*

293

the years but, although he recorded on every major label, he seldom used a girl vocalist on a record.

The great Negro bands produced much fine vocal talent, both male and female. For years Ivy Anderson was as much a part of the Ellington band as Sonny Greer's drums or Johnny Hodges' alto sax. Ella Fitzgerald was so important to the Chick Webb orchestra that she took over as leader when Webb passed away. Billie Holliday began her career as a band vocalist and Dinah Washington got her start with Lionel Hampton. Lena Horne will be remembered best for her singing and recording with Charlie Barnet and Artie Shaw but it was with the Noble Sissle orchestra that she broke into the business.

The use of larger vocal groups was started by Whiteman and Waring but really became a trend in the late thirties. Horace Heidt, perhaps following the pattern set by Waring, and with a sponsored radio show to support the cost, was featuring a large mixed chorus group by that time. It was with Heidt that the King Sisters, four lovely girls from Salt Lake City, first attracted national attention. Also in the Heidt band at the time was guitarist Alvino Rey and since he was married to Louise King the quartet went along with him when he left to form his own orchestra about 1940. Heidt will also be remembered for "Donna and her Don

Juans," a group which included Ronnie Kemper and Art Carney.

The success of Tommy Dorsey with his "Pied Pipers" and Glenn Miller with "The Modernaires" influenced other leaders to augment the vocal department. Throughout the forties trios and foursomes in addition to the featured singles were considered almost necessary to make the musical organization complete. A lot of new groups were formed for this purpose, some of them moving from one band to another intact. A few in an attempt to follow the pattern set by "The Modernaires" and "Pied Pipers," tried their hand at becoming recording and night club attractions on their own.

When the band business recession became a full scale decline the necessity of reducing the payroll usually made the vocal groups number one on the casualty list. By the mid-fifties there were very few leaders who could still maintain a full band plus vocal groups and several had de-emphasized vocals completely.

The question of whether the contribution of the vocalists was greater than the possibility that they distracted from the primary function of providing dance music is still being argued. But there is definitely no question that in the memory of the fans the vocalists have a very warm and secure spot.

HERB JEFFRIES was a headliner with Duke Ellington for many years.

JIMMY RUSHING was Count Basie's great blues singer.
— *Both photos Courtesy of Barney McDevitt.*

RUTH ROBIN was the Phil Harris star in the early 1940s. — *Photo courtesy of M.C.A.*

Lovely PEGGY LEE. — *Courtesy of Barney McDevitt.*

Below, the FOUR KING SISTERS (with Alvino Rey's orchestra), 1943. — *Photo courtesy of Del Courtney.*

EILEEN WILSON sang with Will Osborne and Les Brown before joining the Hit Parade cast on TV. — *Photo courtesy of Don Kramer.*

ROSEMARY CLOONEY became a star after working with Tony Pastor. — *Photo courtesy Hollywood Palladium.*

DORIS DAY at left, singing with the Les Brown band. —*Photo courtesy of Evan Aiken.*

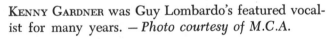

KENNY GARDNER was Guy Lombardo's featured vocalist for many years. — *Photo courtesy of M.C.A.*

BETTY BROWNELL dressed up the Henry Busse bandstand. — *Photo courtesy Barney McDevitt.*

THE YOUNG SISTERS were featured with Ralph Flanagan in the early 50s.
— *Photo courtesy of Hollywood Palladium.*

STUART WADE was another of Freddy Martin's male stars. — *Photo courtesy of Freddy Martin.*

HARRY PRIME when he was Ralph Flanagan's male vocalist. — *Photo courtesy of G.A.C.*

EYDIE GORME's singing career began with Tex Beneke's orchestra. — *Photo courtesy of M.C.A.*

KAY STARR, right, worked both for Charlie Barnet and Joe Venuti. — *Photo courtesy of Capitol Records.*

VAUGHN MONROE and his "Moon Maids." — *Photo courtesy of Vaughn Monroe.*

TOMMY MERCER served several years on the Ray Anthony bandstand. — *Courtesy of Hollywood Palladium.*

"Petrillo says we gotta put two more men on this drum."

Cartoon by Bandel Linn is from an unknown source.

A 1963 news story analyses of Lawrence Welk's success.

— *Courtesy Los Angeles Times.*

In 1955, Lawrence Welk made his first nationwide telecast over ABC network. He had been on locally for two years from the Aragon Ballroom. The dance emporium has since been rechristened the Pavilion. But it was with the start of his 1955 shows that Welk became the national bellwether of the dance bands.

The Aragon soon became the mecca for dancers. The teenagers came, too. Generally, because they were with their parents. Rock and roll was rampant, however, and that's all anyone heard about in connection with youngsters.

Yet this same rock and roll had an insidious quality that was beginning to affect the younger set. Rock and roll had, if nothing else, a beat. And like a John Philip Sousa march or the Pied Piper, it was hard for anyone not to tap his toe to rock and roll and follow it to some extent.

Welk, meanwhile, flourished and so did the Aragon. But the Big Bands were having a hard time meeting expenses. Two top band leaders who were hurting financially met at the Hollywood Brown Derby for lunch one day a couple of years ago. The phenomenal rise of Welk cropped up in the conversation. One of them was bitter over the resurgence of "squaresville" music. The other, older and wiser, commented:

"It's our own fault. We started to play for our own amusement and took the girl out of the boy's arms. Welk put the girl back in his arms."

●

In Summary

"WHATEVER HAPPENED TO the dance bands?"

This was the question posed in the opening chapter and in answer to which a lot of opinions have been given by many people in and out of the trade.

Each individual theory has some degree of evidence to support it.

The economic conditions which existed after the war were generally good. Yet the competition for the spenders' dollar was unusually keen as a great deal of what might formerly have been entertainment money was diverted to buying more tangible things. Spiralling living costs further depleted it and at the same time created travel costs for bands on the road which could only be supported by high guarantees with more operators finding themselves unable to pay these as time went on.

The amusement and cabaret taxes probably did, in many cases, make enough difference to make a prospective spender decide to stay home.

The disc jockeys were certainly a live part of the subject. They were the primary medium through which the "Artists" who replaced bands on the jukeboxes and in the home record collection were built. It would seem, however, that they could have contributed, during the same period, just as much to the building of bands unless something was lacking in the cooperation between the leaders and the jockeys which would have encouraged their support.

Television doubtless contributed to the decline, and in many ways. It made it easy for people to stay home rather than go out. It brought the whole world and its important people into the living room, thereby making top caliber entertainment commonplace. But more directly, it eliminated nighttime radio as a home entertainment medium, simultaneously killing the band remote broadcasts which had once been a very potent band-building medium. Had television been able to perform a similar function, no damage would

have resulted. If nothing else, its unwieldiness made it generally impractical for regular dance location pick-up. The most generous thing which can be said is that it did nothing to build any but a small few of the bandleaders.

In addition to these somewhat generalized theories, individual leaders had the finger of accusation pointed in their direction. Foremost among these was Stan Kenton who periodically throughout the fifties was credited with killing the dance business. Kenton quite readily accepted the blame, but pointed out that he had never either pretended or intended to be a dance band. He blamed operators for billing him as a dance attraction despite his own efforts to schedule nothing but concert performances. He usually topped off such discussions with a few "to the point" comments regarding the contributions of a lot of other people to its demise.

During the span of the declining decade, many of the people who had been part of the era were questioned on the subject and were quoted as having expressed these opinions—

Paul Whiteman—"When they started featuring singers and singing groups and encouraging the crowds to line up in front of the stand instead of dancing, I warned them they were on the wrong track. This may sound strange when you remember that I was the first leader to feature singers. However, I insisted that all of them sing in dance tempo so that they would not distract or interrupt the dancing."

Tom Archer, one of the Middle West's most successful ballroom operators—"I could write a book on why the business died, but I'd lose a lot of friends if I did. Just let my comment be simple—there weren't enough people still playing dance music."

Will Osborne, veteran bandleader—"During the war, good sidemen were so scarce that leaders were forced to outbid one another for their services. In order to keep them once they had them, they started to permit the musical tastes of these men to subordinate those of the leader. In many cases, the band's style was completely altered to accommodate the ideas of the musicians.

"In most cases the style which resulted was not conducive to dancing—dancing became a lost art. The younger generation never learned to dance—they weren't hearing dance music.

"Somehow when the war was over the old spirit couldn't be recaptured and to a large degree this was because there were not enough top musicians around interested in working at the job the way the leaders wanted it done.

"To state it more simply, the business died largely because its people stopped working at it. Their interests died before the public's."

Freddy Martin—"We lost an awful lot of dancers in the years immediately following World War II. The business cannot be revived until we can somehow rekindle that interest."

Art Kassel—"A lot of people blamed television for killing us off. No doubt it did play a part, but it wouldn't have needed to kill us as quickly as it did.

"Basically a lot of these things which affected us developed because the attitude of our unions was at fault. The regulations involved in remote broadcasts made radio stations welcome the simplicity of using disc jockeys. The jockeys did not play band records, but built "artists" instead. This, too, was due in large part to the trouble given by the union to recording companies as a result of which they started to exploit something other than bands."

Lawrence Welk—"Our own success speaks for itself. I believe it came because we never forgot it was the dancers who paid our salaries and we always tried to give them what they came to hear.

"That doesn't answer the question of why the business, compared to what it used to be, amounts to little or nothing. It seems to me it died because people quit really working at it. When I got started it was something we all worked hard at because it was a profession we all aspired to. Now it must have lost its appeal. Too many of the people who are in it now just

want to take out what they can make without putting any real effort into it."

Barney McDevitt — veteran publicity and promotion man — "Bands started playing for themselves instead of the public. No one could dance to what most of them played.

"In addition too many of them tried to coast along on things they had done years before. I know leaders who are semi-active today who brag about not having put a new arrangement into their libraries in fifteen years."

Guy Lombardo—"For us the slump never occurred. We've always had more work offered us than we could handle and we still get good money for it.

"A lot of musicians and even some trade people have made fun of our music over the years. But about ten years ago when people first started to be concerned about the dance band's future I was asked to give some advice to new bandleaders through one of the trade papers. It was my contention then and it is now that bandleaders should not attempt to be educators. People who come to see us pay to be entertained —not educated!"

Meanwhile Stan Kenton was still very much an active participant in the music business but playing the concerts he had always wanted to do, after a brief concession to dance music in a tour made in 1952. His statement in a 1960 newspaper story that the big dance bands had, with the exception of a very few, completely disappeared was all too true. So, too, was his comment that "not many people are interested in coming to a ballroom and dancing any more."

In retrospect it would seem that a lot of people in the business would have done well to heed Kenton's 1950 comments as to what ailed the business. Among other things he had blamed the agencies and operators for having handled all bands in the same manner regardless of style. He pointed out then that only disaster could come from booking bands not styled for dancing into spots catering only to dancers.

In a sense Lombardo and Kenton were saying the same thing, even though their language differed. It was a long time since the 1920s during which any group playing popular music was called a "jazz band" regardless of style. Now two very widely separated styles had been created. Modern

Dick Williams
MIRROR NEWS ENTERTAINMENT EDITOR

JUNE 1958

Bands May Come Back, Says Paul Whiteman

One of the spectacular changes in the entertainment business in the last decade has been the collapse of the popular bands and the rise of the solo singer. The Elvis Presleys, Frankie Laines and Doris Days have largely eliminated the "name bands" which once roved up and down the land.

Many reasons have been advanced to account for the demise of famous old outfits such as Tommy and Jimmy Dorsey, Glenn Gray and the Casa Loma orchestra, Larry Clinton, Benny Goodman, Bob Crosby and others of the swing era of the 30s and 40s.

But Paul Whiteman, who was press-agented into the title of "King of Jazz" back in the 1920s and rode to fame with his concert version of George Gershwin's "Rhapsody in Blue," has his own original reason for the change and it makes sense.

Says Whiteman, who predated all of the bands and has outlived most of them: "I told them, 'boys, you're digging your own graves' when they started featuring their singers and got the crowds ganged around the stand to listen instead of dance. They began to quit playing dance numbers."

Whiteman, who formed his first dance band in 1918 at the Fairmont Hotel in San Francisco, was the first maestro to feature singers. His first ones were Morton Downey and Mildred Bailey.

PAUL WHITEMAN

"But I made them sing in dance tempo," Paul recalled when he dropped by my office for a gab session the other afternoon. "I didn't want to do anything to stop the dancing."

Although he's a little heavier around the midriff and a little more sparsely haired on top, Whiteman with his tiny brush mustache and rotund figure looks much the same as he has for the last 20 or 30 years. He is now one of the stars of "New Faces of 1928," a unique night club venture which comes into the Moulin Rouge tomorrow night after a highly successful Las Vegas run.

Costarring with him are other personalities who became famous for the first time in the 20s including Fifi D'Orsay, Buster Keaton, Harry Richman and Rudy Vallee.

PAUL WHITEMAN expresses his opinions on the status of the band business, 1958. — *Courtesy Los Angeles Mirror-News.*

jazz had become something too intricate to be brought into the supper clubs and ballrooms. Inadvertently the attempt to bring it there had been made and prolonged beyond the point where conclusive evidence was in.

Regardless of whether it was killed or died a natural death as the result of changing public taste, the era of the dance bands is probably dead. The likelihood of its being rebuilt to the heights it once reached is slight since so few factors still exist which made it big.

To those who viewed it firsthand, either from a bandstand or from out front, it was a wonderful era during which all America loved to dance and paid her fiddlers well. The bandleaders of the era enjoyed equal status with movie stars—mingled socially with heads of government—were occasionally elected to high political office—were entertained by millionaires—and a substantial number became millionaires themselves. They exerted a great influence on the wardrobes of the American population and their slang expressions became accepted as part of the nation's language.

No tribute to them could be better expressed than that broadcast several years back by Joe Martin, at that time a disc jockey on radio station KMMF in Grand Island, Nebraska. He is quoted here through the courtesy of Lawrence Welk who heard Martin's broadcast and wrote him for copies.

"Ya' know—it's been said that bandleaders are a big problem . . . to their agencies . . . their followers . . . and their wives . . . to managers . . . ballroom operators . . . hotels and sometimes to each other. Individually and collectively they are cussed and discussed in music circles, at record parties, in barrooms, behind closed doors, and under one's breath . . . from as many angles . . . and with about the same enthusiasm as the daily headlines of the Korean War.

"They make more noise . . . create more cheer, adjust more union disputes, cause more entertainment, hear more grievances, spread more enjoyment, pacify more belligerents, and waste more time under high pressure without losing their temper . . . than any one class we know . . . including Presidents.

"They live in hotels, taxis, tourist cabins, on trains, buses, and a few on park benches . . . they eat all kinds of food . . . drink all kinds of bad water and coffee . . . sleep before, during, and after business . . . with one of the most rigid schedules known to modern man.

"And yet . . . the top band of the nation has a power in society and in the public economy. In many ways they are a tribute to our way of life. They draw more people into happy-go-lucky gatherings . . . they spend more money with less effort and less return than any other group in business. They drop in periodically . . . stay a few moments . . . play a few hours . . . answer more questions . . . ask the least questions . . . put up with more inconvenience . . . and take more guff than any group including the United Nations.

"They introduce new tunes . . . wear out the old ones . . . hire more tuxedos, eat more hamburgers . . . sell more tickets . . . eat more vitamin pills . . . sleep less . . . have nervous breakdowns more often . . . than any other people in the nation. With all their faults . . . they keep America happy . . . and a feeling of happiness in your little old heart . . . and keep human emotions running. More cannot be said of any man."

During the research for the material which has been written into these pages hundreds of people were interviewed. They included important leaders, sidemen, agents, publicity men, ballroom and theater operators, and avid fans who lived in the wonderful era of the great dance bands.

Whenever opportunity permitted it to be fit into the discussions, the following highly controversial question was asked.

"Taking into consideration many things in addition to your personal likes and dislikes as to musical style, if you were asked to name the ten leaders who contributed the most to making the band business the big business it became who would your list include?"

Many were mentioned, but the following names came up with the greatest regularity, and are listed not in an order intended to rate their position of importance, but with some semblance of the order in which they attained prominence. A capsule of the reasons given for their selection is presented with advance knowledge that not all of them will be the same choice as the individual reader's own list of favorites.

1. Paul Whiteman

   For pioneering in the use of well-arranged orchestrations, the use of vocalists whose sole duty was to sing, nation-wide and international tours, for being the first of the really "Big Bands", and because he compensated those who worked for him in a

Tommy Dorsey

Tommy Dorsey is dead. That won't mean much to the bopsters, the progressives and the rock 'n' rollers who dominate the popular music of today. But to those who crowded around the record players and the radios and jammed the theaters and ballrooms of the 1930s and 1940s it means a great music master has passed on.

To them, Tommy was not merely a good musician; he was a band leader with a great talent for getting the best talent. Remember Frank Sinatra when Sinatra was a "voice" instead of a personality? Jack Leonard, Edith Wright, Bunny Berrigan? Remember "Marie", "Who", "The Sunny Side of the Street", "Boogie Woogie?"

These records and those who made them marked a great era in swing music that will survive the wailing chords that now assail the ears. It is sad to see Tommy go. But it is fortunate that most of his best efforts are pressed in wax that will live—and be played —for a long time to come.

Newark Star-Ledger

S. I. NEWHOUSE, Publisher   *Nov. 1956*
GEORGE P. SLOCKBOWER, Associate Publisher

This tribute to Tommy Dorsey probably expressed the feelings of millions.

manner which beneficially influenced the income of all musicians.

2. Jean Goldkette
   For his assistance in advancing many of the things Whiteman started, and for providing a training ground for many of the future top leaders.

3. Fletcher Henderson
   For his pioneering in "big band jazz" with excellent musicians, and his own imaginative arrangements which became the basis for the style of all those who enjoyed success as "swing" bands.

4. Ben Pollack
   For his ability to discover much of the top talent of the era, even though he seemed

unable to hold them together in a band of his own.

5. Guy Lombardo
   For establishing firmly the fact that the melody was important, and for his unwavering courage to stick with a style regardless of "come and go" trends.

6. Jan Garber
   For over forty years of success which began with pioneering in such things as one-night stands, for unequaled ability as a front man, and for never forgetting that the whole thing was a business and as such had an obligation to its patrons including punctuality, good grooming, showmanship, and general catering to the customers' wishes.

7. Duke Ellington
   For long years of maintaining a high standard of musicianship for himself and his orchestra, as a result of which the whole business was inspired to deliver a better product.

8. Benny Goodman
   For touching off the boom which really started "the big band era" and for popularizing the style which set the musical pattern for years to come.

9. Tommy Dorsey
   For making vocal groups important in the building of a band, for outstanding ability to whip a band into shape in minimum time, and for having the first big success with a style combining sweet and swing.

10. Glenn Miller
    For developing the style second only to that of Benny Goodman in terms of lasting effect on the rest of the music world.

There may have been others who enjoyed greater financial return than some of the foregoing list for it includes two or three whose enjoyment of the "sweet taste of success" was very brief or hardly attained at all. But these ten deserve to be labeled as pace setters; they established the styles, trends, and practices which the others adopted.

Whether they set the pace or followed the pattern the leaders of America's dance bands were in the business of making people happy and are worthy of a firm place in the nation's history.

Index

— A —

A. & P. Gypsies, 169*
ASCAP, 175
Aaronson, Irving, 192, 273, 274*
Abbott, Bud, 180*
Accidents, highway, 84, 276-277, 280
Accordion, 16, 23, 136, 232*, 254*
Adams, Ted, 23
Advertising sponsors, 169-185
Adolphus Hotel, Dallas, 195, 205*
Agencies, 38, 69, 80, 198, 214, 233-247, 250, 256-257, 275-276, 302, 304
Akron, 277
Alabamians (Calloway), 31
Alameda, California, 255
Albany, New York, 243-244
Alexander, Williard, 78
Alexandria Hotel, Los Angeles, 10*, 16
Allen, Barclay, 103, 279*
Allen, Bob, 88*-89
Allen, Steve, 230, 268
Allyson, June, 228
Alpert, Mickey, 97-98
Ambassador Hotel Chain, 189
Ambassador Hotel, Los Angeles, 11*, 15, 49*, 52*, 190, 210
American Airlines, 283*
American Broadcasting Co., 185, 300
American Federation of Musicians, 38 128, 130-131, 147-148, 169, 196, 277, 302
American Recording Co., 140
American Tobacco Co., 73, 236
Amsterdam Roof, New York, 15
Amsterdam Theater, New York, 15
Anderson, Ivy, 294
Andrews Sisters, 146, 226*
Anthony, Ray, 103, 105*, 112*-113, 118, 128-129*, 152, 181-182*-183, 205, 213, 230*, 299
Aragon Ballroom, Chicago, 30-31, 48, 57, 84*, 120*, 163-165, 170, 190-191*, 196, 242, 261*
Aragon Ballroom, Santa Monica, 181, 185-186, 192, 218-219*, 300
Arbuckle, Fatty, 249

* Denotes photograph

Arcadia Ballroom, Detroit, 190, 192,
Arcadia Ballroom, New York, 26, 189-190, 192
Archer, Tom, 120, 198, 301
Armstrong, Louis, 29*, 31, 152, 223-224, 231*, 245*, 257
Arnheim, Gus, 49*, 53, 132, 168, 190, 221, 287
Arnold, Murray, 103
Arrangers, 34-35, 53-54, 69, 76-78, 80, 103, 118
Artists Protective Society, 144
Asche, Paul, 31, 80
Associated Booking Corp., 234, 245, 268
Astaire, Fred, 230*
Astor Hotel, New York, 57, 214
Astoria, Oregon, 132, 242
Athens Club, Oakland, 54
Atlanta, 31, 246
Atlanta Footwarmers, 37
Atlantic City, 14*, 18, 22, 26, 28*, 36*, 77*, 188*, 191*, 253*, 288*
Australia, 201
Austria, 201
Avalon Ballroom, Catalina Island, 56*, 86*, 109*, 163, 192, 255
Avodon Ballroom, Los Angeles, 196
Ayers, Lew, 220*, 221
Ayres, Mitchell, 226*

— B —

Babbitt, Harry, 170, 289*
Baer, Buddy, 47, 89
Bailey, Mildred, 284*, 303
Baird, Eugenie, 292
Baker, Wee Bonnie, 77, 143*, 146, 289*
Baker, Mrs. Dorothy, 228
Baker Hotel, Dallas, 195, 278
Baker, Phil, 26
Ballou, Smith, 80
Band-buyer, 237*, 239, 282
Banjo, 9, 15-16, 37, 48, 128, 132*
Bari, Lynn, 213*
Barnet, Charlie, 79, 83, 110, 192, 199*, 205, 208-209, 223-224, 228-229*, 294

Barris, Harry, 44-45*, 50*, 284*, 287, 292
Barron, Blue, 278
Barry, Gene, 287
Basie, Count, 106*, 110, 128, 131*, 257, 263*, 269, 294
Basin Street, New Orleans, 224
Baton Rouge, 205
Bauduc, Ray, 69, 82*
Beiderbecke, Bix, 22*, 30, 45*, 141*, 144, 228
Bellingham, Washington, 193
Beneke, Tex, 97, 102*, 113, 210*, 213*, 215*, 298
Bennett, Lee, 142*, 293*
Bennett, Tony, 287
Benny, Jack, 169-170, 172, 173*
Benson Agency, Edgar, 31
Benson Orchestra, 30
Berigan, Bunny, 90*, 97, 305
Bernie, Ben, 20*, 26, 32, 43, 57, 167, 169*, 189, 218, 244, 250, 255, 263, 265
Bestor, Don, 31, 245*
Beverly Hills, 135, 240
Billboard (magazine), 78, 94, 115, 145*, 150*-151, 154-155*, 158*, 202*, 208*, 234-235*, 244*, 246, 255-256*, 268
Biltmore Bowl, Los Angeles, 255
Biltmore Hotel, Los Angeles, 19, 53, 169, 190
Biltmore Hotel, New York, 15, 189, 195
Bishop, Eames, 246
Black & White Melody Boys (Ray Miller), 26
Blackhawk Restaurant, Chicago, 31, 57, 72*-73, 164, 170, 195, 202*, 234, 253
Blair, Janet, 88*, 287
Block, Martin, 154*-155
Blue Devils (Walter Page), 23
Boles, John, 221
Bossert Hotel, Brooklyn, 57-58*
Boston, 29, 57, 63, 83, 98, 234, 239
Boston *Post*, 37
Boswell, Connie, 146
Boswell Sisters, 222*-223

Boulevard Room, 195
Bouman, John, 45*
Bowering, Jack, 13
Bowers, Gil, 69
Bowes, Major, 54
Boyer, Anita, 291*
Bradley, Will, 256
Bradshaw, Tiny, 243
Brazil, 201
Briglia, Tony, 111*
Brinkley, Dr., 167
Bronson, Art, 23
Brooklyn, 18, 57
Brown Derby, Hollywood, 300
Brown, Les, 68*, 101*, 109, 128, 148, 198, 245*, 257, 268*, 281, 283*, 296
Brown, Steve, 45
Brownell, Betty, 297*
Brunswick Records, 144, 146
Bryce, Elizabeth, 57
Buffalo, New York, 272
Burns and Allen, 170
Burtnett, Earl, 19, 190
Burton, Billy, 248*
Busse, Henry, 16, 45*, 66*, 67, 109, 132-135, 168, 209, 224, 242, 297
Butterfield, Billy, 82*, 207*
Byrne, Bobby, 64*, 83, 284

— C —

Cabaret tax, 198, 301
Cabot, Chuck, 175*, 267*
California, 183, 255, 259
California Collegians, 13*, 19, 59*, 193*
California Ramblers, 12*, 18, 24, 43
California Ramblers Inn, 19
California State Fair, 264*
Call of the North Woods Orchestra (Art Landry), 36*, 37, 248*
Calloway, Cab, 31, 60-61*, 221, 258*, 262
Camden, New Jersey, 140
Camel Caravan, 67, 170
Canada, 31, 201
Capital Theater, Chicago, 42
Capital Theater, New York, 254
Capitol Theater, Washington, 207
Capitol Records, 114, 139-140*, 147, 161, 265, 293
Capone, Al, 40
Carle, Frankie, 88*, 93*, 113, 115*, 136*, 204
Carmichael, Hoagy, 107*, 228
Carney, Art, 88*, 287, 294
Caron, Leslie, 230*
Caruso, Enrico, 139
Casa Loma Orchestra, 9, 30, 60, 63*, 77-78, 95*, 111, 128, 146, 161, 170, 223, 235*, 292, 303

* Denotes photograph

Casa Mañana, Culver City, 178, 269
Casa Mañana, New York, 288
Casino Ballroom, Avalon, 134*
Casino Gardens, Santa Monica, 196, 259
Castle, Lee, 118
Catalina Island, 56*, 86*, 109*, 197*, 255, 259, 266*
Cavalcade of Bands, 183
Cavallero, Carmen, 113, 154, 228
Central Theater, Passaic, N. J., 97
Challis, Bill, 45*
Champagne Music (Makers), 136, 254*
Chapel Hill, North Carolina, 183
Charlotte, North Carolina, 151
Chase Hotel, St. Louis, 195
Checker Inn Orchestra (Jimmie Gallagher), 29
Chesterfield, 170, 172
Chez Paree, Chicago, 195
Chicago, 10, 15-18, 23, 29-31, 37-38, 40-42, 48, 53-57, 68, 72-73, 82-85, 120, 139, 164-165, 170, 190-191, 195, 196, 198, 203, 212, 218-219, 233, 236, 240, 242, 246, 253, 263, 276, 279-280
Chicago University of, Medical School, 234
Chicago World's Fair, 57
Christy, June, 274*
Cinderella Roof, 12*, 19
Claridge Hotel, Memphis, 132, 195, 215
Clarinet, 10, 38, 67*, 76*-77, 126*
Clarke, Buddy, 94, 218, 287
Cleveland, 30, 62, 164
Clinton, Larry, 77-78*, 146, 303
Clooney, Rosemary, 287, 296*
Club 15 Show, 180
Coast Guard Band, 92*
Coca-Cola, 73, 172, 174*
Cocoanut Grove, Boston, 97-98
Cocoanut Grove, Los Angeles, 11*, 15, 18, 48-49*, 52*-53, 84, 125*, 168, 221, 269, 276, 287
Cohen, Harold, 83
Coleman, Emil 26, 57
College Inn, Chicago, 195, 204, 276
Collins, Dorothy, 287
Columbia Broadcasting System, 140, 168*
Columbia Phonograph Co., 140
Columbia Pictures, 223-224
Columbia Records, 131*, 139, 145-146
Columbo, Russ, 57, 286*-287
Commercial music, 43, 113
Como, Perry, 197*, 286*-287
Concert, 110, 124*, 201-205, 302
Coney Island, 37
Congress Hotel, Chicago, 195
Connecticut (state) 132

Connecticut Yankees, 32-33*-34
Consolidated Radio Artists, 234
Cook County Hospital, 234
Cook, Jimmie, 131
Cooke, Doc, 31
Coolidge, Calvin, 251*
Coon, Carleton, 57, 164, 250*
Coon-Sanders Band (Orchestra), 23, 30-31, 57, 73, 162*, 164, 234, 250
Cornet, 19, 74*
Corn Palace, Mitchell, S.D., 203*
Cosmopolitan Hotel, Denver, 196
Costello, Lou, 180*
Costumes, 33*, 35*, 37, 166*, 223
Cotton Club, New York, 27, 60, 167
Courtney, Del, 96*, 132, 181*, 210*
Covington, Warren, 128
Coy, Gene, 275-276*
Creole Jazz Band, 15, 31
Critics, 42-43, 48, 73, 157-159, 228
Crooners, 285
Crosby, Bing, 44-45*, 55*, 60, 66*, 135, 146-147, 153, 221-222*-223, 284*-285, 287, 292
Crosby, Bob, 53, 57-60, 69, 82*-83, 103, 168, 170, 180*, 217, 268*, 292, 303
Crozier, Rube, 45*
Cugat, Xavier, 53-55*, 175
Cullen, Boyce, 45*
Culver City, 269
Cummins, Bernie, 57, 59*
Curfew, 91
Cymbals, 89*

— D —

Dabney, Earl, 10
Dailey, Frank, 73, 80, 98, 113, 122, 183, 196
Dakota, 232
Dallas, 54, 195, 205
Dance Band Magazine, 227*
Dance music, 9-10, 22, 24, 43, 108-109, 118, 128, 198, 301-303
Dance Orchestra Leaders of America, Frontispiece*, 198
Davis, Johnny "Scat", 224*
Davis, Meyer, 15-16, 29, 32, 57-58*, 233-271
Davis, Milton, 16, 31, 43, 271
Day, Dennis, 211*
Day, Doris, 82*, 228, 287, 303
Day, Irene, 93*
Debutantes, 50*, 287*
Decca Records, 142*, 145-146, 151, 153, 160-161, 244, 254
Denver, 23, 60, 63, 196, 201, 234, 274*
Depression, 47-48, 145, 196, 236, 275
Derwin, Hal, 71*
DeSilva, Buddy, 147
Desmond, Johnny, 287
Des Moines, 120, 262

Detroit, 23-24, 29-31, 38, 60, 73, 131, 164, 233, 250
Detroit Club, 30
Dewey, Bob, 152
Dexter, Dave, 147
Dickerson, Carroll, 29, 31
Dieterle, Kurt, 45*
Disc jockey, 110, 122, 132, 144, 147, 153-154*-155, 157, 159, 181, 198, 228, 257, 265, 269, 301-302, 304
Dixieland, 57, 83, 128-130
Dodge Motor Cars, 185
Doernberger, Charlie, 28*
Donahue, Norman, 142*
Donahue, Sam, 118
Donna and her Don Juans, 294
D'Orsay, Fifi, 303
Dorsey, Jimmy, 17*, 22*, 24, 30, 45*, 60-62, 64*-65*, 69, 80, 82*-83, 89, 103, 112*-113, 118, 123*, 128, 132, 144, 146-147, 151*, 154, 161, 168, 174*, 185, 205, 206*, 212*, 214-215*, 218, 223-224, 227*-229*, 234, 241*, 257, 268*, 285, 291-293, 303
Dorsey, Tommy, 22*, 24, 30, 45*, 60-62, 64*-65*, 69, 71*, 73-77, 80, 83-84, 89, 97*, 101, 103, 110, 113, 118, 123*, 128, 132, 141*, 144, 146-147, 151*-153, 155, 161, 168, 170-171*, 175, 181, 185, 192, 196, 201, 212*-214, 215*, 217-218, 223-224, 227, 244, 246, 250, 262, 282, 284-285, 288-292, 294, 303, 305
Douglas, Kirk, 228
Dowell, Saxie, 42*
Downbeat (magazine), 83, 113, 195, 223, 255-256, 268
Downey, Morton, 303
Draft, 84, 97
Drake Hotel, Chicago, 57, 70*, 195
Drake, Johnny, 284
Draper, Rusty, 125*
Dreamland Ballroom, Chicago, 190
Drum, 9, 15, 34, 47, 53, 103-104*, 124, 136*, 294
Duchin, Eddie, 57, 61*, 94, 103, 132, 209, 228, 255
Duchin, Peter, 136*
Dugan, Dixie, 260*
Duke Blue Devils, 68*
Dunham, Sonny, 116*, 118
Durante, Jimmy, 252*, 265
Durium Products Corp., 145

— E —

Earle Theater, Philadelphia, 204*
Eberle, Ray, 97, 172*, 290*, 292
Eberly, Bob, 64*, 82*, 218, 224, 284, 292*
Edgewater Beach Hotel, Chicago, 57, 195

Edison Hotel, New York, 83, 195, 207, 209
Edison, Thomas A., 139
Edwards, Eddie, 57
Egyptian Room, Hotel Brunswick, Boston, 39*
Eisenbourg, Dok, and his Sinfonians, 37
Elgar, Charlie, 10, 31
Elgart, Les, 126*, 152, 159*
Elitch's Gardens, 63, 101*, 201, 215*, 228, 234
Ellington, Duke, 27, 43, 60-61*, 103, 110, 134*, 145, 156*, 159, 167, 201, 273, 294, 305
Ellington Field, Texas, 93*
Ellington, Mercer, 103
Ellis, Frank, 15
El Rancho, Las Vegas, 205
Empire Room, Houston, 216
Ennis, Skinnay, 42*, 84, 100*, 103, 136, 170-173*-174*, 211*
Erickson, Leif, 222*
Erie, Pennsylvania, 273
Essex House, New York, 60
Europe, 10, 29, 60, 84, 201
Evans, Dale, 53, 286*-287

— F —

Facchine, Russell, 246
Fairmont Hotel, San Francisco, 16, 303
Fanchon-Marco, 54
Farley, Ed, 146
Faye, Alice, 89*, 176*, 287
Feather, Leonard, 185
Federal Radio Commission, 144
Fenton, Carl, 30
Ferguson, Maynard, 118
Fields, Shep, 71*, 73, 146, 196, 215*
Fina, Jack, 103, 105*, 113, 265*
Finegan, Bill, 118
Finley, Larry, 246
FioRito, Ted, 24-25*, 30-31, 48, 50*, 145, 164, 166*, 190, 193*, 222*, 250-251*, 252*, 259, 273*, 287*
Fitch Bandwagon, 172, 174*-175
Fitzgerald, Ella, 146, 294
Flanagan, Ralph, 114-116*-118, 128, 152, 201, 218, 280*, 297-298
Fleischmann Hour, 169
Florida (state), 24-26
Fontenelle Hotel, Omaha, 195
Foran, Dick, 227*
Ford, Charles, 142*
Ford, Henry, 43, 272
Ford Motor Co., 157-159
Forrest, Helen, 225*, 290*, 292
Fortui, George, 142*
Foster, Chuck, 118, 207*, 241*
Foster, Stephen, 175

Foster, Stuart, 97
Fountain Inn, Chicago, 10
Fredericks, Bill, 246
Fredericks Brothers, Inc., 234, 246, 254
Freeman, Bud, 43
Freeman, Mona, 265*
Fuller, Earle, 15
Fulton, John, 45*
Funk, Larry, 57

— G —

GAC (See General Artists Corp.)
Gage, Ben, 53
Gale, Moe, 234
Gallagher, Jimmy
Garber-Davis band, 16, 26, 31, 43
Garber, Jan, 15-16, 28*, 31, 43, 56*-57, 83, 94-97, 110-111*, 123, 125*, 142*, 145, 164, 168, 170, 175, 182, 205, 215*, 223*, 228-229*, 240, 244, 246, 255, 271, 292-293, 305
Gardner, Kenny, 296*
Gargano, Tommy, 141*
Gaylord, Charles, 45*
General Amusement Corp., 241*
General Artists Corp., 234, 235, 246-247*, 257
Gennett Records, 141*
Georgia, 277
Georgians (George McCullough), 26
Germany, 151
Gershwin, George, 303
Gerun, Tom, 18
Gibbs, Georgia, 287
Gibson, Julie, 200*
Gigolo, the, 42
Glaser, Joe, 234, 245, 257
Gleason, Jackie, 131, 185, 223, 225*
Glen Island Casino, New Rochelle, N.Y., 62, 80, 190, 196, 228, 284
Goddard, Bob, 135
Gold Coast Room, Drake Hotel, Chicago, 70*
Golden Gate Theater, San Francisco, 108*, 206*
Golden Pheasant, Cleveland, 30, 168*
Goldkette, Jean, 22*, 24, 29-31, 43, 60, 136, 190, 250, 270*, 272, 305
Golf, 26-27
Goodheart, W. E. (Billy), 30, 234, 236, 240
Goodman, Benny, 9, 18, 27*, 43, 57, 63-67*, 74*, 77-78, 83, 94, 96*-98, 123, 126*, 144, 146, 168, 170, 174*, 191-192, 195-196, 199, 207*-208, 218, 223-224*, 228, 244, 282, 290, 292, 303, 305
Gordon, Claude, 130*-131, 266*
Gordon, Gray, 83, 168, 259
Gordon, Jean, 241*

Gorman, Ross, 23
Gormé, Eydie, 287, 298*
Grable, Betty, 222*, 225*, 287*
Graham-Paige, 270*, 272
Granada Cafe, Chicago, 31, 164
Granada Theater, Chicago, 42
Grand Island, Neb., 275, 304
Grand Terrace, Chicago, 31
Grant's Pass, Oregon, 275
Gray, Glen, 9, 60, 63*, 95*, 116, 136, 157*, 161, 168, 170, 174*, 214, 223, 227*, 234, 303
Gray, Jerry, 77, 103, 113-114*, 180*
Grayson, Hal, 132, 251*
Graystone Ballroom, Detroit, 29, 190
Greenwood, Charlotte, 225*
Greer, Sonny, 294
Greyhound, 273*
Grier, Jimmie, 49*-50*, 53, 92*, 94, 103, 132, 135, 167-169, 200*, 212, 223, 251*, 255, 264*
Grier, Margie, 135
Griffin, Merve, 289, 297*
Grofé, Ferde, 34, 45*
Guarantee, 47, 98, 108, 164, 196, 198, 201-202, 234, 242-243, 271, 280-283, 301
Guion, King, 118
Guitar, 37, 54, 60, 84, 95*, 134*, 136*, 209-211, 222, 287*, 294
Gurtler Brothers, 201, 234

— H —

Hadacol, 201
Haines, Connie, 77*, 284-285, 287-288*
Hall, George, 26, 57, 189
Hall, Wilbur, 45*
Hallett, Mal, 21, 29, 57
Halstead, Henry, 220*-221
Hamp, Johnny, 15
Hampton, Lionel, 67, 83, 85*, 110, 245*, 280, 294
Hand, Arthur, 18
Harlem Hot Chocolates (Duke Ellington), 145
Harlem Swing, 275-276
Harmon, Tom, 84-89
Harris, Phil, 15, 51*-52*-53, 89*, 150*, 152, 172-173*-174*, 176*, 190, 266*, 295
Harrisburg, Pennsylvania, 23, 272
Harvard Club, New York, 40
Harvey's Nightclub, Lake Tahoe, 34
Hastings, Nebraska, 23
Haymes, Dick, 287-288*
Haymes, Joe, 62, 73
Haynes, Don, 100*, 103, 228
Hazlett, Chester, 45*
Heath, Ted, 121*

* Denotes photograph

Hefti, Neal, 118
Heidt, Horace, 54-57, 86, 88*, 94-97, 101, 178-179, 183, 196, 204, 223, 244, 294
Heigh Ho Club, New York, 32
Heilbron, Fritz, 142*
Heinz, Lloyd, 47
Henderson, Fletcher, 23, 29-30, 34, 37-38*, 43, 60, 67, 305
Hendricks, Bill, 132
Henie, Sonja, 223
"Hepster's Dictionary", 258*
Herbeck, Ray, 87*
Herbert's Blue-White Diamonds, 34
Herfurt, Skeets, 60, 65*
Herman, Woody, 66*, 69, 83, 100, 104*, 110, 136, 154, 178, 196, 201, 209, 217, 224, 261*
Hickman, Art, 8*, 15-16, 26, 53, 190
Hill, George, 76
Hill, Tiny, 118, 120*
Hilliard, Harriet, 65*, 287
Hillman, Roc, 60, 64*-65*
Hines, Earl (Fatha), 31
Hippodrome, New York, 26
"His Master's Voice", 140
Hit Parade, 296
Hodges, Johnny
Holliday, Billie, 294
Hollywood, 53, 89, 135-137, 154, 168-170, 178, 181, 196, 216-217, 221-224, 227-229, 246, 250, 252, 265-266, 268-269, 287, 300
Hollywood Bowl, 199*
Honolulu, 91
Hope, Bob, 170-173*, 278-279
Horlick, Harry (A. & P. Gypsies), 169
Horne, Lena, 294
Horton, Edward Everett, 225*
Hotsy Totsy Orchestra (Lawrence Welk), 37, 232*
Houston, 195, 205, 216
Howard, Dell, 15
Howard, Eddy, 54, 84*, 102, 110, 136, 148, 152, 218
Howard, Hal, 264
Hunt, Pee Wee, 95*, 128-129*, 152, 214, 228-229*
Hunter's Serenaders, 23
Hutton, Betty, 287-288
Hutton, Ina Ray, 83, 181, 184*, 205
Hutton, Marion, 97, 172*, 207*, 291*
Hutton, Serl, 234
Hylton, Jack, 69*

— I —

Inflation, 280, 301
Inkspots, 146
Iowa, 167, 198, 263, 276
Ipana Troubadours, 169
Ish Kabibble, 170, 284
Italy, 201

— J —

Jackson, Cliff (and his Krazy Kats), 37
James, Harry, 54, 57, 77*-78, 89, 98-99*, 108-109, 118, 124*, 128, 130, 133* 147, 175, 178, 201, 208-209, 217, 225*, 227*, 228, 268-269, 282, 284-285, 288-293
Jantzen Beach, Portland, 122, 239
Jarrett, Art, 88*-89, 195, 203*
Jarvis, Al, 153*, 155, 228
Jazz, 9, 43-44, 73, 110, 113, 128, 198, 302-304
Jefferson Hotel, St. Louis, 195
Jeffries, Herb, 294*
Jenkins, Gordon, 152
Jenney, Jack, 83
Jensen, Mel, 60, 63*
Johnson, Arnold, 60
Johnson, Eldridge, 140
Johnson, Johnny, 22
Johnson, Van, 228
Johnson, Wilbur, 8*
Johnson's Wax, 170
Jolson, Al, 139, 221, 251*
Jones, Isham, 24*, 30, 43, 66*-69, 132, 146, 197, 277
Jones, Spike, 264*
Joy, Jimmy, 136, 259*
Jukebox, 138*-139, 145-146, 151-152, 154, 301
Jurgens, Dick, 53-54*, 83-84*, 86, 103, 110, 163, 174*, 190, 215*, 218, 259
Justice Dept., U.S., 247

— K —

KDKA, 163
KHJ, 178
KMMF, 304
Kahn, Roger Wolfe, 21*, 26, 136, 221
Kaiser, Elmer, 42
Kallen, Kitty, 292-293*
Kansas, 167
Kansas City, 30-31, 47, 57, 164, 190, 196, 234, 269
Kansas City Night Hawks, 22, 57, 162*, 164, 167
Kapp, Jack, 145
Karzas Brothers, 164, 190-191, 254
Kassel, Art, 31, 43, 164, 218, 302
Katzenberger, Al (Katz) and his Kittens, 36*, 37, 141*
Kavelin, Al, 57
Kay, Herbie, 68*, 287
Kaye, Danny, 228, 231*
Kaye, Sammy, 30, 62*, 83, 115-118, 123, 152-153, 168, 183, 211*, 218, 244, 259, 292
Kayser, Joe, 16, 271, 282
Keaton, Buster, 252*, 303
Kellogg's, 252*

310

Kelly, Paula, 291*
Kemp, Hal, 9, 42*, 57, 73, 84, 88*, 164, 275-277
Kemper, Ronnie, 54, 84*, 86*, 88*, 178, 260*, 294
Kenmore Hotel, Albany, N.Y., 243-244
Kenton, Stan, 87*, 89, 98, 110, 124*, 139*, 147, 149*, 185, 196, 201, 274, 278-279, 281*, 293*, 301-302
Kentucky Club, New York, 27
Kentucky Kardinals, 188*
Kettleman, Beldon, 208
King, Al, 57, 240-242
King, Henry, 215*
King, Louise, 294
King Sisters, 146, 294-295*
King, Wayne, 30, 57, 123, 164-165*, 218-219*
Kirk, Andy, 47, 245*
Kirkeby, Ed, 15-18, 237
Knapp, Orville, 29, 72*-73
Knight, June, 53
Korean War, 304
Kraft Cheese Co., 169
Kramer, Don, 68*, 268
Kramer, Karl, 234
Kramer, Maria, 195, 207*, 209*
Krasner, Benjamin, 201
Kreuger, Benny, 30
Krupa, Gene, 77, 83, 110, 124, 144, 158, 228, 271
Kyser, Kay, 20*, 30, 47, 54, 57, 63, 72*-73, 91, 94, 146, 164, 168, 170-171*, 174*-175, 183, 194*, 227*, 253*, 284, 289*

— L —

LaBahn, Kenneth, 276
Lady Esther Serenade, 177*
Lafrano, Tony, 178
Laguna Beach, 19
Laine, Frankie, 303
Lakeside Park, Denver, 63, 194*, 201
Lake Tahoe, 34, 53
LaMare, Nappy, 69, 82*
Lamour, Dorothy, 68*, 216-217, 287
Landry, Art, 35*, 37, 248*
Lane Sisters, 46*, 287
Langford, Frances, 287
Lanin, Sam, 15, 23, 145
Large, Freddie, 31, 142*
Large, Jerry, 142*
Large, Ken, 142*
Las Vegas, 129*, 131-132, 205-208, 303
Laughner, Carol, 51*
Lauder, Harry, 139
Lawford, Peter, 213*
Lawrence, Elliot, 102-103, 113
Lawson, Yank, 69
LeBlanc (Hadacol), 201
Lee, George E., 23

Lee, Linda, 225*
Lee, Peggy, 96*, 287, 292, 295*
Leonard, Ada, 99*
Leonard, Jack, 171*, 285, 305
Lewis, Ted, 11*, 15-16, 37, 43, 63, 146, 192*, 228, 265
Lido Venice, Boston, 63*
Life magazine, 216
Lincoln Hotel, New York, 195
Lindbergh, Charles, 60-62
Lindley, Don, 19
Linz, Austria, 201
Little Rock, 205
Lofner, Carol, 53, 190
Lombardo, Guy, 30-31, 41*, 57-60, 63, 103-107, 115, 123, 127*, 146, 152-154*, 158, 164, 168, 175, 183, 185, 189, 200*, 205, 282, 292, 296, 302, 305
Lombardo, Rose Marie, 292
Lombardo, Victor, 103-104*-107
London (England), 239
Long, Baron, 255
Long, Johnny, 154, 215*
Long-play records, 148
Lopez, Vincent, 26, 32, 57, 70*, 145, 167, 253*, 288
Los Angeles, 15-18, 48, 53, 63, 84, 108, 128, 130, 155, 168, 181, 196, 209-211, 224, 246, 276
Love, Steve, 167
Lowe, Ruth, 83-84
Lowery, Fred, 88*
Lown, Bert, 26, 32, 34*, 136, 145
Lucas, Nick, 287
Luckie, Dick, 34
Lucky Strike, 169-170, 234
Lunceford, Jimmy, 108*, 110, 132, 234*, 257, 262, 277-278
Lund, Art, 287, 292
Lyman, Abe, 11*, 18, 48-53, 80, 132, 190, 251*

— M —

M.C.A. (see Music Corporation of America)
MacDonald, Billy, 91
MacHarg, Eddie, 60-62, 243
Mack, Ted, 54
MacKinney's Cotton Pickers, 37
MacMurray, Fred, 19, 59*, 193
Madera, Calif., 276-277
Magazines, 249
Magnolia Room, Memphis, 215
Malneck, Matt, 45*
Manone, Wingy, 211-212, 245*
Marcellino, Muzzy, 50*-51*, 156, 193*, 222*, 287*
Margulis, Charles, 45*
Marion, N. C., 273
Marion, Va., 273
Mark Hopkins Hotel, San Francisco, 53-55*, 84, 190, 276

Marshall, Reg, 257
Marshard, Jack, 83
Marterie, Ralph, 114, 116*, 152
Martin, Freddy, 57-58*, 73, 83, 103, 123, 125*, 144*, 146, 161, 172, 177*, 181, 218, 252*, 269, 279*, 292, 297, 302
Martin, Joe, (disc jockey), 304
Martin, Rick, 228
Martin, Tony, 53, 287
Mason, Sully, 170
Masters, Frankie, 57, 174*-175
Masterson, Bat, 287
Mathias, Ernie, 178
Matlock, Matty, 69
Matteson, Don, 60
Max the Waiter, 38
Maxwell, Marilyn (Marvel), 107*, 287-288*
May, Billy, 114, 116*, 118- 205
Mayhew, Jack, 45*
Mayhew, Nye, 45*
Mayhew, Robert, 45*

— Mc —

McCarthy, Glen, 216
McConkey Artists Corp., 242*
McConkey Music Corp., 234
McCoy, Clyde, 94, 130*, 154, 198*, 215*
McCullough, George, 26
McDevitt, Barney, 196, 217, 260*, 265*-266*-269, 272-273, 302
McFarland Twins, 245*
McGee, Fibber & Molly, 169
McHugh, Jimmy, 182
McIntyre, Hal, 100*, 103, 132
McKinley, Ray, 64*-65*, 127*-128, 228
McKinney's Cotton Pickers, 30
McLean, Hal, 45*
McNamee, Graham, 165*
Meadowbrook (Frank Dailey's), 73, 80, 98, 113, 122, 183, 196
Medford, Oregon, 240, 275
Megaphone, 32-33*
Mellophone, 8
Melody magazine, 42
Memphis, 54, 111*, 132-135, 190, 195, 215
Memphis Five (Miff Mole), 40
Mercer, Johnny, 139*, 147, 213*
Mercer, Tommy, 299*
Mercury Records, 114, 117*
Meroff, Benny, 31, 42
Merrill, Joan, 227*
Mertz, Paul, 141*
Metronome (magazine), 255-256, 268
Meyer, Vic, 251*
Midway Gardens, Chicago, 190
Milano, Italy, 201
Milford, Kansas, 167

Miller, Glenn, 9, 18, 23, 27*, 39*, 60-62, 65*, 69, 77-81*-83*, 92*, 94-97, 100-103, 127-128, 144, 146, 161, 168, 170, 172*, 190, 195, 223, 227*, 228, 290-292, 294, 305
Miller, Ray, 18*, 26, 37, 43, 251*
Million Dollar Pier, Atlantic City, 28*, 36*
Mills Brothers, 167*, 205, 223, 243
Mills Novelty Co., 139
Mineo, Sal, 228
Minneapolis, 236
Miranda, Carmen, 225*
Mission Beach Ballroom, San Diego, 246
Missouri, 198
Missourians (Calloway), 31
Mitchell, S. D., 203*
Modernaires, 291*-292, 294
Mole, Miff, 18*, 26, 40
Monroe, Vaughn, 83, 110, 178, 183, 201, 207, 244, 299*
Monte Carlo, 12*
Monte, Frank, 131, 201
Montgomery, George, 210*, 223, 227*
Montmarte Cafe, Los Angeles, 19
Moon Maids, 299*
Morehouse, Chauncey, 19
Morgan, David, 134*
Morgan, Jack, 134*
Morgan, John, 103
Morgan, Russ, 17*, 19*, 23-24, 29-30, 69-70*-76, 110, 111*, 113, 123, 134*, 148*, 150-151, 154*, 160-161, 185, 205, 211, 214*, 216, 225*, 244, 262, 278
Morris Agency, William, 234, 244, 246, 257
Morrison Hotel, Chicago, 57
Morrow, Buddy, 114, 116*, 118, 152
Morse, Ella Mae, 147
Moten, Benny, 23, 31
Mound City, Ill., 273
Moulin Rouge, 303
Movies, 48, 60, 221-231, 244, 250, 287
Muehlbach Hotel, Kansas City, 23, 164, 195
Murphy, George, 193*
Murray, Don, 22*, 30, 141*
Mus-Art Management Corp., 242*, 246
Music Corporation of America, 23, 30-31, 53, 69, 78, 84, 106, 135, 164, 185, 234, 235*-239, 240, 242, 244, 246-247, 256, 264, Endsheets*
Musicians' Union (see American Federation of Musicians)
Muskegan, Mich., 146
Musso, Vido, 97
Mutual Network, 172

— N —
National Anthem, 94
National Ballroom Operators' Association, 115, 131, 198, 268
National Broadcasting Co., 166, 168-169, 176, 265
National Orchestra Service, 234, 236*
National Undertakers' Convention, 135
Nebraska, 23, 163, 167, 198, 263
Neighbors, Paul, 118*-119*, 217*
Nelson, Ozzie, 65*, 227*
Networks, 168-187
Newark Star-Ledger, 305*
New Haven, 277
New Mexico, 280
New Orleans, 9, 15, 54, 80, 125, 160, 195, 215, 224
Newspapers, 249
New York, 10, 15-19, 26-32, 34, 38, 40, 53, 57-60, 63, 69, 83, 98, 130, 135, 145-146, 154, 164, 167, 169, 181, 185, 189-190, 195-196, 211, 214, 221, 234, 243-244, 257, 262, 275
New Yorker Hotel, New York 57, 164, 195
New York Zoo, 250
Nichols, Red, 13-14*, 19-27, 39*-40, 43, 63-69*, 74*, 80, 128*, 144, 160*, 168*, 205*, 209, 228, 231, 252*, 255, 277
Noble, Leighton, 73, 109*
Noble, Ray, 62, 69, 80, 86*
Norfolk, Virginia, 243
Norman, Gene, 154*
North Carolina, 275
North Carolina, University of, 20*, 275
North Dakota, 23, 232
North Platte, Nebraska, 275
Norvo, Red, 104*, 245*, 261*, 284
Novis, Donald, 287
Nunn, Clare, 71*
Nutty Boys Club, 232*

— O —
Oakland, 255
O'Connell, Helen, 82*, 185, 224, 287, 292-293*
O'Day, Anita, 287, 293*
Ogden, Utah, 19-22
Ohio, 234
Ohman, Phil, 132
O'Keefe, Cork, 69, 235
Oklahoma City, 205
Old Gold, 167, 170, 173, 221
Oliver, King, 15, 31, 234
Oliver, Sy, 118
Olsen, George, 8*, 15, 18, 26, 32, 56*-57, 73, 192
Omaha, 23, 94, 190, 195, 205, 234, 236, 278

Orange Blossom Band, 30
Orchestra World (magazine), 257*
Oregon, 275
Oriental Theater, Chicago, 212
Original Swanee Syncopators (Hen Youngman), 37
Oriole Terrace, Detroit, 25*, 30
Osborne, Will, 32, 34, 64*, 106*, 166*-167, 180*, 296, 301
Ossman, Vess, 139
O'Toole, Ollie, 88*
Owens, Harry, 90*, 181
Oxley, Harold, 234, 237*, 257, 262

— P —
Pabst Blue Ribbon, 169
Pacific Northwest, 15
Page, Walter, 23
Palace Hotel, San Francisco, 96*, 109, 190
Palace Theater, New York, 57, 192
Palais Royale, New York, 62
Palisades Park, New Jersey, 39*
Palladium, Hollywood, 89, 114*, 119*, 136-137*, 181, 183*, 186, 192, 196, 210*-211*, 213*-214*, 217, 224, 260*, 265, 267*
Palmer House, Chicago, 57, 195
Palmer, Jack, 288*
Palmer, Jimmy, 118, 122*, 207*, 284
Palmer, Lew, 142*
Palomar Ballroom, Los Angeles, 63-67*, 79*, 89, 192, 197*-199*, 209
Panther Room, Chicago, 82*, 195
Paradise Restaurant, New York, 80
Paramount Pictures, 66*, 224, 231
Paramount Theater, New York, 196, 206, 284
Paris, 103
Park Central Theater, New York, 57
Parkersburg, W. Va., 273
Parsons, Louella, 265*
Pastor, Tony, 257*, 296
Pavilion Ballroom, Santa Monica, 300
Paxton Hotel, Omaha, 195
Payne, John, 225*
"Payola", 157
Peabody Hotel, Memphis, 52*, 195
Peanut vending machine, 60-62
Pearl, Ray, 118, 121*, 242, 261*, 264*
Pearl, Warren, 243
Pekin Theater, Chicago, 10
Pelham Heath Inn, New York, 22
Penner, Joe, 169
Pennsylvania (state), 23, 234
Pennsylvania Hotel, New York, 57, 195, 207, 214
Pennsylvanians (Waring), 29
Perella, Harry, 45*
Perkins, Red, 23, 49*, 236*
Perry, Mario, 45*

* Denotes photograph

Personal appearances, 189-219, 282
Perth Amboy, N.J., 277
Petrillo, Jimmy,
    94, 110, 147-148, 151, 157
Philadelphia,
    23, 29, 103, 140, 203, 272
Philip Morris, 179, 183
Phillips, Lib, 23
Phillips, Teddy, 118, 120*
Phonograph, 138*-139
Piano, 9, 15, 27, 37-38*, 57, 93, 103,
    136*, 223*, 228, 249, 287*
Pied Piper (of Hamelin), 255, 300
Pied Pipers, 84, 290*, 294
Pieper, Leo, 118, 242
Pingatore, Mike, 16, 45*, 75*
Piqua, Ohio, 19-22
Pittsburgh, Pa., 23, 163
Pla-More Ballroom, Kansas City, 122
Plantation Ballroom, Los Angeles, 192
Player piano, 139
Plugger, song, 179, 182
Politicians, 250
Pollack, Ben, 18, 27*, 31, 43, 57, 63,
    69, 80, 145, 191*-192, 228, 262,
    305
Port Arthur, Texas, 54
Portland, Oregon, 15, 239
Powell, Dick, 287
Powell, Teddy, 223, 245*, 287
Power, Tyrone, 228
Presley, Elvis, 303
Press agent, 250, 257-264*
Prime, Harry, 298*
Proctor & Gamble, 185
"Progressive jazz," 110, 185
Prohibition, 38, 48, 62, 236
Prom Ballroom, Twin Cities, 203
Publicity, 249-269

— Q —

Quadling, Lou, 53-54
Quicksell, Howdy, 141*
Quodbach, Al, 31, 164

— R —

RCA-Victor, 114, 138*, 140, 145-146,
    152-153, 183
RKO, 221-224
Rackmil, Milton, 145
Radio, 23-24, 29, 32, 37, 48, 57, 60,
    73, 80, 83, 86, 103, 110, 115, 122,
    132, 135, 139, 144-145, 157, 162-
    187, 189, 244, 249-250, 256, 269,
    278, 282, 287, 301-302
Radio Melody Masters (Elmer
    Kaiser), 42
Ragtime, 9-10
Rainbow Ballroom, Los Angeles, 192
Rainbow Gardens, Denver, 192
Rainbow Rendezvous, Salt Lake City,
    192
Ravazza, Carl, 53
Ray, Johnny, 152

Raye, Martha, 288
Recording (records), 16, 23, 32, 48,
    53, 60, 76, 80, 83, 110, 113-114,
    132, 138*-161, 189, 249, 282, 292
Rector's Novelty Orchestra, 15
Redman, Don, 60
Reed, Tobe, 172
Reed, Tommy, 118
Reichman, Joe, 85*, 132, 178, 269
Reisman, Leo,
    29, 39, 43, 57, 135, 291*
Re-issues, 159
Reser, Harry, 145
Rey, Alvino, 95*, 103, 294-295
Reynolds, R. J. Co., 170
"Rhythm and blues," 157
Rhythm Boys,
    168, 221-223, 284*-285, 287, 292
Rhythm Jugglers, 140*
Rice Hotel, Houston, 195, 216
Rich, Buddy,
    103-104*, 113, 118, 124*
Rich, Freddie, 26
Richman, Harry, 303
Riley, Mike, 146
Rinker, Al, 44-45*, 284*, 292
Riverview Park Ballroom, Chicago, 42
Road trips, 271-283
Robbins, Gale, 287
Robbins, Ray, 241*
Robin, Ruth, 295*
Rock and Roll, 122, 157, 300
Rockford, Ill., 271
Rockwell Agency, Tommy, 80
Rockwell-O'Keefe Agency,
    69, 234-235*, 243
Rockwell, Tom, 235
Rodemich, Gene
Rodin, Gil, 69, 82*
Roe, Douglas, 142*
Rogers, Buddy,
    41*, 57, 80*, 196, 207*
Rogers, Elizabeth, 101
Rogers, Roy, 286
Rogers, Shorty, 118
Romero, Cesar, 223-225*, 227*
Roosevelt Grill, New York,
    31, 63, 127*
Roosevelt Hotel, New Orleans,
    80, 160-161, 195, 215
Roosevelt Hotel, New York,
    57, 164, 189, 195
Rose, Billy (Music Hall, New York),
    63
Rose, David, 207*
Rose, Vincent, 19
Roseland Ballroom, New York,
    15, 29-30, 69, 78, 89, 98, 190,
    216*-217*
Ross, Doc, 57
Ross-Renton Farms, New Jersey, 57
Roth, Otto, 164
Royal Canadians, 31, 41*

Royal Palms Orchestra, 14*, 22
Rush Medical College, 234
Rushing, James, 294*
Russell, Andy, 287
Russell, Jane, 287
Russell, Mischa, 45*
Russo, Danny, 30-31, 48, 190

— S —

Sacramento, 53, 132, 175, 278
St. Francis Hotel, San Francisco,
    15, 48, 51*-54*, 190, 200
St. Germaine, Kay, 53, 287
St. Joseph, Mo., 263, 271
St. Louis, 125, 135, 178, 195
St. Regis Hotel, New York, 53, 190
Salt Lake City, 196, 209, 294
Salzburg, Austria, 201
Sanders, Joe, 57, 164, 242*, 250*
San Diego, 246
San Francisco, 15-18, 48, 53, 84, 109,
    128, 132, 190, 200, 206, 275-276,
    303
San Francisco World's Fair, 15
San Joaquin Valley, 276
San Mateo, 240
Santa Barbara, 16
Santa Monica, 192, 196
Sargent, Kenny, 111
Satterfield, Tom, 45*
Sauter, Eddie, 118
Sauter-Finegan orchestra, 118-119
Savitt, Jan, 83, 132, 223, 245*
Savoy Ballroom, New York,
    29, 60, 190
Saxophone, 17*, 19, 24, 32, 34, 37,
    54, 59*-60, 72, 79*, 102*, 104*,
    107, 120*, 123*, 193, 209, 218,
    271, 281, 294
Schutt, Arthur, 19*
Scott, Cora Lee, 51*
Scranton Sirens, 17*, 24
Seattle, 251
Selmer Instrument Co., 37
Senter, Boyd, 23, 80
Senter Park, Neb., 23
Shamrock Hotel, Houston, 216
Shaw, Artie, 9, 29, 76*-77, 83, 94,
    101, 123, 146, 170, 207*, 223, 282,
    291, 294
Sheet music, 23, 248
Sherman Hotel, Chicago, 82*, 195, 204
Sherman's College Inn, Chicago,
    57, 195
Shore, Dinah, 146, 210*
Short, Al, 42
Shoup, Don, 142*
Shreveport, La., 205
Silver Slipper, New York, 57
Simms, Ginny, 170, 227*, 287, 289*
Sinatra, Frank, 77*-78, 84, 103, 113,
    284-285, 288*, 305
Sissle, Noble, 294

Skelly Gasoline, 166
Slack, Freddie, 64*, 147, 245*
Sousa, John Philip, 300
South America, 201
South Dakota, 263
South, Eddie, 31, 245*
Southmore Hotel, Chicago, 31
Spanier, Muggsy, 43
Speakeasies, 38, 62
Specht, Paul, 15, 19*, 23-24, 29, 31,
    43, 69, 76, 132, 163-164
Spivak, Charlie,
    29, 69, 83, 93*, 123, 207*, 229*
Spotlight Bands (Coca Cola),
    172, 174*
Stabile, Dick, 103, 284
Stacey, Jess, 82*
Stafford, Jess, 41*
Stafford, Jo, 287, 291
Standby musicians, 196
Starr, Kay, 287, 298*
Steele, Blue, 24
Stein, Dr. Jules, 30, 69, 164, 234, 236
Stevens, E. F. Jr., 146
Stevens Hotel, Chicago, 57, 85*, 195
Stevens, Roy, 113
Stewart, Jimmy, 103, 228
Stone, Butch, 281*
Stordahl, Axel, 171*
Straight, Charlie, 10, 26*, 30
Strand Theater, New York,
    83, 214, 216
Strasburg, North Dakota, 23
Strike, 147-148
String bass, 15, 37, 136*, 214
Strong, Benny, 267
Struckfaden, Charles, 45*
Sunset Cafe, Chicago, 31
Sweatman, Wilbur, 10
Swing (magazine), 284
Syncopating Five, 14*, 22
Syncopation, 9
Syncopators, 31

— T —
Tacoma, Washington, 100*
Taft Hotel, New York, 57, 190, 195
Taft, Jim, 60
Tag lines, 168
Talking pictures, 221
Tape recording, 151
Tate, Erskine, 10, 31
Teagarden, Jack,
    57, 75*, 90*, 136, 190, 285, 293
Teenagers, 107*
Television, 115, 118, 122, 131, 136,
    157, 178, 181*-187, 189, 196, 246,
    287, 292, 301-302
Tennessee (state), 278
Territory bands, 23, 37, 47, 118-122,
    128, 168, 202, 271, 275

* Denotes photograph

Terry, Don, 118
Texas, 54-57, 132, 216
Texas Centennial, 195*
Thayer, Lyle, 238, 246
Theme songs, 167-168, 178, 214
Thornhill, Claude, 58*, 94, 99*, 103
Three Cheers, 287
Times Square, 93*, 216
Tiomkin, Dimitri, 268
Tobin, Louise, 292
Tom Dor Enterprises, 244, 246
Torme, Mel, 287
Trafficante, Michael, 45*
Tremayne, Paul, 57
Trianon Ballroom, Chicago, 56-57,
    122, 164, 170, 188*, 190, 194, 196,
    242, 254, 261*
Trianon Ballroom, Cleveland, 62*, 190
Trianon Ballroom, Los Angeles, 190
Trianon Ballroom, Seattle, 190
Trombone, 15, 17*, 24, 37, 40-41*,
    60, 83, 90, 116*, 123*, 134*, 137*,
    214*, 217, 228, 262
Trotter, John Scott, 42*, 84
Trumbauer, Frankie,
    18*, 26, 30, 44*, 45*, 271
Trumpet, 15-16, 29*, 37, 54, 66*, 67,
    78, 101, 116*, 198, 200-209, 214,
    223-224, 228
Tuba, 37, 60, 272-273
Tucker, Orrin, 75*, 77, 94, 103, 143*,
    146, 183*, 289
Tucker, Tommy, 212-214, 256*
Tucson, 209
20th Century-Fox, 225*, 228
Twin Cities (Minnesota), 203
Two Black Crows, 139

— U —
U.S.O., 90*, 94, 101-103, 278
Underworld, 38-40
Universal Pictures, 221, 226
Utah Hotel, Salt Lake City, 196

— V —
Vallee, Rudy, 32*-33*-34, 92*, 94,
    144-145, 165*, 167, 169, 220*-221,
    227*, 263, 272-273, 282, 285, 303
Van, Gloria, 218
Variety (magazine)
    44-45*, 115, 255, 256
Vaudeville, 10, 15-16, 19, 26, 54, 195
Venice Ballroom, California
    18, 178, 192
Venice, Italy, 201
Venuti, Joe,
    22*, 30, 83, 178, 209-211, 214, 278
Vibraphone, 85*, 104*
Victor Records, 114, 116, 138*-140
Victor Talking Machine Co., 140
Violin,
    9, 15-16, 37, 51, 101, 215, 287

Virginia Beach, 74*
Vocalists, 32, 46, 50*-51*, 60, 65, 68,
    73, 77, 83-84, 88, 96*, 101*, 116*,
    146, 152, 181, 185, 222, 224, 249,
    281, 284- 299, 301, 303-304

— W —
WABC, 32
WCAU, 103
WDAF, 23, 164
WGN, 73, 253-254
WNAX, 23, 167
WWM, 164
Wade, Jimmie, 31
Wade, Stewart, 297*
Waldman, Herman, 52*, 54
Waldorf-Astoria, New York, 57, 195
Walker, Leo, 125*, 238, 264*
Waller, Fats, 237*
Wallichs, Glenn, 147, 293*
Walsh, Jimmy, 53
Ward, Helen, 292
Waring, Fred, 15, 23, 29, 46*, 144,
    154, 170, 173*, 265, 272-273, 287,
    294
Waring's Banjatrazz, 15
Warner Brothers Vitaphone, 221
Wasescha, Warren, 125*
Washington, Dinah, 294
Washington, D. C., 207, 278
Washingtonians (Ellington), 27
Washington (state), 251
Way, Sterling, 211*
Webb, Chick, 294
Weber, Kay, 60, 65*, 292*
Weeks, Anson, 53-55*-60, 190, 195,
    204*, 276-277, 286
Weems, Ted, 30, 40*, 132, 136, 140,
    144, 148-151, 154, 170, 197*, 215*,
    286-288*
Weidemeyer's Orchestra, 248*
Weiss, Seymour, 80, 160, 195, 215*
Welk, Lawrence, 16*, 17*, 23, 37,
    91*, 123, 136, 167, 181, 185-186*-
    187*, 218, 232*, 254*, 259, 270*,
    272, 283, 300, 302, 304
Wesley's Levee Loungers, Dave, 132*
Western Union, 238*, 262*, 268*
West Virginia, University of, 234
White, Alice, 251*
White, Dick, 142*
White, George, 19
White, Josh, 139
Whiteman, Loyce, 50*, 287
Whiteman, Paul, 10*, 15-18, 26, 30-
    31, 34, 43-44*, 53, 57-60, 63-67,
    75*, 123, 140, 144, 147, 154*-155,
    167-170, 185, 188, 190, 221, 224,
    227*, 272, 282-284, 286, 292, 294,
    301, 303-304
Whittemore, Jack, 246

314

Wiedoeft, Herb, 12, 19
Wiedoeft, Rudy, 19, 32, 34*
Wildroot, 178
Williams, Dick, 303
Williams, Griff, 51*, 53, 55*, 85, 132
Williams, Mary Lou, 67
Williams, Murray, 209
Wilson, Eileen, 296*
Winchell, Walter, 135, 249, 255
Wonders, Ralph, 236
Wood, Lou, 59
Woolworth's, 275

World War I, 234
World War II, 84-109, 135, 174-175,
   178, 194, 224, 243, 277-278, 282,
   301-302
Wright, Edythe, 171*, 285, 288, 305
Wylie, Austin, 30

— Y —

Yale Bowl, 92*
Yancey Hotel,
   Grand Island, Nebraska, 275
Yankton, South Dakota, 23, 167

Yerkes, Harry, 32, 233
Yoder, Walt, 66*
Young, Austin, 45*
Youngman, Hen, 37
Young Sisters, 297*
Youth Opportunity Show, 183

— Z —

Zentner, Si, 137*
Ziegfeld, Florenz, 15
Ziegfeld Roof, 10, 15
Zucker, Stanford, Agency, 234